THE URBAN GENERAL PLAN

Chandler Publications in

POLITICAL SCIENCE

VICTOR JONES, *Editor*

THE URBAN

GENERAL PLAN

By T. J. KENT, Jr.

PROFESSOR OF CITY PLANNING
UNIVERSITY OF CALIFORNIA, BERKELEY

WITH A BIBLIOGRAPHIC ESSAY
ON THE URBAN GENERAL PLAN

By HOLWAY R. JONES

HEAD SOCIAL SCIENCE LIBRARIAN
UNIVERSITY OF OREGON, EUGENE
(FORMERLY, CITY PLANNING LIBRARIAN,
UNIVERSITY OF CALIFORNIA, BERKELEY)

COMPANY / SAN FRANCISCO

Distributed by:
Science Research Associates, Inc.
259 East Erie Street, Chicago, Illinois 60611

A Subsidiary of IBM

The charts and maps that appear on the following pages are the work of Mrs. Eve Kemnitzer: xv, 14, 36-37, 92-93, 111, 114-115, 149, 155, 164-165, 172-173, 175, 178-179

Library of Congress Catalog Card No. 64–14294
Printed in the United States of America

To Mary, and to Tom, Steve, and Dave—

whose strong desire for better and more beautiful cities
has always refreshed me,
and whose practical interest in civic action to improve their own city
has always inspired me.

CONTENTS

ILLUSTRATIONS

I know no safe depository of the ultimate powers of society but the people themselves; and if we think them not enlightened enough to exercise their control with a wholesome discretion, the remedy is not to take it from them, but to inform their discretion by education.

THOMAS JEFFERSON

. . . politics is the slow public application of reason.

THEODORE H. WHITE

PREFACE

THE LEADERS of America's cities have never before been so aware of pressing problems and great opportunities. Postwar experience with the surging tide of urban growth has produced an entirely new generation of civic, professional, and political leaders who have had, in effect, on-the-job training in city planning. Today, these citizens are acutely aware both of the shortcomings and of the powerful momentum of the postwar city-rebuilding and suburban-tract-development programs, characterized during the 1950's by large-scale urban-redevelopment projects, metropolitan freeways, and fringe-area subdivisions. They are now re-examining, with a critical eye educated by complex postwar experiences, the dreams of the 1930's for better cities.

In this context, the urban general plan for the physical development of a community is a subject of great fascination for students, practitioners, and professors of city planning. It has a similar appeal for a significantly large proportion of those citizens who have participated directly in the work of democratic municipal self-government. Thus, in addition to its use as a textbook for students of city planning and for students in the related fields of architecture, landscape architecture, engineering, law, political science, public administration, community organization, sociology, and urban-land economics, I hope that *The Urban General Plan* will be of use to the individual members of citizen study groups such as the city-planning and related committees of local chambers of commerce, service clubs, professional societies, political parties, and the League of Women Voters. It is my hope, in particular, that city councilmen, city-planning commissioners, mayors, and city managers will find the ideas in this book directly related to one of their major areas of responsibility, and that they will find it stimulating and of practical value.

The Urban General Plan focuses on the legislative uses (Chapter III) and the characteristics (Chapter IV) of the plan. The discussions of local government, the role of city planning, and alternative plan concepts (Chapter I) are intended only to provide an adequate context for the material that follows. Thorough consideration of these important, related topics is beyond the scope of this book. Likewise, I do not attempt to cover the history of city planning, although I judge it necessary to discuss in detail (Chapter II) the general-plan concept embodied in the 1928 Standard City Planning Enabling Act and to present my view of the historical context and consequences of the Act. In Chapter V, I take up the contents and organization of the general-plan document.

For several reasons, I discuss only the *urban* general plan, meaning the general plan of a *municipal* government. Consideration of the county general plan and of the general plan for a metropolitan region is deliberately excluded. Certain of the uses of the urban general plan would apply to county and metropolitan-region plans. But some uses would not and some additional uses would be involved. Therefore, while municipal governments throughout the United States do have a common need for general plans and while my ideas may be generally applicable to the needs of such governments, I make no claims of applicability with regard to types and levels of government other than municipal.

Interest in metropolitan governmental and physical-development problems has increased greatly since 1950. These subjects are and have been for many years of special interest to me. Hence, in concentrating on the needs of municipal governments, I do not wish to give the impression that I am unaware of the needs of the great metropolitan communities that are growing and reshaping themselves with such powerful vitality on every continent of the world today. (For a discussion of basic relationships between municipal and metropolitan governments, see *Report of Royal Commission on Local Government in Greater London, 1957–60,* Her Majesty's Stationary Office, Cmnd. 1164. My own views concerning these relationships are set forth in my essay "City and Regional Planning for the Metropolitan San Francisco Bay Area," Institute of Governmental Studies, University of California, Berkeley, 1963.) In *The Urban General Plan,* I have chosen to concentrate on the needs of municipal governments because these governments exist today; because they are the only general governments directly responsible for govern-

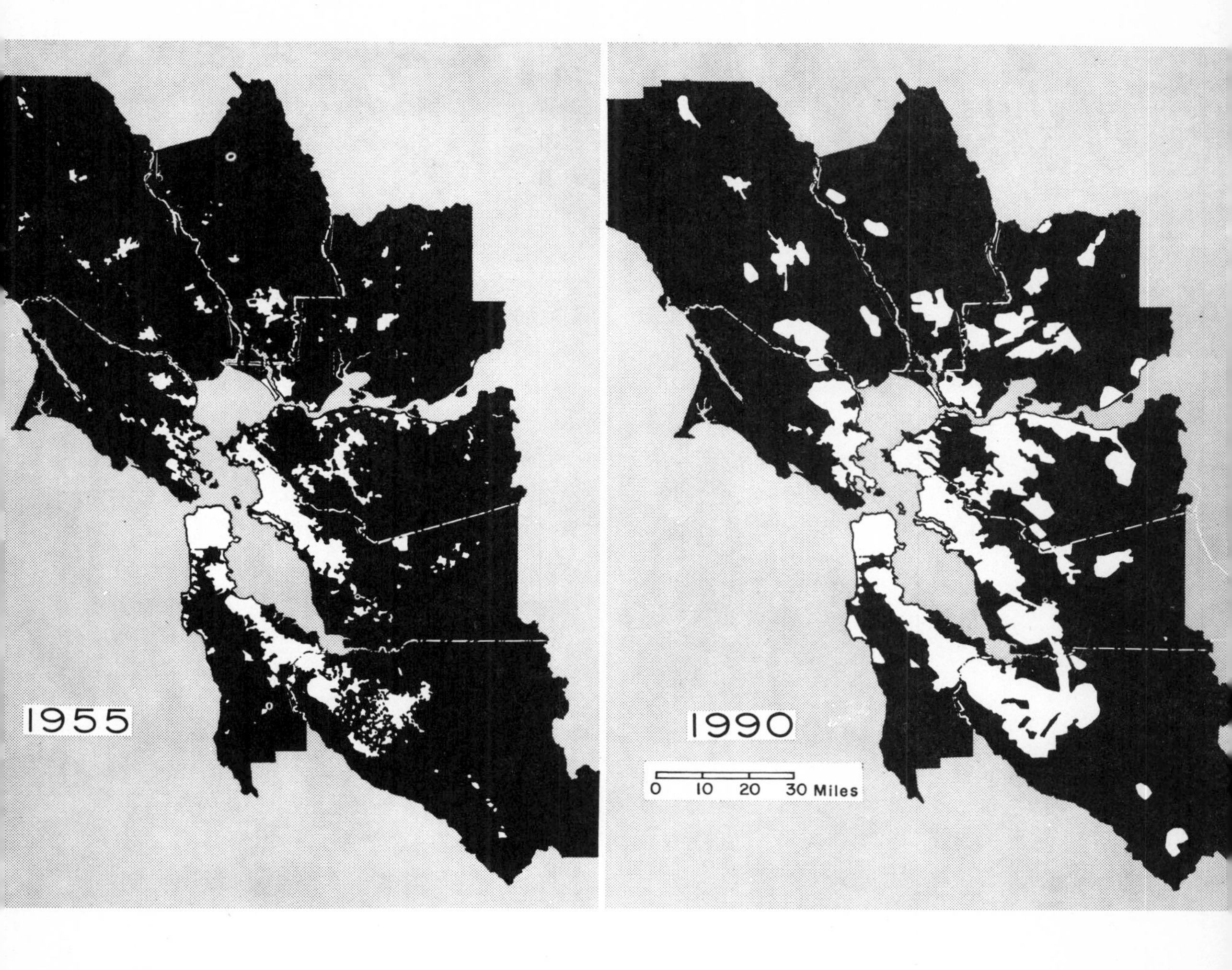

METROPOLITAN EXPANSION AND MUNICIPAL GOVERNMENTS

It is anticipated that between 1955 and 1990 the population of the metropolitan San Francisco Bay Area will have increased from 3,000,000 to approximately 7,000,000 persons. This tremendous population growth can be expected to accelerate the outward physical expansion of the metropolitan community and the intensive redevelopment of the central cities in a manner similar to that which has characterized post-World War II urban growth throughout the world. It can also be expected that, regardless of the success or failure of contemporary efforts to create some form of metropolitan government, there will continue to be a significant increase in the number of municipal governments within metropolitan areas in the United States, and in the authority of these governments over physical-development activities. During the twenty-year period between 1940 and 1960 in the San Francisco Bay Area, the number of municipal governments increased from 67 to 83. By 1990 there probably will be more than 100 municipal governments in the Bay Area.

ing physical-development activities; and because, as metropolitan governments suited to our American political traditions gradually come into being—as they must—I believe that our municipal governments should and will be retained and strengthened, and that they will increase in number.

I began to practice city planning in 1939 and have been actively engaged ever since, in one capacity or another, in preparing, using, and revising general plans for the physical development of cities—large, small, medium, and metropolitan in size. My academic colleagues describe me as a "doer," rather than as an "observer." Consequently, although I have been able to read and travel widely and have an intense interest in comparative studies of city planning, local government, and local politics, it is natural for me to express my ideas in the form of advocacy. I hope that the reader will not be put off by this method of presentation, and that the ideas that are presented in the following pages will be accepted, modified, or rejected on their own merits.

ACKNOWLEDGMENTS

I WISH TO express my appreciation to the many professional colleagues and civic leaders with whom it has been my privilege to work in the metropolitan San Francisco Bay Area during the past twenty years. I am especially indebted to Corwin R. Mocine and James A. Barnes, Berkeley city-planning directors from 1949–55 and 1955 to the present, respectively. I have benefited greatly from their practical knowledge of city planning and municipal government, and have been influenced by their ideas throughout the entire fifteen-year period of our collaboration in the preparation and use of the *Berkeley Master Plan*. (A full account of the Berkeley experience is being prepared by Warren M. Campbell for publication in the Inter-University Case Program series. Mr. Campbell's excellent manuscript presents additional evidence with which to judge the validity of the general-plan concept as I have defined it.)

I am particularly indebted, also, to Alan Black. As a city-planning graduate student at the University of California in 1959–60, he clarified for me some of the basic features of the general-plan concept and he summarized, far better than I had been able to, the context within which the concept must be seen to be fairly judged. With his permission, I have drawn freely from his excellent thesis, "The Functions of the Urban General Plan" (Masters Thesis, University of California, Berkeley, 1960), particularly in the preparation of chapters I and III. As an intellectual collaborator in the task of putting ideas into words, I wish to express my admiration for his abilities and to acknowledge my debt to him.

Francis Violich and Melvin M. Webber, University colleagues, have for many years been actively working on aspects of the general-plan concept that are of special interest to them. Their ideas have influenced me, as have the challenging questions raised by my other colleagues, Catherine Bauer, Donald L. Foley, and Mellier G. Scott, Jr. Contacts with other professors and work with several outstanding city-planning graduate students since 1948 have contributed much to my thoughts about the urban general plan.

I am indebted to Professor Victor Jones for his encouragement; and to Mrs. Sallie Walker and the members of her staff for the final typing of the manuscript and for effectively handling many other important details and arrangements. It would be impossible to name all the others who have helped me.

I wish to express a special word of appreciation to Mr. Holway R. Jones for his very kind permission to include in this book, with minor changes, his excellent bibliographic essay on the urban general plan.

T. J. KENT, JR.

Berkeley, California
August, 1963

THE URBAN GENERAL PLAN

INTRODUCTION

IN 1911 Frederick Law Olmsted, Jr., in a statement presented at the third National Conference on City Planning, described the urban general plan in the following terms:

We must cultivate in our minds and in the mind of the people the conception of a city plan as a device or piece of . . . machinery for preparing, and keeping constantly up to date, a unified forecast and definition of all the important changes, additions, and extensions of the physical equipment and arrangement of the city which a sound judgment holds likely to become desirable and practicable in the course of time, so as to avoid so far as possible both ignorantly wasteful action and ignorantly wasteful inaction in the control of the city's physical growth. It is a means by which those who become at any time responsible for decisions affecting the city's plan may be prevented from acting in ignorance of what their predecessors and their colleagues in other departments of city life have believed to be the reasonable contingencies.

Today, more than half a century later, it would be difficult to obtain agreement among the leaders of the profession on Olmsted's definition of the purpose and scope of the general plan. Ideas about the political and technical purposes and the substantive scope of the general plan, and the basic physical elements of the community that must be dealt with in the general plan, have evolved largely through the practical experience of preparing and using plans; they have not been based on extensive theoretical thinking. City planners continually refer to the general plan, but they rarely define it or explain its purposes and uses. Although there are certain basic similarities in most of the published general-plan documents, these similarities result from practices handed down from one city planner to another, rather than from the existence of any widely accepted conceptual basis.

It is also apparent from these general-plan documents that there are disagreements on important questions concerning the general plan: Should the plan represent goals or forecasts? How technical should it be? How general should it be? Should it include cost estimates? Whom is it primarily intended to serve? Should it be adopted, and if so, by whom? Should it be published? How often should it be reconsidered and amended? Should it attempt to be at the same time both flexible and firm?

The validity of the basic general-plan concept itself is questioned by some of the leaders of the city-planning profession today. These leaders suggest that since it is not possible to foresee the needs of the future scientifically, it is dangerous to prepare a plan and misleading to suggest that it is possible to do so.

Despite the questions, uncertainties, and misgivings within the city-planning profession, municipal governments must continue to govern and to act. Every year an increasing number of city councils prepare and use long-range general plans to assist them in determining their short-range physical-development programs. I believe that the preparation and maintenance of the general plan is the primary, continuing responsibility of the city-planning profession. It will continue to be our most significant contribution to the art of local government.

The ideas presented here are based on more than twenty years of experience, mainly in the metropolitan San Francisco Bay Area. I first gained a clear understanding of the reasons why a municipal government ought to have a general plan while I was a graduate student at the Massachusetts Institute of Technology in 1942. Convictions concerning the essential physical elements that should be dealt with in the general-plan document developed as a result of my experiences as a member of the city-planning staff, and later as Director of City Planning, in the City of San Francisco.

The belief that the municipal legislative body must be acknowledged as the principal client of the plan and the emphasis I give to the idea that the basic policies of the plan must be distinguished from the general physical-design proposals of the plan result mainly from fifteen years of experience in Berkeley, first as a citizen member of the City Planning Commission from 1948 to 1957, and subsequently, from 1957 to the present, as an elected member of the City Council. Berkeley has a council-manager form of government; San Francisco has a strong-mayor form of government.

Since 1948 I have been a teacher, and my ideas, consequently, show the influence of academic debates with colleagues and students and the practical experiences of students following graduation. I have also been stimulated by the general-plan work carried out by the staffs of several of the larger cities in the United States whose policies have been shaped by professional colleagues I have known since my student days.

I believe that we now have sufficient practical experience to attempt to define the general plan and delineate its specific uses and characteristics. City planning has made remarkable progress, but it has not reached the goals expected of it. We need only look at our cities to realize this. Nearly sixty years of experience and experimentation with general plans have produced only modest achievements. What may be a workable general-plan doctrine is just now appearing on the horizon. If it crystallizes and proves to be generally applicable, the effectiveness of city-planning programs will be greatly enhanced.

The discussion of ideas in the following pages to some extent depicts an ideal state of affairs which will never be realized in any community. I intend, however, to present a concept of a general plan that can be used in an actual American city, and not in a utopia. Although I make generalizations to which there will be some exceptions, the general-plan concept I advance represents an attempt to formulate a realistic doctrine which takes practical considerations into account. The effects of politics, personalities, and human traits and weaknesses are considered. It is acknowledged, however, that the city-planning process advocated here will not be easy to apply and will not always function smoothly.

Some of my proposals may not seem to advance the cause of the professional city planner; they involve restraint and discipline on his part. I seek to advance the cause of better cities, of more effective physical-improvement policies and action programs, rather than the cause of the city planner. I attempt to do this by clarifying the needs of the city council in its role as the city builder of our era and, therefore, as the primary client of the city-planning profession.

I 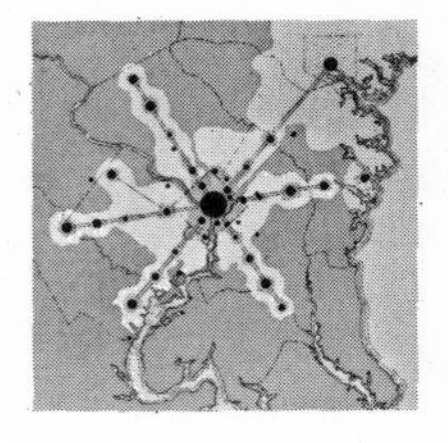

MUNICIPAL GOVERNMENT, CITY PLANNING, AND THE GENERAL PLAN

THE WAYS in which the general plan for the physical development of a community should be used cannot be considered in a vacuum. It is not possible to make sweeping generalizations about how the plan should be used without considering in a single context one's beliefs about municipal government, city planning, and the general plan. There must be an integrated system of ideas in which each part supports and is supported by the other parts. The uses of the plan are dependent upon beliefs as to the substantive scope of city planning, the place of city planning in the structure of local government, the primary client of the general plan, and the basic technical and political realities which make necessary a long-range physical-development plan of some sort.

If the plan is to serve the specific needs of the particular people who have to use it, it is essential to make a judgment as to who should be considered the most important user—the primary client—of the plan. This judgment is of paramount importance in determining the uses, since the different users will have varying and sometimes different needs.

If the chief executive is the primary client of the general plan, then a particular set of uses will be predominant. If the city-planning commission is an independent body, this will influence the uses of the plan. If the plan is simply a forecast, this fact will affect the uses. In similar fashion, the uses of the general plan influence its characteristics and the contents and organization of the general-plan document.

In this chapter I take up first the salient points about municipal government and city planning which have shaped my ideas on the primary client, the uses, and the characteristics of the general plan. The brief overview of municipal government and city planning is followed by a discussion of my own general-plan concept. This chapter and the historical perspective presented in Chapter II establish the context for the subsequent exposition of the legislative uses and characteristics of the general plan and the contents and organization of the general-plan document.

FORMS OF MUNICIPAL GOVERNMENT

In medium-sized and large American cities today there are two major forms of municipal government structure which have great vitality: that in which the chief executive is an elected mayor who is independent of the legislative body, and that in which the chief executive is a city manager appointed by the legislative body. These may be called the "strong-mayor" and "council-manager" forms, respectively.[1]

The strong-mayor form is patterned after the organization of state governments and the federal government. It assures a system of checks and balances by separating the legislative body and the chief executive and dividing the governing powers between them. It also makes possible strong political leadership by the mayor. This form of municipal government is common in cities in the Northeast, and it is used elsewhere in the United States in most of the large cities.

The council-manager form is an innovation of this century which was sparked by the reform movement brought on by widespread corruption in municipal government. It gained acceptance rapidly and is now widely used by medium-sized cities throughout the country. It has achieved its greatest popularity in California.

The strong-mayor governments of the dozen or so American cities having more than three-quarters of a million population may be considered by some readers to be in a special category. Most students of American gov-

[1] See *The Municipal Year Book* (Chicago: The International City Managers' Association, 1313 E. 60th St., 1963) for complete information on the major groupings of the 17,997 American municipalities by size of population and type of governmental structure.

ernment who accept the premise that it is possible to have a single government for a city with a population of 750,000 or more that is also "local," find themselves seeking constantly to strengthen the position of the elected chief executive and his professional advisors at the expense of the legislative body. Indeed, at the present time there are no prominent advocates of the idea that the city council of a large city, like every other responsible legislative body, should be expected to define and state the basic policies that its specific legislative acts are intended to implement. On the other hand, no serious student of democracy has ever advocated the abolition of the city council—it has always been taken for granted that a "committee" of directly elected fellow citizens is needed to legislate on behalf of the entire citizenry, even in the big cities. Thus, while the general-plan concept may not seem suited to what some judge to be the specific needs of the governments of our major cities, the concept does suggest that there is a way to bring about the open formulation, completion, and use of a coherent physical-development policy in those major cities—such as New York, Los Angeles, and Chicago—where strong mayors and their professional advisors have no such policy as is evidenced by a general plan.

There are forms of municipal government which do not include a strong chief executive, either elected or appointed. The "weak-mayor" form, in which the city council takes the place of a single chief executive, is common in small cities. A significant proportion of the cities in the United States still use the "commission" form, in which the legislators also serve as the heads of administrative departments; however, this form of municipal government is declining in popularity.[2]

In considering the general-plan concept set forth in this book, it is not necessary to anticipate changes in the formal structure of local government below the level of the city council. Since the primary uses of the general plan as I define them are legislative in nature, I believe these uses have general applicability, now and in the future, wherever the political philosophy of any society places final responsibility and authority for community policy-making and lawmaking in the hands of an elected group of citizens.

American citizens, within the context of the distinctive traditions of

---

[2] Regardless of the ways in which local governments are organized, I believe we will continue to see an increase in the number of citizens directly involved in local government on official and semiofficial boards and commissions and a steady increase in the significance of local partisan political activity. I also believe we will see the emergence of an "executive group" which will take the place of the single chief executive, at least in practice if not, for some time, in theory.

their respective state governments, will continue to experiment with different forms of local government. Regardless of the present dominance of the two forms—strong-mayor and council-manager—that have attempted to institutionalize a strong executive separated from the legislative body, the need for city planning and the general plan will continue.

The legislative uses of the general plan for physical development as defined in this book may seem especially appropriate to the council-manager form of government. However, the ideas presented are not intended to be viewed as an argument in support of the council-manager form. These ideas do reflect the rise of this concept—and its contemporary appeal and vitality, despite criticism and setbacks—and represent an attempt to learn from it, as well as from other, older concepts of local government. The main object of this book is to clarify the nature and purposes of the general plan for physical development that is needed by municipal governments regardless of the differences in their formal structure.

CITY MANAGEMENT AND THE COUNCIL-MANAGER FORM

The council-manager form of municipal government elevated the city council to the unchallenged leadership of local government and concentrated full authority and responsibility in the council. Under this form of government it was assumed that the chief executive would be a professional administrator, a subordinate appointed by the council and charged with carrying out its wishes. This assumption stimulated the development of the profession of city management. It also gave rise to the central-management concept of public administration, in which all administrative departments are responsible solely to the chief executive, and the chief executive is the spokesman for the entire administration. Thus, the appointed chief executive theoretically can be held responsible for coordination of all policy-implementation measures.

The original concept of city management held that the city council should decide all matters of policy and the city manager should decide all matters of administration. However, experience has shown the separation to be unrealistic. The city council has had to concern itself with administration—as by law it is required to do—and the city manager has always played a major role in the formulation of policy. The "expert" status of the city manager has given him more influence than was anticipated. It now seems reasonable to some students of democratic local government to consider the city council and the city manager as partners in governing, with the council having the last word in cases of conflict.

In general, the council-manager form has proven to be notably successful in a relatively short time in bringing about honest and apparently efficient local government. However, there are certain dangers in the system, one being too great a centralization of power in appointed chief executives and another being the tendency of forceful city managers to confuse and weaken the authority of city councils. As with every system of human organization, personalities have much to do with how the system operates in actual situations. It probably will take another generation or two to bring about effective solutions to the already apparent contradictions and flaws in the central-management theory as applied to local self-government.

Some city councils, through neglect or ignorance, have virtually ceded their power to their city managers. Some managers have attained dominance over their councils from the unquestioning faith that the councils put in them. Occasionally city managers have proven to be skillful in the political arena and have become the political bosses of their communities—for a time.

These practices are contrary both to the council-manager concept and to the principles of democratic self-government. The city manager is not directly responsible to the people. Final and effective authority for major policy decisions should reside only in those citizens—the members of the elected legislative body—who are directly answerable to the people. City councils must exercise their rightful prerogatives and must assert their supremacy over their city managers. It is the duty of the city manager to help his city council to perform its most important duties thoroughly and well.

On the other hand, the fact that the city manager serves at the pleasure of a political body sometimes may make him unduly sensitive to the city council and may cause him to weaken in his role as a professional man. A weak manager, of doubtful professional integrity, is as unsatisfactory as a politically strong manager. The city manager must satisfy the dominant majority of the council to maintain his position. Because he must, particularly if the council has no effective minority, some managers fail to stand up for their department heads when professional recommendations conflict with purely political considerations; instead, they try to quash disputes and present an image of a harmonious, smoothly functioning administration. "Don't rock the boat" is their motto. I believe that constructive controversy is natural and essential in democratic political affairs. There will always be understandable differences of opinion and judgment among professional men. These differences should be expected—indeed, looked for and encouraged—and should be easily and openly expressed to the council.

I believe that some of the most important features of the council-manager form will be retained during the next evolutionary development of municipal government, although there will be some changes of fundamental importance. Changes will be required by the reality of widespread partisan political activity in local affairs and by the realization that the manager should not permit himself to become a political leader. Democratic government at the local level will always, by definition, be pluralistic to a considerable extent; citizen commissions and principal department heads must have access to the council on an equal footing with the city manager when natural differences of political and professional judgment are evident and when a judgment has been made by the council that it must debate an issue vigorously to educate the community and maintain control.

City managers have been a tremendous boon to both city councils and city planners. However, the argument is still heard that the training and orientation of the city manager predispose him to take a short-range view. He is pictured as a man of action, rather than as a man of ideas. Supposedly, he is not apt to be sympathetic to the kind of long-range policies which concern city planners. While there is, I believe, some truth to these claims, they do not qualify as valid generalizations. The central-management concept places great reliance on long-range planning of all kinds. City managers obviously should be concerned with the future, and most experienced and successful city managers have established their reputations very largely as results of their ability to help their councils formulate and use long-range policies.

THE CITY COUNCIL

Regardless of the form of government, the city council is, and should be, the principal legislative and policy-making authority of municipal government. It is the city council that must enact legislation and make important decisions every week at its regular meetings, ranging from broad policies to minute details.

Under a council-manager municipal government, there is no question as to the formal supremacy of the council. Under a strong-mayor government, it is true that the mayor is directly responsible to the people and that he often has a platform of broad policies and definite projects. However, the council still passes the laws, is responsible for final action on the budget and the capital-improvement program, sets the tax rate, and is, without question, the final policy-making authority. The political power and initiative that can be exercised by the mayor give him a key role in the formulation of the policies finally acted upon by the council; but the mayor's primary responsibilities are those of a chief executive. Dominant members of the council usually serve several terms, making the council more stable and not so liable to the drastic policy changes which may occur when one mayor succeeds another.

For practical reasons, once a community has increased in population beyond a certain size, the people do not govern themselves directly, but do so through representatives whom they elect. The people exercise their control when they vote for their representatives, normally every two years. They also express their will directly at bond-issue elections and on other questions subject to the referendum. Citizen participation is to be encouraged at all times, so that the councilmen will be informed of the views of their constituents. However, the councilmen should be leaders of the community and should use their own best judgment of the public interest, rather than rely on public-opinion surveys, straw votes, or the protests voiced at hearings. Similarly, they should not permit themselves to be unduly influenced by the views and political pressures expressed and exerted by nonelected community leaders. It is their duty to govern on behalf of the entire community, and not just of special groups.[3]

Many attempts have been made to dissipate the power of the city council. One approach has been to establish a host of independent government bodies, such as the hundreds of special-purpose districts found in California. Such situations have inevitably produced confusion and conflict. They make effective coordination and control of local government difficult. It would be better to place all of the functions of local government under the control of the municipal government and its legislative body.

Another drain on the council's authority has been the creation of semiautonomous commissions and agencies within the over-all structure of city government. Often city charters deliberately provide for such arrangements. One example has been the independent city-planning commission. Such efforts tend to produce a multiheaded government in which authority and responsibility are harmfully diffused.

One motive behind this whittling away at the council's domain is to enhance the position of the "experts" in the government. When a specialized

---

[3] Every community has a political structure which can be distinguished from its formal governmental structure. The general-plan concept presented in this book takes this duality into account. It is assumed that there will continue to be an increasing interest by individual citizens in municipal affairs, and that this will gradually create a situation in which the influential leaders of both the formal and informal governing groups will find it in their interests to develop, control, and use a general plan to guide the physical development of their community.

agency is relatively independent of the council, its professionals and technicians enjoy more freedom. These people are often afraid that their supposedly impartial judgments will be subject to the political maneuverings of the council; they want to be "above" politics.

Again, I would like to emphasize that it is contrary to the political philosophy of democracy to place government in the hands of administrators who are not directly responsible to the people. Career administrators become dangerous when they begin to assume that they are able to interpret the public interest better than the legislative body. No matter what the field of the public official, his work will involve important value judgments which offer valid subject matter for public debate.

While the city council should make the final determinations of municipal policy, this view does not imply that the council should make policy alone and unaided. Quite the contrary. The chief executive plays a prominent role in initiating and recommending policy, while other municipal officials also advise the council. Furthermore, interested and influential citizens participate in policy-making by expressing their wishes and opinions to the legislators.

The concentration of authority in the city council places it in a decisive role. The success or failure of the entire local government will depend largely on how well the council does its job. The councilmen must accept their responsibility and strive to live up to their challenge. Therefore, the key question is whether or not the councilmen are to be trusted with this responsibility.

It is true that the performance of councilmen is often disappointing. Many councilmen are elected not on the basis of their ability or their views, but on the basis of their popularity. Many councilmen seem to be mediocre: they straddle the fence, they try to please everyone, they are afraid or unable to face reality when it is unfamiliar to them. There are some who are even worse, who display bigotry, stupidity, inexcusable ignorance, and favoritism.

On the other hand, there are many capable and intelligent councilmen who are doing excellent jobs. They have integrity and they influence and lead their fellow councilmen and fellow citizens. Councilmen do not always rely on their administrators for ideas; they conceive and initiate sound proposals on their own far more frequently than is generally realized. Not infrequently it is apparent to close observers that legislators have stronger convictions and are willing to go further than administrators. Although it is not generally recognized, the leaders of practically every city council are influential primarily because of their intelligence, knowledge, logic, and personal leadership, and not because of their political affiliations.

Disenchantment with councilmen causes many people to develop a deep distrust of city councils. Distrust stimulated the attempts at the turn of the century to weaken the power of the council and to insulate much of the government from it. Distrust is reflected in the post-1900 charters of many cities. This viewpoint shaped the early philosophy of the American city-planning movement and had a dominant influence on the practice of city planning until after World War II.

I do not think the solution to this problem is to attempt to deprive the city council of its authority. The effective and democratic functioning of municipal government requires that authority and responsibility be clearly visible. The city council can be made to work effectively by clarifying its most important duties and procedures.[4] City councils spend too much time on routine matters, which they must act upon formally as required by law. On the other hand, many important policy issues are never brought before the council in a way that can be understood, openly debated, and clearly decided. Instruments should and can be developed which will assist the council in accepting its responsibility and exercising its authority. The general plan for physical development, as defined in this book, is such an instrument.

THE ROLE OF CITY PLANNING IN LOCAL GOVERNMENT

City planning has had to find its place in the complex, constantly evolving institutions which are American local government. Different beliefs concerning human nature and the practical validity of the democratic philosophy of government which is part of our heritage have led to different proposals concerning the place of city planning in municipal government. In general, there are three different concepts of the role of city planning. They are discussed under the following three headings:

(1) An Independent Activity of the City-Planning Commission
(2) A Staff Aide to the Chief Executive
(3) A Policy-Making Activity of the City Council

---

[4] Most councilmen want to and are sincerely trying to do a good job, although their attempts under present conditions may at times seem abortive. The only answer to the problem for one who has faith in democracy is to help the councilmen to do their jobs better. Often they do not understand simply because no one has devoted himself to the task of teaching them how to perform their most important duties. To a great extent, councilmen learn their jobs from the administrators they work with, and sometimes these administrators are poor teachers. It is the responsibility of every professional in city government to educate his council and to assist them in performing their jobs properly.

(1) An Independent Activity of the City-Planning Commission

This concept holds that city planning should be independent and insulated from the mainstream of political and administrative affairs. The city planner is seen as a technical expert who should not be subjected to political influence. The body in charge of city planning is the citizen commission, which is semiautonomous. The commission is usually given some control over the city council by the requirement of a greater-than-majority vote of the council to overrule a recommendation by the commission. This concept reflects a basic distrust of the city council.

The independent-commission concept of the role of city planning predominated during the years prior to World War II, and it is still held by many city planners, especially those whose experience has been limited to the larger cities with the strong-mayor form of government. The San Francisco, Cleveland, and Philadelphia city-planning agencies are current examples of this approach to city planning. The authors of the 1928 Standard City Planning Enabling Act, especially Alfred Bettman and Edward M. Bassett, believed in the concept of the independent city-planning commission. Bassett said of the master plan: "It should be kept within the four walls of the city planning commission." [5] The 1928 Act, which is examined in detail in the next chapter, had a great influence on city-planning legislation throughout the country; consequently the organization it prescribed, with an independent citizen planning commission, is still in common use. The Act, which was prepared as a model, was adopted by many state legislatures and cities during the early 1930's.

One able and experienced contemporary proponent of the independent-commission concept is John T. Howard. His views are not as extreme as those of the pioneers of the city-planning profession, but he does believe, as they did, that the city-planning commission should be the primary client of the professional city planner.[6] He recognizes the importance of city planning to the council, but argues that the council does not have enough time to give it the attention that it must have.

Rexford G. Tugwell has been another strong advocate of the independent-commission concept. His view of the planning agency as a "fourth

[5] Edward M. Bassett, *The Master Plan* (New York: Russell Sage Foundation, 1938), p. 142.

[6] See John T. Howard, "In Defense of Planning Commissions," *Journal of the American Institute of Planners,* Vol. 17, No. 2 (Spring, 1951), pp. 89–94.

THE ROLE OF CITY PLANNING IN MUNICIPAL GOVERNMENT

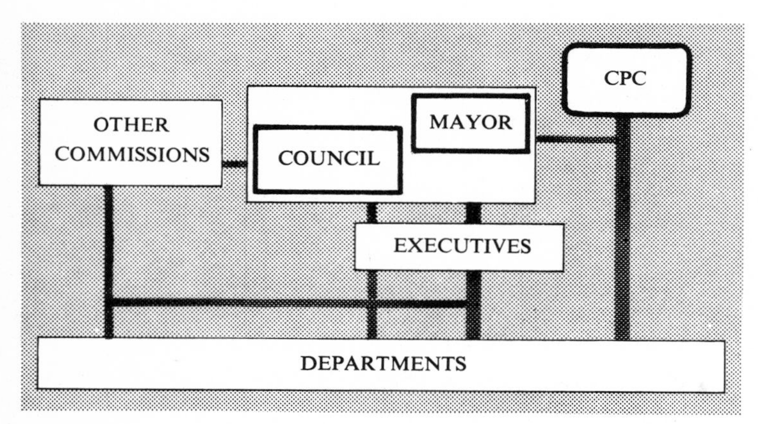

1. AN INDEPENDENT ACTIVITY OF THE CITY-PLANNING COMMISSION

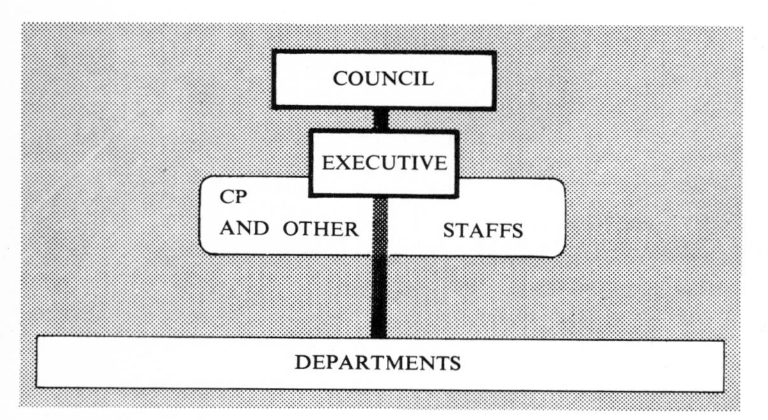

2. A STAFF AIDE TO THE CHIEF EXECUTIVE

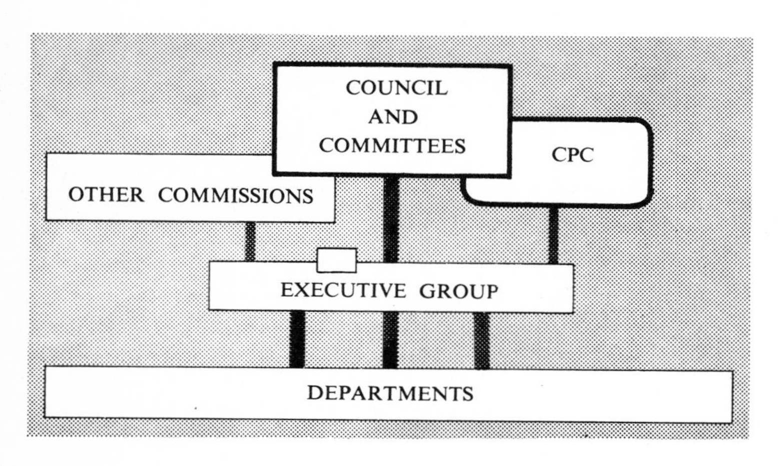

3. A POLICY-MAKING ACTIVITY OF THE CITY COUNCIL

power," in addition to the executive, legislative, and judicial powers set forth in the United States Constitution, has had much influence. Tugwell was very distrustful of both city councils and chief executives. He also was opposed to any subject-matter limitation on the scope of the planners.

The heyday of the independent city-planning commission came to an end in the 1940's when permanent professional staffs began to be established throughout the country. The assertion of control over the independent commissions by the appointing authorities—either the city council or the mayor—came with the increases in budgets and influence of the commissions. In the minds of some observers, the change was significantly speeded up by the publication in 1941 of Robert A. Walker's study [7] of thirty-seven city-planning commissions. Walker's conclusions constituted a telling indictment of the independent commission, which he showed was not doing the job it was supposed to do and was not having much effect on community development. Walker advocated, in effect, the elimination of the citizen planning commission.

(2) A Staff Aide to the Chief Executive

Walker favored the second concept of the role of city planning, under which the planning director is a staff aide to the chief executive and the planning commission advises and assists the planning director. Today this is the most popular view among city planners, particularly in council-manager cities, where the chief executive is appointed, not elected. The staff-aide concept is actually an outgrowth of the central-management idea, and it is incorporated in most public-administration texts.

According to the staff-aide concept, the planning director is a full-fledged department head who reports to the chief executive. The planning director is a confidential advisor to the chief executive and a member of his cabinet. The chief executive is regarded as the head planner of the administration and presents all planning matters to the city council. The planning director is regarded as the executive's lieutenant in charge of central planning and research activities. The scope of the planning agency advocated by Walker has no subject-matter limits; it is as broad as the scope of city government.

Under the arrangement advocated by Walker, the city-planning commission is largely superfluous, although in practice it continues to exist. There

[7] Robert A. Walker, *The Planning Function in Urban Government* (Chicago: University of Chicago Press, 1941). Second Edition, 1950.

are, in fact, no clear-cut examples of the organization for planning as advocated by Walker. Most council-manager cities have attempted, unsuccessfully, to move in the direction of this concept at one time or another, but there are no longer any recognized advocates of this concept in its pure form. Some central-management advocates regard the commission as an advisory body to the planning director, and some, as an advisory body to the chief executive. The staff-aide concept also views the planner primarily as a technical expert. It implies that planning is too esoteric to be comprehensible to city councilmen except as interpreted to them by the chief executive. However, this concept recognizes the practical implications of planning and the need to bring planning into closer contact with the everyday affairs of city government.

(3) A Policy-Making Activity of the City Council

The third concept holds that the city council is the primary client of the city-planning agency because it is the final policy-making authority in municipal government. This is my belief, and it is upon this concept that I base my definition of the primary uses of the general plan. At present, a minority of the city-planning profession holds this view.[8]

The concept of the role of city planning as a policy-making activity of the city council regards the city council not only as the body which must be relied upon to make all the final decisions on major policy questions, but it also regards the members of the council as being capable of understanding what it is that they must do if effective civic-improvement programs are to be developed and sustained. The city-planning commission in this concept is advisory to the council, and the professional director and staff are advisory to the commission. The city-planning director presents the recommendations of the commission to the city council.

The chief executive's importance is recognized, and the city-planning director and staff also serve and advise him. Thus, the city-planning director has two bosses, the city-planning commission and the chief executive. I be-

[8] I have advocated this concept since 1954 when I described its main component ideas to the Fourth Biennial Institute of Mayors and Councilmen held by the League of California Cities in a statement entitled "Guiding City Development: A Major Responsibility of the City Council." (See published *Proceedings of the 1954 Institute.*) In this concept the scope of the city-planning agency is limited to matters concerned primarily with the general physical development of the community; it assumes that the need for long-range planning to meet financial, social, and other community problems, when recognized, will lead to the establishment of separate, parallel, and cooperating planning agencies.

lieve that this dualism formalizes relationships that cannot be avoided or eliminated. These relationships must be recognized and, indeed, encouraged if the city-planning activities *of the council* are to be as effective as I believe most city councils and most chief executives want them to be. The Berkeley city-planning agency is a good example of this form of organization.[9]

This concept places city planning in the mainstream of government by putting it in the hands of the city council. Fixing the responsibility of the council for city planning should be beneficial to both the city planner and the city council. It gives the city planner and the city-planning commission a much greater chance of having their proposals understood and realized. It helps the city council, which must make a number of important decisions at every weekly meeting affecting the physical development of the community.

The policy-making concept supports centralization of power and the concentration of this power in the city council. It necessarily assumes confidence in the councilmen and the belief that they are competent to understand and decide on city-planning matters. This concept accepts the fact that city planning is as much political in nature as it is professional and technical.

This concept of the role of city planning holds that the city-planning commission is not autonomous; it is subordinate to the council, but it does have a role of vital importance. The commission serves as the principal advisor of the council on all city-planning matters of major importance. The commission must be trusted and respected by the council, which requires that the commissioners be appointed by and serve at the pleasure of the council. Like councilmen, the commissioners are laymen, but they devote much more time and attention to city planning and in time acquire an understanding of the technical aspects of city planning.[10]

The city-planning director is regarded as the principal advisor of the commission. He is also the chief administrator of the city-planning depart-

---

[9] A complete description of this organization, and of the important role played by City Manager John Phillips in creating it over a ten-year period, is included in a case study of the *Berkeley Master Plan.* The manuscript, by Warren Campbell, describing this study is scheduled for publication in 1964 in the Inter-University Case Program series.

[10] I believe that the commission, although its members may not be councilmen, should view its role as being that of a "committee of the council" on city-planning matters in order to indicate clearly the close tie between the two bodies while at the same time emphasizing the superior role and responsibility of the city council. I also believe that if the membership of the council is increased significantly, as is typical of most cities in Europe, the commission ought to be replaced by an actual committee of council members.

ment. The proposals of the staff should go from the city-planning director through the commission to the city council.

The city-planning director must also work closely with the chief executive and seek to coordinate city-planning activity within the over-all administrative program of the city government. The chief executive must be regularly informed in advance concerning all items on the commission-meeting agendas. The chief executive should be consulted on controversial proposals before they are presented to the city-planning commission. However, the executive should not dictate what goes to the commission. After the commission and the chief executive have considered all proposals, there is no reason why they should not submit opposing recommendations to the city council. The council is capable of understanding why officers and agencies under its control will, at times, have different points of view and recommendations for them to consider. The council will welcome this kind of direct relationship on major issues and will be able to make its final decisions better understood because of the open debate that precedes them.

The general-plan concept outlined in this book is based on the premise that the city-planning process should be designed to involve directly and continuously the city council and the city-planning commission, and not just the city-planning staff and the chief executive.

THE GENERAL PLAN DEFINED

A definition of the general plan for the physical development of a community is appropriate at this point, although the meaning of the phrase as I use it will become clearer and sharper as the exposition proceeds. I advance this definition: *The general plan is the official statement of a municipal legislative body which sets forth its major policies concerning desirable future physical development; the published general-plan document must include a single, unified general physical design for the community, and it must attempt to clarify the relationships between physical-development policies and social and economic goals.*

"Master plan" is the traditional phrase, while sometimes "city plan" and "comprehensive plan" are used. Essentially, the phrases are synonymous with "general plan," but each has subtle connotations of its own. I began to use "general plan" in 1948 because it seemed to give a more accurate emphasis to the broad policy nature of the plan. This phrase is now widely used.

There are three basic physical elements of the urban environment which are dealt with in virtually every published general plan: land use, circulation, and community facilities. Land use refers to the use of *private* property for commercial, industrial, and residential purposes. I prefer to identify the land-use section of the plan as the "working-and-living-areas section" because this phrase emphasizes basic human activities, rather than the convenient but frequently misleading method of simply classifying the way land is used. The phrase "land use" is also confusing because it has been used to refer to all physical elements dealt with in the plan, since community facilities and streets are, in fact, uses of land. The section of the plan dealing with the circulation element is concerned primarily with the street-and-highway system and the public-transportation routes and stations. The community-facilities section of the plan deals with the variety of *public* activities that involve physical development, such as schools, parks, playgrounds, and the civic center.

I believe that the general plan also should include sections on a civic-design element and a utilities element. The section on the civic-design element should focus on the major physical features and policy decisions of the plan which are the result of aesthetic judgments. The section on the utilities element should deal with water supply, drainage, sewage disposal, and other utility systems insofar as the other physical elements of the plan depend on them.

In addition to these five physical elements, with which every community is concerned, each city has particular needs which may call for additional sections in its general-plan document. There might be sections devoted to historic districts or to areas designated for comprehensive redevelopment. The *Berkeley Master Plan,* for example, has special sections dealing with waterfront development and with the campus of the University of California in Berkeley.

With respect to presentation, the general-plan document should include a comprehensive large-scale drawing of the general physical design of the whole community and a written summary describing the major policies and proposals of the plan. A statement of community goals, including a description of the primary and secondary social and economic roles that the city is to play in the region, should be a key feature of every general plan.

Most existing plan documents include overviews of essential background material concerning population, the local and regional economy, the geographic setting, and the historical development of the community and its government in relation to city planning. The plan document also should include an assessment of the present conditions in the community, pointing out major problems and issues. The opportunities and needs of the future should be discussed. Assumptions and forecasts should be stated.

The bulk of the plan document should consist of a full description of the proposals, standards, and principles which are intended to guide physical development toward the desired goals. These four things—goals, proposals, standards, and principles—are crystallized in the unified general physical design of the plan. From them will emerge the basic, major policies of the plan that should be plainly stated in the summary, together with the major physical-design proposals and a schematic drawing of the general physical design.

Policies are the most important ingredients of the general plan. *A policy is a generalized guide to conduct which, although subject to modification, does imply commitment.* To me, therefore, there can be no such thing as a flexible plan, since there can be no such thing as a flexible policy in relation to physical development. A so-called "flexible" plan is no plan at all. A policy carries no legal force; it is not irrevocably binding. A specific decision to act is not a policy; it should, however, be based on and express a policy. A standard dictionary defines policy as "a settled or definite course . . ."

The relationships between the major physical-design proposals of the plan and the most important city-planning standards and principles used in making the plan should be stated. It is not possible to make a plan that does not express significant value judgments concerning standards, such as the desirable size of elementary-school sites, or concerning principles, such as the desirability of separating industrial activities from residential districts. Because city-planning standards and principles are not scientifically determined and because they have a major and direct impact on the final set of physical-design proposals in the plan, the value judgments and relationships that are implicit should be made as explicit as possible.

Since there can be no plan without decisions rejecting certain alternatives and adopting others, and since the understanding and support necessary to implement the plan require constant explanation of the reasoning expressed in the final plan, the major alternatives that were considered and rejected by the legislative body should be described in the plan document. Finally, there should be—and usually is in existing plans—a separate section devoted to a general discussion of the methods by which the plan will be carried out.

As an expression of desirable physical development, the general plan is an affirmation of goals. It is not a prediction, although its policies and proposals, which express its physical-development goals, to be reasonable, should be within the range of what is judged to be possible. The general plan is a statement of willful intention.

The general plan is not a program. It states the desired ends, but does not specify the means for achieving them. Thus it should not include schedules, priorities, or cost estimates; these things can be handled in implementary documents which spell out the means for achieving the desired ends. The general plan should have inspirational value; it should not be inhibited by short-term practical considerations. The fact that it is inspirational does not mean that the plan will be impractical. Every long-range plan must be based on judgments concerning the relative necessity and relative feasibility of overcoming short-range practical objections.

It is not correct to view the general plan as an ideal picture of the community at some date in the future. Because of the incremental, gradual nature of community development, no fixed date can apply to all the goals, policies, and proposals expressed in the general plan. Because of the dynamic character of the subject matter of the plan and, therefore, of the plan itself, the end-state depicted is ever changing, always moving into the future well ahead of the present.

City planners today talk about all sorts of plans, and some would make a number of different plans integral parts of the general plan for physical development. There are city planners who talk about the financial plan, the economic plan, the social plan, the public-services plan, all reflecting fundamentally different conceptions concerning the substantive scope of city planning. A comprehensive-policies plan has been suggested which would include all of these plans and, by implication, others such as a school-curriculum plan, since it is an expression of public policy of paramount importance to the future of the community. Some planners talk about an urban-form plan, looking fifty years into the future, while others talk about a middle-range, detailed, community-renewal plan, the latter having a time lead of ten to fifteen years.

I have no doubt that some of these concepts will prove to be useful and that the useful concepts will emerge as new policy-control instruments. However, for the purposes of this book, I am concerned only with the general plan that focuses on the physical development of a community and looks at least twenty to thirty years into the future. City plans of this sort, in one form or another, always have been and always will be essential for every responsible municipal government. This is the kind of plan widely used, in one form or another, in cities in the United States today.

I do not think any other plans should be included in the general plan for physical development. However, since the general plan for physical development will increasingly be related more closely to other long-range policy and short-range program-control instruments which prove to be as necessary and as workable as the general plan is for its specific and limited uses, city planners, in cooperation with other planners in municipal government, will naturally be concerned with efforts to clarify the relationships between such control instruments.

Above all, the general plan for physical development should not include such detailed documents as the zoning ordinance, the capital-improvement program, and detailed district-development plans. These detailed implementary documents must be kept separate to avoid confusion of their distinctive features with the more important features of the general plan.

THE CLIENT OF THE GENERAL PLAN

The general plan must be formulated so as to be useful to many clients. However, since their needs will vary and at times be in conflict, it is necessary to determine the primary client of the plan—the client whose requirements must be met first. The different views on the primary client of the plan follow from the different concepts of the role of the city planning in local government.

Those who believe in the independent city-planning commission think that the general plan should be designed primarily for the use of the commission. If the plan is to be adopted, it should be adopted only by the commission. This was common practice during the early period of the development of city planning. Under this arrangement, the city council is required to refer all physical-development matters to the commission for its recommendations. But, according to Bassett, "The commission and not the plan should be the advisor of the legislative body and the various departments." [11] The plan is for the guidance of the commission only, and need not ever be published and made generally available.

Those who see the city-planning director as a staff aide to the chief executive think the general plan should be shaped to serve the chief executive. The staff-aide concept has not been put into practice; there is no published general plan that has been designed expressly for the use of the chief executive. Although there are exceptions, experience indicates that the typical chief executive does not want a long-range plan to follow that will be publicly identified as his plan; he wants recommendations from the city planners on specific proposals. Thus, the staff-aide concept of the role of city planning usually emphasizes the idea that the plan must be "flexible," and avoids all

---

[11] Bassett, *The Master Plan,* pp. 67–68.

attempts to establish a unified set of objectives and a definite physical design for the community toward which current actions may be directed.

There are city planners who believe that the principal client of the plan should be the professional staff. This idea does not fit into any of the three concepts of the role of city planning presented earlier. However, it seems to be gaining popularity, perhaps because many city planners are uncertain as to their role and because some of the leaders of the profession today do not believe it is possible to make a useful plan for a city in view of the technological, social, and economic changes that make any kind of long-range planning so difficult. Those who hold this view usually also consider city planning to be too technical to be understood by laymen, including those laymen who become city councilmen. They also tend to believe that the city planner is best suited to interpret the public interest. Some want planning to be isolated from politics. Others believe that planning is highly political and that the planner should be a behind-the-scenes politician. Planners who hold these views sometimes prepare plans for themselves to use as a basis for making recommendations to the city-planning commission or chief executive, but they do not reveal their plans.

I believe that the city council should be the principal client of the general plan, and that the plan should be prepared for active use by the council. This belief follows from my belief that city planning is primarily a policy-making activity of the city council. Every important physical-development policy with which municipal government is involved must eventually come before the city council for final determination and action. Effective city planning cannot be sustained without the responsible participation of the council.

The general plan, thus, should be conceived of primarily as a legislative-policy instrument, rather than as a complex technical instrument to be understood only by the professional staff and possibly some members of the city-planning commission. In reality, every city-planning decision of significance must sooner or later be made in the council chamber; such decisions cannot be made in the city-planning office. The men who initially formulate a plan must follow through and present it, with its controversial judgments exposed, to the members of the council in terms that are understandable to the council. The professional planners must seek to make their technical findings and professional judgments convincing to the councilmen.

Some planners would not even show the general plan to the council, but most planners now recognize that the council must be involved with the plan in some way. One concept—erroneous in my opinion—is that the general plan is a kind of ideal picture which the council can look at when making decisions. Councilmen can compare their own judgments against the staff-made plan, but they can disagree with it whenever they wish. I believe that the general plan is not something for the council to compare its policies with; it should contain the policies of the council. If the council finds that it disagrees with the plan, it should change the plan.

Some city planners argue that councilmen do not have the time to acquire understanding of a plan, much less decide what should go into it. It is true that deliberation over the general plan will occupy much of the councilmen's time; but, from the viewpoint of the community as a whole, this is one of the most important subjects to which the council should regularly devote its attention.

Another argument some city planners pose against council control and official adoption of the general plan is that this procedure will make the plan static (that it will "ossify" the plan, to use a favorite word of Bassett). It is true that ossification would be fatal for the plan. At all times the plan should reflect the current policies of the council. The plan must change when the policies change.

Admittedly, some legislators deliberately shun their responsibility for determining policy. They do not want to commit themselves to long-range policies which might prove bothersome or embarrassing later. They want to reserve the option to make all decisions on an *ad hoc* basis without regard for consistency. They call this *ad hoc* procedure "deciding an issue on its merits." This attitude increases the opportunities for favoritism and allows councilmen to decide an issue by counting up the potential votes on both sides.

From my own experience with city councils, I believe that most councilmen do want to be reasonable—they do, in other words, want to deal with problems and needs by establishing long-range policies and maintaining consistency in their actions in order to make some tangible progress. They feel an acute need for a guide in passing on the diverse, complex physical-development matters that come before them every week. A frequently voiced question at council meetings is: "What is our policy on this kind of matter?" Often this is answered by referring to previous decisions, regarded as precedents, on similar matters. It would be better answered by referring to well-thought-out policies expressed in the form of a general plan.

The general plan answers this need of councilmen for a policy guide on physical-development matters. It will inevitably compel commitment or opposition to its policies. It will severely limit the latitude of action by legislators who cannot learn to think of the long-range implications of their actions. But once the general plan has been understood and adopted as a result of favorable action by a majority of the members of the council, it will provide a written and graphic record of the policies and the definite physical design on which the council has agreed. The general plan will then become the basis upon which the council will gradually shape a positive physical-improvement program that the entire community will understand and implement.

THE PURPOSES OF THE GENERAL PLAN

The statement in this section of the broad purposes of the general plan for physical development derives from my own concept of the plan. The purposes are not all necessarily peculiar to the general plan; some are also the purposes of city planning in general and of local government in general. The fundamental purposes which the general-plan process is intended to achieve are as follows:

(1) *To improve the physical environment of the community as a setting for human activities—to make it more functional, beautiful, decent, healthful, interesting, and efficient.* This purpose is in accord with the broad objective of local government to promote the health, safety, morals, order, convenience, prosperity, and general welfare of the community. These phrases are customarily associated with the police power; they actually pertain to all acts of government.

(2) *To promote the public interest, the interest of the community at large, rather than the interests of individuals or special groups within the community.* The comprehensive nature of the general plan contributes to this purpose, for it facilitates consideration of the relationship of any question to the over-all physical development of the entire community. Because the plan is based on facts and on studies that attempt to be thorough and impartial, it helps to prevent arbitrary, capricious, and biased actions. The contributions of the plan to democratic, responsible government help to safeguard the public interest.

(3) *To facilitate the democratic determination and implementation of community policies on physical development.* The plan is primarily a policy instrument. The plan constitutes a declaration of long-range goals and provides the basis for a program to accomplish the goals. By placing

the responsibility for determining policies on the city council and providing an opportunity for citizen participation, the plan facilitates the democratic process.

(4) *To effect political and technical coordination in community development.* Political coordination signifies that a large majority within the community is working toward the same ends. Technical coordination means a logical relationship among the physical elements dealt with in the plan and the most efficient planning and scheduling of actual improvements so as to avoid conflict, duplication, and waste. Effective coordination of such a complex subject requires a unified, integrated plan if the physical elements of the environment are to be managed without costly conflicts of function and if the political forces of the community are to deal with controversial development issues, including the plan itself, in a constructive manner.

(5) *To inject long-range considerations into the determination of short-range actions.* In effect, this purpose is intended to achieve coordination through time, to attempt to make sure that today's decision will lead toward tomorrow's goal. The extensive use of forecasts and the establishment of long-range goals are significant features of the general plan. The plan represents an effort to add the important time dimension to the decision-making process.

(6) *To bring professional and technical knowledge to bear on the making of political decisions concerning the physical development of the community.* This purpose is intended to promote wiser decision-making, to achieve informed, constructive government. Through the general plan, the special knowledge of the professional city planner is brought into play in the democratic political process.

II

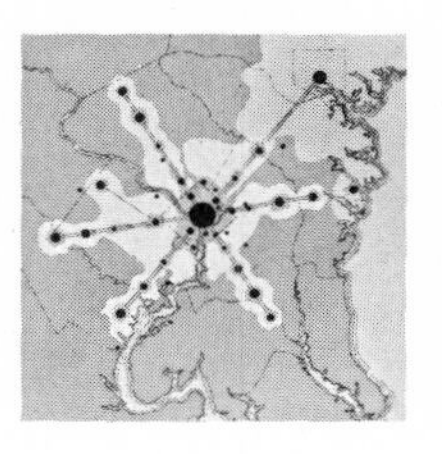

FIFTY YEARS OF EXPERIENCE WITH THE GENERAL PLAN

IN THIS chapter an attempt will be made to develop a historical perspective that will enable us to understand the significance of the first fifty years of experience and experimentation with the general plan. We turn our attention first to the initial concept of the general plan as it was formulated by Frederick Law Olmsted and Alfred Bettman in response to the needs of the municipal government officials who sought their advice during the period between 1910 and 1930. During these years mayors, councilmen, and civic leaders throughout the United States first became aware that municipal governments alone were responsible for guiding the over-all physical development of their communities, and that this responsibility was going to remain, of necessity, in their hands.

The general-plan concept embodied in the 1928 Standard City Planning Enabling Act is examined next. A full appreciation of the basic ideas expressed by the authors of this historic "crystallization" is essential. The 1928 Act was widely adopted by cities throughout the United States and was one of the major causes of the confusion that characterized city-planning practice with respect to the general plan during the 1930's and 1940's.

General-plan experience following World War II is then reviewed briefly, and an attempt is made to understand the lessons of fifty years of experimentation in the United States with the general-plan concept. The conclusions thus drawn provide the basis for the new approach and redefinition of the general-plan concept suggested in this book as to the primary client, legislative uses, and characteristics of the urban general plan for the physical development of a community.

THE OLMSTED CONCEPTION OF THE GENERAL PLAN

Among the early leaders of the American city-planning profession, Frederick Law Olmsted, Jr., stands out as a most remarkable man. Born in 1870 and introduced by his father, a great landscape architect and pioneer city planner, to the challenge and opportunity of the new profession, Olmsted was mature and ready for the great surge of municipal reform and city-planning work that came just after the turn of the century. His city plans and his writings on the subject of the general plan are marked by their simplicity, their logic, and their expression of quiet confidence in the natural desire and ability of the American people to greatly improve their cities once they understood how this could be done. To Olmsted, the need for a general plan in carrying on the never-ending task of governing the physical growth and development of a city was taken for granted. He was a superb spokesman for the new profession in explaining what the general plan was concerned with, how it should be used, and the essential physical elements with which it should deal.

In 1911, in a statement presented to the National Conference on City Planning, Olmsted described the scope of city planning and the subject matter of the general plan in the following words:

> The fact is we are concerned with a single complex subject, namely, the intelligent control and guidance of the entire physical growth and alteration of cities; embracing all the problems of relieving and avoiding congestion—congestion of people in buildings and of buildings upon land, congestion of transportation facilities or of recreation facilities, congestion in respect to the means of supplying light, air, water, or anything else essential to the health and happiness of the people, but also embracing in addition to the problems of congestion, each one of the myriad problems involved in making our cities year by year, in their physical arrangement and equipment, healthier, pleasanter and more economical instruments for the use of the people who dwell within them in carrying on that part of the work and life of the world which is not to be done in the open country.

Having thus described and defined the subject matter of the general plan in terms that are as appropriate today as they were more than fifty years ago, Olmsted went on to state his understanding of the major political and technical purposes of the general plan. The general-plan concept worked out by Olmsted may be restated in contemporary terms as follows: The governing groups of every city sooner or later will recognize the technical necessity and the obvious political advantages of guiding the physical growth and development of their community in accordance with a general plan. This plan, which will be long-range and, as a necessary consequence, general in nature, will deal comprehensively with all significant aspects of the physical environment. It will deal with the physical elements involved in the general location and extent of (a) the working-and-living areas of the city; (b) the community facilities judged to be necessary and desirable in relation to the commercial, industrial, residential, and civic activities provided for in the working-and-living-areas section of the plan; and (c) a circulation system designed to accommodate the anticipated movement of people and goods within the city and within the larger region of which the city is a part.

Olmsted's concept plainly recognized that the plan could not avoid dealing with important controversial issues that would be of direct concern to the governing groups, however they might be organized, and that because of this some procedure would have to be worked out to keep the plan up to date and in accord with the judgments of the leaders of the community at any given period, while at the same time assuring the maintenance of a public record of other significant ideas that might prove to be acceptable in the future.

THE BETTMAN GENERAL-PLAN CONCEPT

A few years after Olmsted spoke at the 1911 Conference, Alfred Bettman became interested in city planning and began his long and constructive association with the city-planning profession. Mr. Bettman was born in 1873, studied law at Harvard, and was active before World War I in the municipal reform movement in his home city of Cincinnati. His experience as city solicitor in the successful reform administration in Cincinnati made him aware of the need for city planning. Following the war, his interest in the new profession was reawakened and, while he continued to practice law, city planning gradually became the dominant interest of his life.

By the end of the 1920's, Alfred Bettman had become one of the acknowledged leaders of the city-planning profession. His broad intellectual interests and educational background, his sustained local experience as a Cincinnati civic leader, and the wealth of experience that he had gained throughout the United States as an expert on the subject of city-planning legislation led him to formulate and advocate definite ideas about the scope, uses, and nature of the general plan. He and Olmsted undoubtedly were influenced and stimulated by one another, but Alfred Bettman was pre-eminently a man who thought things out for himself. What he had to say concerning the general plan at this period in his career is, therefore, of great significance. Speaking before the Twentieth Annual National Conference on City Planning in 1928, he said:

> A city plan is a master design for the physical development of the territory of the city. It constitutes a plan of the division of the land between public and private uses, specifying the general location and extent of new public improvements, grounds and structures, such as new, widened or extended streets, boulevards, parkways or other public utilities and the location of public buildings, such as schools, police stations, fire stations; and, in the case of private developments, the general distribution amongst various classes of uses, such as residential, business and industrial uses. The plan should be designed for a considerable period in the future, twenty-five to fifty years. It should be based, therefore, upon a comprehensive and detailed survey of things as they are at the time of the planning, such as the existing distribution of existing developments, both public and private, the trends toward redistribution and growth of population, industry and business, estimates of future trends of growth and distribution of population and industry, and the allotment of the territory of the city in accordance with all such data and estimated trends, so as to provide the necessary public facilities and the necessary area for private development corresponding to the needs of the community, present and prospective.

Bettman's description of the general plan specifies more exactly than the 1911 statement by Olmsted the essential physical elements to be dealt with in the general plan. Bettman's concept is similar to Olmsted's in that it assumes the same subject-matter focus for the plan; it assumes the same general purposes that the plan must be designed to serve; it calls for the same qualities of generalness and comprehensiveness.

Because of the basic agreements expressed by these two outstanding leaders of the city-planning profession, it might have been expected that no serious weaknesses would develop in the general-plan concept that had been defined and put into practice between 1910 and 1930. As a result of an unfortunate combination of circumstances, however, just as the profession was about to enter its first major period of expansion during the 1930's, the lessons of the initial years of experience that were distilled in the Bettman-Olmsted general-plan concept were ignored, misinterpreted, or actively challenged by the next generation of men and women who entered the profession at this time. And as we shall see, the uneven way in which the practice of city planning was developing also caused Bettman and Olmsted themselves, as members of the committee that wrote the 1928 Standard City Planning Enabling Act, to contribute to the confusion that characterized the general-plan work of the 1930's and 1940's.

1930–1950: TWENTY YEARS OF CONFUSION

While Olmsted and Bettman and their colleagues in the young profession prior to 1930 were seeking to clarify their ideas about the general plan, they found themselves at the same time unavoidably engaged in what is now recognized as the second continuing phase of city-planning work. Following the formulation of a general plan, the next step in any sustained city-planning program calls for work on detailed proposals aimed at carrying out the plan. The existence of established municipal departments responsible for the design, construction, and administration of the proposed publicly owned projects that were included in every general plan kept the attention of city-planning commissions in connection with these features of the plan focused where it should have been—at the general physical-development-policy level. But the situation was completely different with regard to general-plan proposals concerned with private property.

Without any recognized public program or regular department of municipal government concerned with the privately owned working-and-living areas of the city—areas that combined amount to approximately one-half of the total land area of every city—it was only natural for most city-planning commissions and their professional advisers to move directly from the general-plan level to the detailed, regulatory level for the working-and-living-areas element of the physical environment. This was done during the 1920's at the request of city councils throughout the United States and resulted in the creation of what we now know as zoning ordinances. The emphasis given to this necessary activity at this particular time in the evolution of American city planning was the primary cause of a twenty-year period of confusion as to the basic purposes and nature of the general plan. There were other factors that contributed to what now may be seen as a temporary but unfortunate diversion of the city-planning profession from its principal task. But of all the causes for the uncertainty during the 1930's and 1940's as to the basic purposes and nature of the general plan—and, indeed, of city planning itself—the confusion between the zoning plan and the working-and-living-areas section of the general plan was paramount.

In order to appreciate the extent to which the remarkable pioneering work on the general-plan concept was obscured, it is helpful to consider in detail the definition of the general plan that is expressed in the 1928 Standard City Planning Enabling Act. I have, therefore, used the Act as the basic context in which to view and judge the major controversies and competing ideas that developed during the twenty-year period following its publication. Both Olmsted and Bettman were members of the committee that prepared this influential document. This fact alone, when one becomes fully aware of the contradictions expressed in the Act, is illuminating evidence of the difficulties that confronted the profession during this stage of its development in fashioning its principal concepts and policy instruments.

The 1928 Standard City Planning Enabling Act was prepared by a nine-man committee appointed by Secretary of Commerce Herbert Hoover from among the nation's most experienced and outstanding members of the city-planning profession. In his Foreword to the final report which presented the suggested Standard Act, Mr. Hoover clearly described the purpose of the undertaking and the main ideas expressed in the Act:

In several hundred American cities planning commissions are working with public officials and private groups in order to obtain more orderly and efficient physical development of their land area. They are concerned partly with rectifying past mistakes, but more with securing such location and development of streets, parks, public utilities, and public and private buildings as will best serve the needs of the people for their homes, their industry and trade, their travel about the city, and their recreation. The extent to which they succeed affects in no small degree the return, in terms of practical usefulness now and for years to come, of several hundred million dollars of taxpayers' money spent each year for public improvements, as well as the value and serviceability of new private construction costing several billion dollars each year.

The drafting of a standard city planning enabling act based on a careful analysis of the wide experience gained by these numerous local efforts was undertaken three years ago by the advisory committee on city planning and zoning of the Department of Commerce, in response to many requests. A State legislature, in adopting such an act, grants to cities the authority deemed necessary for effective planning and prescribes certain conditions as to planning organization and procedure.

The advisory committee members have each had many years of first-hand experience in coping with local planning problems, both as local citizens and in connection with the leading national business, professional, and civic groups which they represent. During their three years' work in drafting this act they have made laborious researches into legal problems and have consulted with expert planners, members of planning commissions, municipal officials, and other interested persons throughout the country.

The report recommends, first, a clearly defined permanent planning branch in the local government, in the form of *a commission which formulates a comprehensive plan and keeps it up to date. The commission* then *advises the legislative and executive branches of the municipality,* and the public, as to the importance of the plan and promotes conformance to it *in the laying out of new streets, the construction of public works and utilities, and the private development of land.* Close attention was given to every detail here, as elsewhere in the act, that would help make good planning popular and effective . . . [Emphasis added.]

It is vital for the reader to recognize the significance of the Standard Act and the great positive contribution that it made to the development of the American city-planning movement. In using it to illustrate and explain the difficulties of the city-planning profession during the 1930's and 1940's, I hope that the reader will attempt to appreciate as fully as possible the historical context within which the Act was conceived.

The 1928 Standard Act specifies as the principal duty of the city-planning commission the preparation, adoption, and maintenance of a long-range, comprehensive, general plan for the physical development of a city. In explaining the primary purposes of the plan, the manner in which it was to be used, and the nature of the plan, the authors became involved in all of the major questions that are dealt with in this book.

In the following discussion of the difficulties that developed in the application of the Standard Act general-plan concept during the turbulent depression, defense, and wartime periods, the problems that confronted the experienced consultants and the directors of the newly established city-planning departments of the time have been grouped under the following five headings:

Problems caused by—

(1) Confusion Between the Zoning Plan and the Working-and-Living-Areas Section of the General Plan
(2) Piecemeal Adoption of the General Plan
(3) Lack of a Specific Definition of the Essential Physical Elements to Be Dealt with in the General Plan
(4) Basic Questions as to the Scope of the General Plan
(5) Distrust of the Municipal Legislative Body

(1) Confusion Between the Zoning Plan and the Working-and-Living-Areas Section of the General Plan

The authors of the Standard Act believed that in order to promote

and protect the general welfare of citizens living in urban communities it was essential for municipal governments to assume positive responsibility for guiding the growth and development of the physical environment of the city. In Section 7 of the Act, which is titled "Purposes in View," the basic reasons why a general plan is needed and justified are expressed as follows:

The plan shall be made with the general purpose of guiding and accomplishing a coordinated, adjusted, and harmonious development of the municipality and its environs which will, in accordance with present and future needs, best promote health, safety, morals, order, convenience, prosperity, and general welfare, as well as efficiency and economy in the process of development; including, among other things, adequate provision for traffic, the promotion of safety from fire and other dangers, adequate provision for light and air, the promotion of healthful and convenient distribution of population, the promotion of good civic design and arrangement, wise and efficient expenditure of public funds, and the adequate provision of public utilities and other public requirements.

With the broad governmental purposes expressed in the preceding passage thus assumed and clearly stated as the basis for city planning and the general plan, the authors of the Standard Act described the general, comprehensive, and long-range nature of the plan in footnotes 31, 32, and 44 [1] in the following terms:

. . . The planning commission's function . . . is to make a general design as to location [of the physical elements of the city], which it is especially competent to do in view of its knowledge of the needs of the city and the probable trend of the city's future growth . . .

"a master plan": By this expression is meant a comprehensive scheme of development . . .

. . . Planning is intended to be a process whereby the larger lines and directions of future public and private development will be influenced and to some extent controlled . . . [The master plan] should be designed to cover a long period of years . . .

In these explanatory footnotes the intent of the authors is clearly expressed: The municipal government needs a plan that can be used as a

[1] Because of the special nature of the Standard Act, many of the most important ideas contained in the Act are fully explained only in the footnotes of the original report on the Standard Act. To simplify the references in the text above, and in the following pages, the footnotes are identified by referring to them directly as they are numbered in the report.

guide in governing public and private developments in the city, and the plan, or over-all design for the layout and physical development of the city, should be long-range, comprehensive, and general. But although this conception of the general plan is clearly and repeatedly presented in the detailed footnotes throughout the document, the language of the proposed official Act also specifically includes the zoning plan among the list of subjects that are considered appropriate for inclusion in the general plan.

A zoning plan is a specific and detailed regulatory device used to control the use of private property. It must always be detailed rather than general, and many of its proposals must, necessarily, be concerned with a period of time that will be much shorter than the long-range period that must be dealt with by the general plan. As will be shown, the importance of distinguishing between the general plan, which must be long-range, and, therefore, general in nature, and the endless number of specific, detailed, and short-range projects, plans, and regulations that are based on the general plan and are intended to carry it out, but which are not part of the plan, was fully understood by the authors of the Act. Why, then, the zoning plan was included in the official text of the Standard Act as a section of the general plan is extremely difficult to understand. In any case, this basic contradiction was written into the Act, and, because of the great influence that the Act had on this particular question during the 1930's and 1940's, it is important to know exactly what the specific provisions of the Act contain.

In Section 6 of the text recommended for legislative adoption, under the title of "General Powers and Duties," the authors described the general plan in the following language:

. . . It shall be the function and duty of the commission to make and adopt a master plan for the physical development of the municipality, including any areas outside of its boundaries which, in the commission's judgment, bear relation to the planning of such municipality. *Such plan,* with the accompanying maps, plats, charts, and descriptive matter *shall show* the commission's recommendations for the development of said territory, including, *among other things, the general location, character, and extent* of streets, viaducts, subways, bridges, waterways, water fronts, boulevards, parkways, playgrounds, squares, parks, aviation fields, and other public ways, grounds and open spaces, the general location of public buildings and other public property, and the general location and extent of public utilities and terminals, whether publicly or privately owned or operated, for water, light, sanitation, transportation, communication, power, and other purposes; also the removal, relocation, widening, narrowing, vacating, abandonment, change of

GENERAL PLAN—1953

- Downtown
- Major Shopping; Business and Services
- Light Industry
- General Industry
- Institutions and Open Areas
- Low-Density Residential
- Medium-Density Residential
- High-Density Residential

THE GENERAL PLAN AND THE ZONING PLAN

The major land-use section of San Francisco's long-range physical-development plan was adopted by the City Planning Commission in 1953. As shown above, the 1953 general-plan proposals called for drastic changes in the existing zoning map. A new zoning map and new regulations were adopted in 1960. Although many important general-plan proposals were effectuated by the new zoning ordinance, the long-range and general nature of some of the most important plan proposals means that there always will be distinct differences between the general plan and the zoning ordinance.

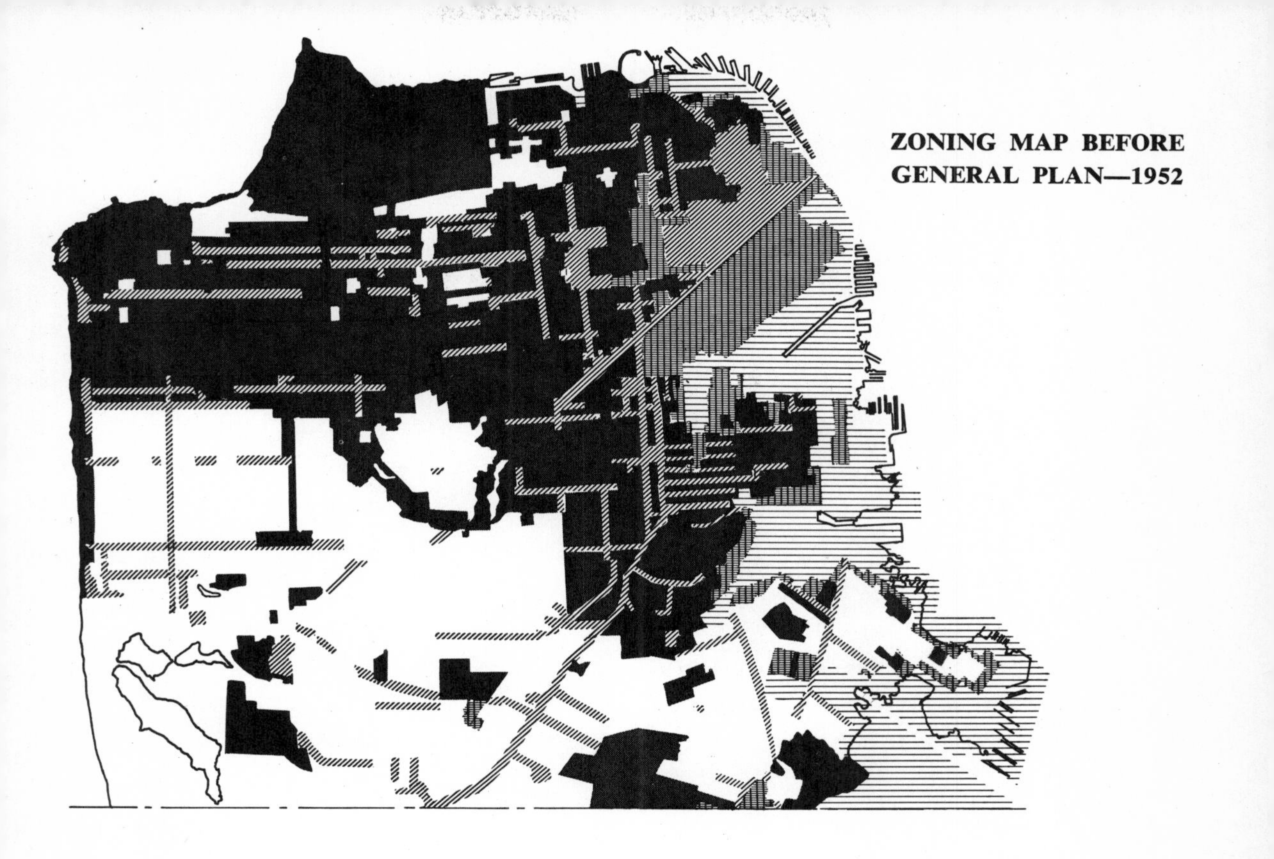

ZONING MAP BEFORE GENERAL PLAN—1952

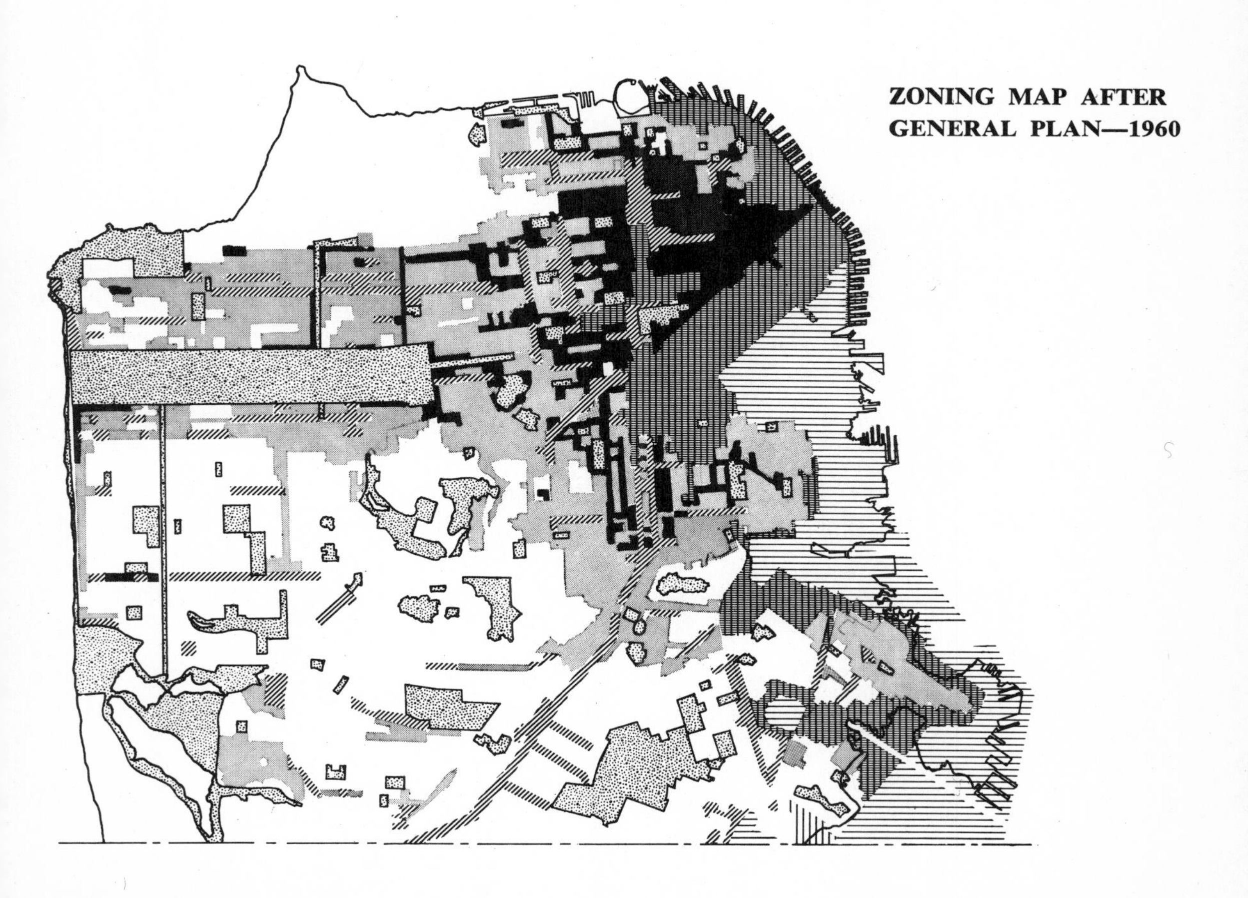

ZONING MAP AFTER GENERAL PLAN—1960

use or extension of any of the foregoing ways, grounds, open spaces, buildings, property, utilities, or terminals; *as well as a zoning plan for the control of the height, area, bulk, location, and use of buildings and premises.* [Emphasis added.]

This official definition of the general plan is explained in four footnotes that are of particular importance. In the first footnote the authors state flatly that the zoning plan is to be included as an integral part of the general plan; and in the second, third, and fourth footnotes, they contradict themselves and state that the general plan must remain general; that it cannot accomplish its principal objectives if it becomes detailed; and that zoning is simply one method of carrying out the general policies dealing with private property that are set forth in the working-and-living-areas section of the general plan.

The first point is made in footnote 35:

"among other things": The enumeration of the kinds of matters with which a city plan should deal which follows these words, is purely illustrative and in no sense meant to be exclusive. The power given to the city planning commission is to make recommendations for the physical development of the entire territory covered by the plan, and, whether the specific phase of that development happens to be mentioned in this section or not, the power to deal with the whole field still rests with the commission. The list included in the text of the act might be helpful to a new city planning commission in undertaking its work; but they are all illustrations only and not comprehensive.

By emphasizing their intent to be only illustrative in the official text, the authors make it clear that while subjects other than those listed may be appropriate for inclusion in a general plan for a particular community, those subjects that are listed in what is, in effect, a legislative definition of the general plan definitely are considered to be appropriate. Since the zoning plan is specifically mentioned, and since zoning has always dealt with the privately owned land areas that make up the working-and-living areas of the city, anyone inexperienced with the practice of city planning and not fully aware of the overriding importance of the requirement that the general plan remain general, would naturally assume that the authors of the Standard Act believed that the specific and detailed zoning plan was to be considered as the working-and-living-areas section of the general plan. This, in fact, is what actually happened in hundreds of cities throughout the United States between 1930 and 1950.

To me, however, it is inconceivable that Mr. Olmsted, Mr. Bettman, and the other members of the committee meant to be understood in this way.

The following quotations taken from footnotes 36, 31, and 41, respectively, describe the relationship between the zoning plan and the general plan that has finally been recognized—after many years of confusion and harmful experience—by most of the leaders of the profession and by the city-planning commissioners and city councilmen in those cities that have pushed ahead during the past ten to fifteen years with the job of fashioning a useful instrument—the general plan—to assist them in the complex task of governing the physical growth and development of their communities.

In footnotes 36 and 31 the authors describe the essential quality of generalness that the plan must have:

"general location and extent": These words have very great importance. They indicate the demarcation of the commission's functions. As pointed out in the general discussion of the commission's powers and duties, it is not intended that the planning commission shall include in the master plan such exact details of location or engineering plans and specifications as will come to be needed when the public improvement or building is to be actually constructed.

. . . This act is based on the theory that a planning commission should view all . . . phases of a city's development in a broad and comprehensive fashion . . .

By emphasizing the meaning of the words, "general location and extent," and by emphasizing the significance of their inclusion in the legislative definition of the general plan, the authors seem to be saying that because of the vital importance of the characteristic of generalness that the plan must have, the zoning plan cannot be considered as equivalent to the basic, general proposals that will form the working-and-living-areas section of the general plan. Indeed, in footnote 41, which discusses the constitutional basis for the general plan, the following language is used which states flatly that zoning is a method of carrying out the general plan:

. . . Many of the phases of . . . carrying out the plan . . . as, for instance, zoning legislation . . .

The only logical implication of this statement is that zoning legislation, which requires a precise and specific citywide plan of land-use zones and detailed regulations for each zone, obviously cannot and must never be considered an integral part of the general plan itself.

It may be that the phrase "zoning plan," when used in the Act to illustrate one feature of the general plan, was meant to refer to a longer-range and nondetailed version of the precise zoning-district map which is an essential part of zoning legislation. However, this critical point was not discussed. The need for emphasizing the distinction between the fundamentally different uses of the working-and-living-areas section of the general plan and the uses of the zoning ordinance is nowhere evident in the Act. In any case, the fact is that for more than twenty years following publication of the Act, the subordinate relationship of the zoning ordinance to the general plan was obscured. Many zoning ordinances were adopted without an awareness of the long-term implications of overzoning, strip zoning, strict separation of land uses, and the segregation of residential districts by lot sizes. Cities everywhere in the United States today are confronted with serious economic and social problems as a result of the failure to distinguish between the task of defining general-development objectives and policies in the form of a general plan and the task of regulating, by means of detailed zoning legislation, the use of private property.

The purpose of the preceding discussion, it must be emphasized, has been to document one of the specific sources of the confusion concerning the nature of the general plan that developed during the 1930's and 1940's. There are compelling historical explanations of the difficulties that confronted the authors of the Standard Act that justify the decisions they finally made. The facts are, however, that uncertainty and confusion did characterize the technical general-plan work of the profession following the publication of the Act, and that for more than two decades there was no agreement on the vital necessity of distinguishing clearly between the zoning plan and the working-and-living-areas section of the general plan. Even today, despite the legislative definitions of the general plans that have been enacted by local and state governments since World War II, despite the promulgation of an "official" federal definition of the urban general plan that is crystal clear, and despite formal approval in 1952 by the Board of Governors of the American Institute of Planners of what is, in effect, an official policy statement of the city-planning profession on this question, all of which express exactly the same point of view on this particular issue that I have expressed here, there are still many individuals within the profession and among the thousands of citizens serving on city-planning commissions and city councils who do not understand that the inclusion of the zoning plan in the general plan will effectively destroy the latter's usefulness as a general policy instrument.

(2) Piecemeal Adoption of the General Plan

In the light of experience subsequent to preparation of the Standard Act, it is clear that a second major weakness of the general-plan concept as defined by the Act was caused by the endorsement that the Act gave to the idea of piecemeal adoption of the plan. The Act repeatedly stresses the unified nature of the plan and the vital importance of organizing the city-planning program in such a way as to assure the completion of the plan as an entity. Yet the authors compromised with the realities of small staffs and of pressing city-development problems that were undeniably evident in the 1920's in a way that led—inevitably, it now appears—to one of the worst features of American city-planning practice during the two decades following publication of the Act.

The procedure suggested for adoption of the general plan is spelled out in the official text in Section 8:

> *Procedure of Commission: The commission may adopt* the plan as a whole by a single resolution or may by successive resolutions adopt *successive parts of the plan,* said parts corresponding with major geographical sections or divisions of the municipality or with functional subdivisions of the subject matter of the plan . . . [Emphasis added.]

The words "parts of the plan" in the suggested official text of the Act are then discussed in footnote 42:

> The city plan is an organic whole, every part of which, whether considered territorially or as to subject matter, is organically interrelated with every other part. That means that every part needs to be studied with these interrelations in mind. However, while the comprehensive or master plan should be envisaged and treated as an organic single unity or whole, there may be no imperative necessity for withholding the completion and publication of parts as they are finished to await the conclusion and publication of the whole. By part may be meant a territorial part; that is, that the plan of one of the major geographical divisions or sections of the city, as, for instance, the territory on one side of a river which divides the city into two sections, may be completed and published previous to the completion and promulgation of the plan of the whole city. "Part" may also relate to subject matter, as, for instance, the completion of the major thoroughfare part of the plan and its publication previous to the completion of the park part or recreational part or railroad part. The territorial part selected should have, in and of itself, some logical basis; and nothing less than the whole of one subject matter, such as major streets, should be treated as a part. *Moreover, any such part adopted before the completion and adoption of the whole plan should be clearly recognized and treated as a part which is being adopted and published in advance pending the completion of the plan, and always as a part, the significance and usefulness of which depends on its relation to the other parts.* [Emphasis added.]

The logical and practical intent of the authors is made very clear in this added explanation which, it must be emphasized, is not a part of the recommended formal legislation. Once the Standard Act was adopted and put into practice in numerous cities throughout the United States—which happened very quickly—the clarifying footnotes were forgotten, and the authorization in the formal text of the Act itself permitting piecemeal adoption of the plan without any qualifications was taken at its face value. Hundreds of city-planning commissions began the complex job of city planning by authorizing the preparation of piecemeal plans, and once these separate "plans" were adopted, the commissions promptly lost sight of the other key general-plan sections that were needed to provide a logical basis for the one or two piecemeal plans that had been adopted.

Street systems initially received most attention in general plans. Cities throughout the country during the 1920's and 1930's adopted "comprehensive" thoroughfare plans that were, naturally, dependent for their validity on the unstated land-use and mass-transit proposals and assumptions made by the city-planning consultants and local staff members who had prepared them. During the years that followed, these partial plans came to be labeled as master plans. Thus, parts of the circulation sections of many general plans were transformed into master plans of thoroughfares. The illogical reasoning expressed by this use of the term "master plan" led innumerable city-planning commissions to postpone indefinitely—in many cases for twenty to thirty years—the completion of the other essential sections of the general plan. Needless to say, many of these commissions were advised by members of the city-planning profession who had been misled by their own illogical interpretation of the Standard Act on this point.

The only alternative that apparently was considered by the authors of the Act was an "everything or nothing" approach—a requirement that would have specified the completion of all of the key sections of the general plan before permitting the adoption of any single separate section. The mandatory-referral provisions of the Act did restrain the city-planning commission from active participation in the work of municipal government until such time as the general plan or pertinent sections of it had been adopted. If the Act had not permitted piecemeal adoption, the mandatory-referral requirement, it now seems in retrospect, would have provided the spur necessary to obtain the support needed to complete the plan.

Preparation and adoption of the general plan as a whole in preliminary form, pending completion of the careful studies needed to do the job thoroughly, would have been a far more practical and reasonable alternative than the piecemeal-adoption procedure which was accepted.

This, in fact, is the procedure many cities have finally adopted after living with inadequate partial plans for many years. The successful completion and effective use of such "interim" or "preliminary" general plans in recent years, followed up by revisions based on subsequent studies and working experience sufficient to transform preliminary plans into fully developed general plans, has suggested the ideas on procedures for general-plan adoption and annual review and amendment that are called for in Chapter III of this book.

In many ways, the situation that has been briefly described here concerning the results of the piecemeal-adoption procedure authorized by the Standard Act is comparable to the now settled but recently very active controversy over the relationship of the zoning plan to the general plan. The issue is settled, but the effects of the confusion linger on. For, although the unity of the essential physical elements that must be dealt with in the general plan is now widely appreciated among professional practitioners and citizen commissioners and councilmen, there still are cities, some advised by members of the city-planning profession, authorizing the preparation of separate sections of the plan for subsequent piecemeal adoption.

(3) Lack of a Specific Definition of the Essential Physical Elements to Be Dealt with in the General Plan

The authors of the Standard Act consciously attempted to exclude from the formal text of the recommended legislation a specific definition of the essential physical elements to be dealt with in the general plan. On this issue, unlike their decision on the issue of piecemeal-adoption procedure, they failed to elaborate on the reasons for their decision. It apparently was the intent of the authors of the Act to encourage every city-planning commission to define the key physical elements to be dealt with in the general plan in its own way. Indeed, for more than twenty years—during the 1920's and the 1930's—this point of view was championed by Mr. Bettman. During this period, the possibility seems to have been almost completely overlooked by Mr. Bettman and other leaders of the profession that legislation authorizing the preparation and use of a general plan which did not specify at the very least the essential physical elements to be dealt with in the plan might enable and encourage illogical city-planning programs to gain support in the name of comprehensive city planning.

As a matter of fact, despite a specific statement in the explanatory footnotes of the Standard Act that says an express definition of the general plan is not deemed necessary or desirable, when the members of the committee finally reached the point in the Act where it became necessary to explain in legislative language what was meant by the master, or general, plan, they were compelled to write a definition. The specific language constitutes, undeniably, a definition that actually does specify the essential physical elements that a plan must deal with if it is to serve its purpose as a comprehensive general plan that can be used to guide the physical development of a community. Thus, by saying one thing in the footnotes and actually doing the opposite in the formal text of the proposed legislation, the Standard Act added to the confusion and uncertainty of the period on the fundamental question as to what constituted the basic physical elements to be dealt with in the general plan.

The relevant provisions of the Act on this issue are included in Section 6, titled "General Powers and Duties." The first sentence of this section of the Act states that it is the duty of the city-planning commission to make and adopt a master plan. At this point in the text the attention of the reader is directed to footnote 32, which says:

> *"a master plan":* By this expression is meant a comprehensive scheme of development of the general fundamentals of a municipal plan. *An express definition has not been thought desirable or necessary.* What is implied in it is best expressed by the provisions of this section which illustrate the subject matter that a master plan should consider. [Emphasis added.]

The next sentence of the formal text attempts to "illustrate the subject matter that a master plan *should* consider." This sentence reads as follows:

> . . . (the) plan . . . *shall* [emphasis added] show the commission's recommendations for the development of said territory, including, among other things, the general location, character, and extent of streets, viaducts, subways, bridges, waterways, waterfronts, boulevards, parkways, playgrounds, squares, parks, aviation fields, and other public ways, grounds and open spaces, the general location of public buildings and other public property, and the general location and extent of public utilities and terminals, whether publicly or privately owned or operated, for water, light, sanitation, transportation, communication, power, and other purposes; also the removal, relocation, widening, narrowing, vacating, abandonment, change of use or extension of any of the foregoing ways, grounds, open spaces, buildings, property, utilities, or terminals; as well as a zoning plan for the control of the height, area, bulk, location, and use of buildings and premises . . .

This legislative "definition" of the general plan may be paraphrased in contemporary terms as follows: The master or general plan *shall* include, among other sections on physical elements judged by the city-planning commission to be necessary to the particular requirements of the community: (a) a section on working-and-living areas (which the Standard Act, as we have already seen, unfortunately confused with the zoning plan); (b) a section on community facilities; and (c) a section on circulation. In other words, having just said that they did not believe an express definition of the general plan should be included in the Act, the authors then found it necessary to write an "illustrative" definition that included the word "shall" as applied to the subject matter of the three key physical elements to be dealt with in the plan.

There are several possible explanations for this contradiction. Despite what is said in the explanatory footnotes, the decision to attempt consciously to omit what could be called an express definition of the general plan from the Act probably was the result of basic differences of opinion among the individuals in the group that drafted the document. We know from his later writings that one of the members of the committee, Edward M. Bassett, believed that the scope of the plan should be precisely delimited, and that the component parts of the plan should be specified. We also know that Alfred Bettman during this period of his career argued that anything that might come to be known as a "standard definition" of the general plan might lead city-planning commissions throughout the country to do their work in a perfunctory way, without really thinking for themselves, and hence might cause them to ignore the special problems, features, and opportunities that characterize every community. Thus, one who is aware of the unavoidable limitations and problems of committee authorship might draw the conclusion that Mr. Bassett wrote the legislative definition of the general plan that is in the Act, that Mr. Bettman wrote the footnote saying that no express definition was thought desirable or necessary, and that they each succeeded in qualifying the other's words sufficiently so that they could agree to sign the final document. It is very important, however, that we also remind ourselves that at the time the Standard Act was being written the city-planning profession itself had not, as yet, been able to complete a representative number of general plans for cities throughout the United States. Hence, while there was broad agreement on the subject matter and major purpose of the general plan, there probably was no easy, natural agreement among a substantial majority of the leaders of the profession, based on common practical experience, as to how to define in legislative language what were then, as they are today, the essential physical elements that must be dealt with in the general plan.

The harmful reality and widespread extent of the *non*general, *non-*

comprehensive, and *non*long-range work done as a result of the inability of the city-planning profession to define its principal instrument can be verified by a visit to any city hall in the country. The record of the 1930's and 1940's speaks for itself. Detailed zoning ordinances and piecemeal plans that were unrelated to even the sketchiest framework of a general plan were the familiar products of the times. Not until the huge backlog of postponed public works forced the issue immediately after the end of World War II did we rediscover the essential physical elements that must be dealt with in the general plan and face up to the necessity of describing them in straightforward language suitable for use in formal legislation. By this time, Mr. Bettman had changed his point of view, and during the period between 1940 and 1946 he made one of his most important contributions to the development of the city-planning profession—a formulation of an "express definition" of the general plan which will be considered at the end of this chapter.

(4) Basic Questions as to the Scope of the General Plan

The three "soft spots" in the general-plan concept as expressed in the Standard Act that have just been considered are concerned with questions that to a great extent have been resolved as a result of the pressures of experience. On each issue it is still necessary for clarifying definitions of the general plan to catch up with and reflect accepted good practice. But today there is, once again, a direct relationship between general-plan theory and general-plan practice on these points. It does not seem unrealistic to anticipate that there will be, therefore, a consolidation of experience subsequent to World War II that will (1) clearly distinguish the general plan from the zoning plan, (2) require adoption of the general plan as an entity rather than piecemeal, and (3) spell out in legislative language a firm definition of the essential physical elements to be dealt with in a general plan for physical development.

We now must acknowledge the existence of a challenge to the general-plan concept that is still very much alive. This is the challenge posed primarily by social scientists, public administrators, and the architect-planner advocates of "total design" to the self-imposed limitation of the scope of the plan to questions of general physical development.[2]

[2] There are several able and active proponents of the points of view held by the groups I have identified. In the subsequent discussion I have in mind the principal arguments made by Dr. Rexford G. Tugwell as a social scientist, Professor Robert A. Walker as a public administrator, and Professor Henry Fagin as an architect-planner.

Between 1930 and the present time two main arguments have been made against the idea that the general plan should continue to be limited in scope to questions of physical development. The first argument advocates greater breadth, the second, greater depth. They raise questions that are fundamental and that must, therefore, be acknowledged and answered. They agitate the minds of students and professors, in particular. On the other hand, they have no large significance for men and women of the city-planning profession who have had sustained experience in municipal government and who are motivated primarily to improve the physical environment. Practitioners of all professions understand the need for subject-matter limitation and for distinguishing general policy questions from specific, detailed, short-range action proposals.

The first argument—the "breadth" argument—may be summarized as follows: Since every general physical-development plan is admittedly based on judgments concerning social and economic objectives and factors, and since the physical environment is, also admittedly, of second-order importance—a means to an end, not an end in itself—the physical-development focus of the plan should be broadened to enable the plan to become "truly comprehensive." Only in this way, it is argued, can urban governments be as rational as possible in comprehending and determining the complete set of policies—social, economic, physical, and fiscal—needed to govern wisely.[3]

The response to this challenging argument is, of course, not directed against reason and wisdom. Olmsted and Bettman and their works exemplify reason and wisdom. The early advocates of the general physical-plan concept simply assumed that a number of governmental policy-control instruments would always be needed—such as the annual budget, the capital-improvement program, the personnel-classification system, and the school curriculum —and that, given the limitation of the land resources of the city, it would be sensible to add to these a long-range plan for the physical development of the community. The contemporary advocates of the general physical plan likewise assume that there will continue to be a number of governmental policy-control instruments that will be practical; they assume that the general physical plan is one such instrument; and they are working, together with others, to develop additional control instruments, such as the community-

[3] See Rexford G. Tugwell, *The Place of Planning in Society,* Puerto Rico Planning Board Technical Paper No. 7, 1954, San Juan, Puerto Rico; and "The Fourth Power," in *Planning and Civic Comment* (Washington, D. C.: 1940).

renewal program and public-policy statements concerning intergroup and race relations, as the need and practicality of such instruments become clear.

The response of the traditionalists, however, does not seem reasonable to the advocates of the "truly comprehensive" approach to governmental planning. They wish to create a superior staff group of professional planners who will prepare and maintain a "comprehensive-policies plan." [4] In advocating this, they have confused the continuing need for a general physical plan, and have failed to make a case directly for the new and different concept that they seek to have considered. How did this confusion develop?

Shortly after the publication of the 1928 Standard Act the nation was plunged into the depression of the 1930's. The special attention and emphasis given to social and economic problems during this period was quickly reflected in the work of the city-planning profession and led directly to disagreements and confusion as to the scope of the general plan.

For reasons that were plainly stated, Olmsted and Bettman and the other authors of the Standard Act believed that the subject matter of the general plan should be limited to the major issues of physical development that were confronting cities. This view was questioned by many of the younger men who entered the profession in the 1930's and was challenged by the activities and publications of the National Resources Planning Board which were concerned with national and regional resources and socio-economic development problems as well as questions having to do with the development and improvement of the nation's cities. The NRPB, as it came to be known, undoubtedly made a major contribution to the development of the city-planning profession in the United States during the most active years of its existence (1932 to 1942). Many of today's leaders of the profession gained their initial experience as junior staff members in the regional offices of this creative and controversial New Deal agency. But the work of the NRPB and the influence of many of its senior officers resulted in what now seems to me to have been an unnecessary diversion of the creative energies of the city-planning profession.

The main theme that ran through the criticisms of the Standard Act philosophy on the scope of the general plan during this period may be expressed as follows: In order to plan logically for the future physical development of a city, it is necessary to make plans also for the financial, social, and economic factors that are affected by, and that, in turn, them-

---

[4] See Henry Fagin, "Organizing and Carrying Out Planning Activities Within Urban Government," *Journal of the American Institute of Planners,* Vol. 25 (August, 1959).

selves limit and control, the physical development of the city. Put in more general terms, this argument says that since everything in the urban community is related to everything else, it is illogical to attempt to make a plan for only one aspect of the community. Put another way, this argument seems to say that each of the traditional, limited-scope policy-control instruments—the long-range financial plan, the annual budget, the five-year capital-improvement program, the social and economic policies of the community, however stated, and the general physical-development plan—should be conceived of as a separate section in a single, ultracomprehensive plan.

The impact of this point of view on the practices of the city-planning profession reached its peak during the immediate period following World War II when full-scale city-planning programs were being organized throughout the country for the first time and new staffs were being recruited. Many social scientists interested in urban problems joined these staffs and participated actively in the internal office debates that resulted from the necessity to translate the theoretical notion of the general physical plan into practical reality in order to solve obvious and pressing problems. In those cities where plans were actually produced during the first postwar decade, such as Cincinnati, Cleveland, Detroit, San Francisco, and Seattle, the question as to the scope of the plan was invariably decided in favor of the physical-development focus advocated by the Standard Act. In a significant number of other offices that were and still are well organized and well directed, however, no general plans of any sort have been completed, and the issue is still being debated.

It is now generally recognized that, regardless of the outcome of the arguments concerning the technical feasibility and political acceptability of a truly comprehensive plan to be prepared by a unified central staff of professional planners—a plan that will deal directly with race relations, tax policy, mental health, and community welfare in addition to over-all physical development, capital improvements, and community renewal—there will always need to be at the very least a general plan that focuses on physical development, just as the budget and the long-range fiscal plan focus on the subject matter of financial resources. Whether or not city planners of the Olmsted-Bettman tradition will find themselves subordinate members of a larger consolidated professional planning group remains to be seen. The appeal of this concept of consolidation can be expected to grow, however, and the argument against the physical-development subject-matter focus of the Standard Act general-plan concept that springs from it will be confronting us for many years to come.

A related argument against limiting the scope of the general plan to physical development also grew out of the nonphysical, or completely comprehensive, point of view that gained support among some city planners during the depression years of the 1930's, a point of view that was carried over into the first decade following World War II. This idea attacked the very notion of any broad-gauge plan at all. Social scientists and public administrators, joined by anti-general-plan city planners,[5] argued that the very existence of any such plan, regardless of its subject-matter focus, was harmful. These men advocated the concept of continuous, flexible planning by a professional central-management and planning group without any limitation as to subject matter, and without a requirement to produce what they judged would be the inhibiting and distorting device of a "completed" plan or series of plans. The argument that continuous planning by a professional staff group without the requirement of a stated comprehensive plan or series of subject-matter plans makes control of the basic policies of the staff by the city council impossible does not seem to have been fully appreciated by the proponents of the continuous, comprehensive-planning approach.

The failure of city governments during the 1920's to establish permanent professional city-planning staffs so that the consultant-prepared general plans for physical development that were developed during this period could be kept up to date and, hence, kept useful, was one of the legitimate causes of the attacks on the general-plan concept by the advocates of what may be termed the continuous, comprehensive-planning point of view.[6] The authors of the Standard Act were very much aware of this criticism and of the harm that could result from a general physical plan that was not kept up to date. In footnote 8, which explains the provision of the Act that authorizes municipalities to make, adopt, amend, and carry out a general plan for physical development, the authors of the Standard Act state:

The act contemplates that the planning commission shall not only make the plan but also have a strong influence in protecting the plan against departures and in getting the plan carried out. . . . While the making of the comprehensive master

[5] See Adams, Howard, and Greeley, *Report to the Board of City Planning Commissioners, City of Los Angeles, on the Los Angeles City Planning Department, 1956* (Cambridge, Mass.: November, 1956) for documentation. The well-financed, and in many respects outstanding, program of the Los Angeles City Planning Department, established in 1941, has yet to produce even a preliminary general plan for physical development.

[6] See Robert A. Walker, *The Planning Function in Urban Government* (Chicago: University of Chicago Press, 1941). Second Edition, 1950.

city plan is the main initial piece of work to be undertaken by the planning commission, the completion of that plan does not represent the completion of its work. On the contrary, the second main and equally important stage of its work commences with the adoption of the master plan. This stage is continuous and permanent, being the continuous process of adjusting the actual physical development of the municipality to the plan, and also the continuous elaboration of the plan and adjustment of the plan to new situations as they arise . . .

Despite the emphasis given in this explanatory note to the necessity for continuous physical planning once the initial version of the general plan has been completed, the Olmsted-Bettman Standard Act tradition is still criticized as one that gives too much emphasis to the idea of a fixed plan and not enough emphasis to the idea of continuous planning. In fact, the Standard Act gives equal emphasis to the need both for a plan and for a program of continuous city planning. It specifically calls for continuous review and revision in view of the political role assigned to the plan as one of the major policy-control instruments of the municipal government.

The contemporary practice of city planning is, unfortunately, still subject to legitimate criticism as a result of a repetition of the practices of the 1920's. Many of the smaller cities that took advantage of the city-planning financial-aid program of the federal government between 1954 and 1962, prior to the time when grants were available for continuous planning activities, undertook programs that called for completion of general plans without adequate provision for the establishment of a continuing city-planning program. As a consequence, the reasonable argument against spending money on a useless plan continues to be heard. But despite this resurgence of bad practice, and despite the continued support being given to the city-planning programs of several of our major cities that are led by city planners who do not believe in the necessity of a city plan, a general plan limited in its scope and definiteness to a general physical design has been a necessary and useful device in an ever-increasing number of American cities where the political leaders have assumed direct responsibility for the basic policies being used to guide the physical-development activities of their communities.

The second main argument—the "depth" argument—against the scope of the Standard Act general-plan concept contends that the requirement that the plan remain general is inhibiting and impractical. In recent years, among those who do realize that a general plan for physical development is needed, controversy has developed around the idea that the plan must not be permitted to become precise and detailed. It may be said that the same sort of confusion caused by the failure to distinguish between the detailed zoning plan for all privately owned land and the working-and-living-areas section of the general plan is now reappearing as a result of the failure to maintain a distinction between the capital budget for public works and specific public projects and improvements suggested by the plan and the broad policies and general citywide physical-design proposals expressed in the community-facilities and circulation sections of the plan.

Experience has shown that as soon as a community completes its general plan, serious consideration will be given to the most pressing problems dealt with by the plan. In the 1920's these were the problems caused by the anarchy of unregulated use of that part of the city that was privately owned. After the mechanics for coping with this situation were crudely worked out and accepted, general-plan proposals that dealt with public projects came into the spotlight. By 1945 the nation had been through defense and war periods that had caused the postponement of essential municipal public works for almost a decade. Thus when, following World War II, city-planning programs got under way and general plans were completed, the widespread tendency to convert the plan into a specific blueprint for public capital improvements, including in many instances detailed financial programs, was understandable. This tendency, which confused the continuing need for a general statement of citywide physical-development policy, was expressed in the first definition by the federal government, prepared in 1950, of the scope of the urban general plan. It also found expression in England when, also for the first time, the national government found it necessary, as a result of the 1947 Town and Country Planning Act, to specify in the form of official regulations the exact contents of the city- and county-development plans that had to be prepared by all local governments by 1950. In both cases, the higher-level governments required the inclusion of short-range and detailed plans and programs in the official set of documents that had been intended, initially, to assure the formulation and use, by local governments, of long-range plans for physical development.

Today we are able to see the results of the debates and controversies that have been and continue to be concerned with the scope—the breadth and depth—of the general plan for physical development. Although each of the two main points of view discussed still has its adherents among the members of the profession, the sustained practice of city planning in large and small cities throughout the United States since the end of World War II has demonstrated that the realistic needs of the governing groups in every city include the need for a plan (1) that focuses on the major issues of physical development; (2) that outlines a single, definite, unified general design for the principal elements of the physical environment; and (3) that, by remaining general in nature, enables a clear focus to be maintained on the long-range policies and physical design that are required if there is to be a functionally logical and politically fair basis for the ever-increasing variety of detailed regulations and public projects that must be designed and implemented by municipal governments.

(5) Distrust of the Municipal Legislative Body

Of all the major ideas that were combined to form the general-plan concept that found its expression in the Standard Act, the idea that the principal client of the plan should be an independent, appointed, citizen commission rather than the directly elected members of the city council seems to be the one that was and continues to be more widely taken for granted in most parts of the country than any of the other key ideas. I believe that this idea, although not considered controversial at the time, was based on a fundamental misinterpretation of the requirements of democratic self-government. It permitted the confusion on technical general-plan questions to continue for a much longer period than would have been the case if the city-planning profession had not been shielded from direct public inquiry by a citizen commission trained to think of itself as superior to and independent of the city council. Needless to say, it also directly influenced the very nature of the general plan itself, leading in most instances away from the idea that the plan should focus on the major issues of physical development and toward the conception of the plan as a detailed and increasingly precise scheme to be seen and used only by the members of the city-planning commission and its professional staff.

The political and governmental authority of the public body for whom any major policy-control instrument is prepared has a very great influence on the nature and form of the instrument. It now seems obvious that not until a definite new decision is reached as to who really must be recognized by the city-planning profession as the principal client of the general plan will we be able to design, present, and maintain the plan properly for the combined political and technical uses that it must serve if it is to meet the practical, working needs of the client.

Before we examine in detail the reasons given by the authors of the Standard Act for attempting to create a nonpolitical public body while at the same time attempting to avoid a specific requirement that this body present its basic policies in the form of a unified general plan, I believe my own views should be restated. Personal judgments and values are of critical importance on this question. The decision one makes on this issue dictates one's definition of the uses and characteristics of the general plan.

I believe that the Standard Act concept was based on the assumption that the members of the city council could not, realistically, be expected to be competent to determine and maintain a wise policy to use as a basis for governing physical development. The Act, therefore, called for an independent citizen commission to do this necessary and important job. It was also assumed by the authors of the Act that the task of preparing and maintaining the general plan would continue to be very complex, technically. The Act, therefore, imposed no requirement that the general plan should ever be publicly presented or described in its entirety, although it was assumed this should and would be done eventually. Hence, two major assumptions made by the authors of the Standard Act, one based on political considerations and the other based on technical considerations, led citizen commissioners and professional city planners alike to accept—and in many instances to advocate—the idea that the general plan as a unified entity did not ever have to be made available, either to the city council or the citizens of the community. These assumptions, although understandable in the historical context of the 1920's, no longer can be considered realistic or reasonable. If they are rejected, as I propose, and replaced (1) by the belief that the city council, and only the city council, should be the principal client of the general plan, and (2) by the judgment that the technical complexity of the general plan is not such that it is impossible to make the plan understandable, available, and amendable, then several of the most important characteristics of the general plan as suggested by the Standard Act will necessarily have to be modified.

The convictions and basic assumptions that led the authors of the Standard Act to define the relationship of the city-planning commission to the city council in the way that they did are openly presented and discussed in the explanatory footnotes of the document. The official text simply spells out the conclusions that logically follow from these judgments.

The specific proposals in the text of the Act that define the membership, role, and authority of the city-planning commission with which we must now become familiar may be summarized as follows: Since a general plan is needed so that the physical development of the community can be governed in a way that is both thoughtful and fair, a city-planning commission should be appointed by the mayor, without confirmation by the council, to prepare and maintain such a plan. Six of the nine members of this commission should be outstanding civic leaders whose terms of office should be such that no mayor, directly, or council, indirectly, during their terms of office, would be able to change a majority of the members of the commission. Six-year, overlapping terms are suggested, and removal procedures are spelled out that are intended to assure the tenure of the citizen commissioners. The remaining three commissioners are to be men who will become members of the commission by virtue of other positions they occupy, namely, the mayor, one of the chief administrative officers of the government who is to be designated by the mayor, and a member of the city council to be selected by the council.

The commission is charged with the primary duty of preparing, adopting, and maintaining the general plan, and is given a staff that is responsible to it exclusively and is, therefore, intentionally independent of the regular administration. The general plan is not to be adopted by the council.

Once the commission has adopted the plan, all proposals affecting physical development that must be acted upon finally by the city council must first be referred to the commission for review. After the council has received a report from the commission presenting its views on the proposal as to its relationship to the general plan, the council may act. However, if the council wishes to approve a proposal that the commission has recommended against, the council is permitted to do so only if two-thirds of its full membership votes to overrule the commission.

In the 1960's, more than thirty years after the publication of the Standard Act, after more than sixty years of municipal reform, and after a general post-World War II reawakening of citizen interest in civic and political activity at the community level, many of the cities that are still operating with the organization for city planning called for by the Standard Act have either ignored the intent of the ordinances or charter provisions under which they have been operating or they have already made major changes in their basic city-planning organization legislation. Ways have been found to remove entire commissions whose members were hostile to newly elected political leaders, and councils have united to overrule commission recommendations based on a general plan that they had never seen and that, as a natural consequence, they did not understand. During recent years, the facts of political life have reminded the American people convincingly that final power to enact laws, to raise and spend money, to control or significantly influence the appointments to citizen commissions that as a political reality can never be more than advisory, and to define by ordinance or control in other ways the organization and specific functions of such commissions, resides in the hands of the elected representatives of the people—the members of the city council. Even in the largest cities with strong-mayor governments, city councils are rediscovering their powers, although some are still being manipulated by well-intentioned reform mayors or behind-the-scenes political bosses. In a system of representative democracy it has always been considered a fundamental principle that lawmaking, taxation, final action on all capital improvements, and the formulation of public policies to guide actions in these matters are direct responsibilities of the legislative body. Why, then, did the authors of the Standard Act attempt to go against this principle?

The reasons given in the Act in answer to the question posed above are, as usual, plausible and persuasive, as the reader will see for himself when he considers the five explanatory footnotes presented below. In footnote 10, which presents the opening argument for an independent commission, the authors say:

> . . . the planning function is quite different and distinct from the legislative function. The city council represents the people of the city for the length of the term for which it is elected and during that term is to be deemed to possess the qualification for and has its time and energies taken up with the problems of current legislation and current control of the public moneys. The making of a plan or design for a long period of future years, a period which will cover the incumbency of many successive councils, is an entirely different type of work, raises problems which involve different factors, and requires different qualifications. The board which has this work in charge should be free form the pressures of purely current problems. Consequently council, by virtue of the very nature of its functions and by virtue of its term of office, does not have the qualifications, the time, or the political status which would make it an appropriate body for this long-term planning work. That work needs to be intrusted to a board or body specially chosen for the purpose and given a place in the structure of the government specially appropriate to the nature of this planning work. Later provisions of this act and later notes explain the mutual relationships between the planning commission, the plan, council, and current developments.

Having thus stated the reasons for attempting to create an independent commission as free as possible from the political influence of the elected representatives of the people, the Act then proposes six-year, overlapping terms for the members of the commission and describes the reasons for this decision in footnote 20:

> *"six years":* The principle which explains this period is that the terms of members of the planning commission should so overlap the terms of councilmen and of the officials of the city administration that, in the first place, the whole planning commission will not go out when a city administration or council goes out and, in the second place, that no city administration shall during a single term have the power to name a majority of the members of the planning commission . . .

Next, in explaining the provision of the Act that calls for adoption of the plan by the commission only, the authors say in footnote 44:

"adoption": Planning is intended to be a process whereby the larger lines and directions of future public and private development will be influenced and to some extent controlled. It should be designed to cover a long period of years, much longer than the term of office of any single city council, including the city council which is in office at the time of adoption of the plan or any part of it. Legislation is designed to meet pressing and immediate needs, whether it takes the form of penal legislation controlling persons or property or whether it be fiscal legislation expending public funds. The two functions, planning and legislation, are important and essential to the efficient working of city government, but they are quite different from each other and involve differing considerations, differing points of view, and differing talents and interests. The two functions, therefore, need to be reposed in two separate bodies, one called in this act the planning commission and the other the council.

Furthermore, a city council is elected for a specific term during which it is the representative of the people. Beyond that term it is not the representative of the people, and its legislation, therefore, should be restricted to the matters which require decision and enactment into law and action during its specific term. For these reasons the plan should not be required to be submitted to or approved by council. Each council will finally determine the public improvements for which moneys are to be expended during its term, and as to each council the plan will have the legal status given to it in the later section of the act, a status which does not finally bind council. In other words, in the end the planning commission cannot bind council. To pass upon the plan itself, however, is, for the above reasons, not within the appropriate functions of council; and a requirement that the plan be submitted to and approved by council will have many disadvantages. For instance, in case of a political overturn a latter council might be hostile to the plan as the work of its overturned predecessor . . .

Finally, the "two-thirds" procedure specified in the Act which limits the freedom of the council to legislate on all physical-development and general-plan matters once the commission has adopted the plan is explained and justified in footnotes 46 and 52:

"Legal status of official plan": This section is one of the most important of the act. Numerous matters are constantly before council for decision. Some of them may represent a departure from or violation of the city plan. Others may represent matters upon which the city plan contains no light but which involve a major planning problem. As council proceeds from week to week with its work, pressed by all sorts of pressures to pass this, that, or the other measure, there is great danger,

especially in the early stages of the planning movement in any city, that the city plan may come to be ignored or given rather casual attention. Consequently, the State planning legislation should devise a means whereby, from the time there is a city plan or a substantial part thereof, all matters which involve location of public buildings, improvements, utilities, etc., should receive city planning consideration; that is, full consideration of their bearing upon the city plan. The requirement contained in the text appears reasonable and adequate and has worked well where it has been adopted. It provides that in the case of any improvement in which the planning problem is involved the opinion of the planning commission must first be asked. If the planning commission approves, the council will be free to proceed with whatever affirmative vote is required by the general law governing it. If the commission disapproves, there naturally ensues a reconsideration, with probably a full discussion between council and commission. Council retains the power it should have, namely, the power to decide in the end; but in order that this decision may be after full consideration of the planning problem and of the relation of the proposed improvement to other city developments, the requirement of a vote of two-thirds of council is reasonable and justified.

"overrule": When a specific improvement has been submitted to the commission after the comprehensive plan has been adopted and the commission disapproves, the council should not be allowed to overrule such disapproval except by a substantial majority. It is, therefore, provided that such action shall be by not less than two-thirds of the votes of the entire membership of council and not merely a majority of two-thirds of those who happen to be present on a given day. Such a provision militates against hasty action, when a bare quorum might be present, and will also necessitate full discussion and the members going on record where important action is to be taken.

The two principal points that are made in these footnotes may be restated in this way: First, since councilmen are elected for relatively short terms, and since immediate political pressures are always present and dominant in their minds, they cannot be expected to have any long-range objectives or policies of their own that will serve as a logical basis for the decisions they must make every week on so-called short-range matters. Second, since the situation just described is assumed to be true and unavoidable, some way must be found to force these politicians to permit a group of wiser men, whose tenure the council is not supposed to control, to make a general plan for the city and to limit the freedom of the council to legislate on all matters affecting the physical development of the community.

The underlying judgment here seems to be one of almost complete distrust and lack of confidence in the ability of the members of the city council to be reasonable. The combination of this distrust and lack of confidence with an undue concern about the technical complexity of the plan-making job and the job of keeping the plan up to date led the authors of the Act to attempt to create a nonpolitical public body, which was the objective of many reformers during the first decades of the century, and, without really wanting or intending to do so, to free this body from accountability by consciously excluding from the Act any specific definition of the essential physical elements to be dealt with in the general plan and by consciously permitting piecemeal adoption of the plan with no provision requiring publication of the plan in its entirety in any form.

As will be shown in the next section of this chapter, Mr. Bettman himself by 1945 had changed his mind concerning the need for "an express definition" of the general plan that could be understood and adopted by the city council, and, shortly after his death in 1946, the post-World War II revision of the Cincinnati general plan, which he had done so much to make possible, was itself adopted by the city council after it had been summarized and made widely available in a form that was understandable to the general citizenry.

During the past fifteen years an ever-increasing number of city councils throughout the United States has taken formal action on the general plans prepared by their commissions. Many leading members of the city-planning profession, however, are still strongly opposed to this procedure on both practical and theoretical grounds.[7] As a consequence, relatively few general plans have been prepared with the city council as client in mind. Thus, since 1950 a large number of hybrid general plans have been completed, prepared by professional staffs competent in their ability to grasp and deal with the essential technical facets of the plan, but unconcerned and unclear in their thinking as to who would eventually have to understand, control, and make use of the plan in governing the physical development of their cities. In my judgment, no way can be found to keep the council from exercising effective control over the city-planning commission and the general plan once the leaders of the council become aware, as they inevitably will, of the significance of the commission and the general plan. As a consequence, I believe an attempt must now be made to encourage and assist the council to be as wise and as fair as is possible by placing the general plan firmly in its hands, in a form suited to its unique role as the primary policy-making and governing body of the community.

---

[7] See John T. Howard, "In Defense of Planning Commissions," *Journal of the American Institute of Planners,* Vol. 17, No. 2 (Spring, 1951), pp. 89–94.

AFTER WORLD WAR II: REALITIES AND CRYSTALLIZATION

In the preceding pages I have attempted to single out and describe the most important problems that developed as a result of the efforts of city planners, city-planning commissioners, and city councilmen to make use of the general-plan concept expressed in the Standard Act during the twenty-year period following the publication of the Act in 1928. The practice of city planning in the United States during these two decades was unavoidably experimental. In a historical sense, the practitioners of this period were occupying strange territory in a hurry and, as a result of their difficult experiences, they were making it possible for the next generation to see more clearly where to build anew the foundations of the profession.

By the end of the 1950's, many medium-sized council-manager cities had joined the larger strong-mayor cities in establishing permanent city-planning programs and professional staffs. Practitioners everywhere began to see that the experience following World War II with the technical city-planning job had clarified the essential physical elements to be dealt with in the general plan. City councils and mayors began to assert their political supremacy and control over the supposedly independent city-planning commissions. A new crystallization of basic city-planning concepts was beginning to take place.

During the first decade following World War II, two realities imposed themselves on the prewar trends that had caused the confusion and uncertainty in the use of the general-plan concept of the Standard Act. First, as a result of the slow but sure effects of the municipal reform movement, cities throughout the country established permanent professional city-planning staffs and began to give continuous, thoughtful, top-level attention to the job of understanding and guiding the physical development of their communities. And second, at the same time, as a result of the pressing demands created by the wartime postponement of essential public works, by the tremendous postwar growth of our cities and metropolitan regions, and by the natural urge to do constructive tasks after the years of destruction caused by the war, city governments changed from negative to positive their approach to the job of city planning. Whether they realized it or not, the mayors, councilmen, and city-planning commissioners of America's cities following World War II no longer thought of patching up bits and pieces of the urban environment. The reality of the demand for, and the obvious interrelatedness of, the postwar freeway, urban-redevelopment, off-street-parking, school, recreation, and metropolitan rapid-transit projects, coupled with the need for a complete overhaul of the twenty- to thirty-year-old original zoning plans that had been used to govern postwar private development in the central business districts, industrial areas, and residential neighborhoods and suburbs, forced civic leaders in American cities everywhere to change their point of view toward city planning. As a result of these two major changes, most of the newly established city-planning staffs were pushed into the job of working out some kind of over-all scheme for the physical development of their cities that could be used by the leaders of their governments to relate in a reasonable way the major postwar public-works projects to one another and to the proposed new zoning plans. The years of skeleton staffs, of major concern with the administration of crude, first-stage zoning ordinances, and of illogical and misleading piecemeal plans had passed. The first great period of general-plan work and of thorough testing of the general-plan concept had begun.

Between 1945 and 1960 general plans were prepared and published, in one form or another, by the cities of Cincinnati, Detroit, Berkeley, Cleveland, and Seattle. These plans were comparable in their subject matter, in the basic physical elements with which they dealt, and in their general characteristics. They expressed, in effect, a reassertion of the Olmsted-Bettman concept of the general plan on these points. This is not surprising when it is realized that the professional staffs and directors concerned were influenced to a great degree by the ideas and experience of Ladislas Segoe, one of the outstanding city-planning consultants in the United States.

Mr. Segoe, an engineer by training, was one of the principal professional staff members involved in the 1925 Cincinnati general-plan effort, which led to one of the first sustained comprehensive city-planning programs in the United States. Beginning in 1925, Mr. Segoe and Mr. Bettman were closely associated in their professional careers. During the decade following World War II, when the first major opportunities for the widespread practice of city planning throughout the United States materialized, Mr. Segoe was the principal figure in the profession providing the link between the general-plan concept as worked out by Olmsted and Bettman and the ideas that were tested and developed by the post-World War II general-plan programs in cities throughout the country. Perhaps the most important and influential expression of Mr. Segoe's outstanding technical competence was made indirectly, by Mr. Bettman, during the 1940's when Mr. Bettman adopted one of Mr. Segoe's most important ideas and changed his position on the question of whether or not an express definition of the general plan should be included in city-planning enabling legislation.

In 1928, Mr. Bettman was, as we have seen, one of the leading proponents of the "no express definition" policy. After years of experience following the publication of the Standard Act, he reversed his position. In 1945, under the sponsorship of the American Society of Planning Officials, he published a draft of a model urban-redevelopment act which included an express definition of what by that time had been rediscovered as the essential physical elements with which the general plan must deal. His definition reads as follows:

> The planning commission is . . . directed to make . . . a master plan of the municipality . . . which shall include *at least* [emphasis added] a land use plan which designates the proposed general distribution and general locations and extents of uses of the land for housing, business, industry, communication and transportation terminals, recreation, education, public buildings, public utilities and works, public reservations and other categories of public and private uses of the land.[8]

In contemporary terms this definition may be rephrased to read: The general plan of the municipality must deal with, as an absolute minimum, the following three essential physical elements: (a) working-and-living areas, (b) community facilities, and (c) circulation. The most significant feature of the general plans that were prepared by Cincinnati, Detroit, Berkeley, Cleveland, and Seattle was their positive acceptance and use of the Bettman-Segoe postwar conception of the essential physical elements to be dealt with in the general plan. The fact that Mr. Bettman's change of position on this point was endorsed, in effect, by the American Society of Planning Officials was of major significance because the executive director of the Society, Mr. Walter Blucher, by 1945 had become one of the most influential and respected leaders of the city-planning profession.

There were many other cities that "learned by doing," without the advice of consultants, how to prepare and use general plans. Needless to say, it took most of these cities longer to get under way and they made many time-consuming and costly detours. It must also be acknowledged that there were and still are a significant number of cities with active, sustained city-planning programs that have not completed general plans, including some that have not yet even begun that task of preparing a general plan. Some of these cities, including Los Angeles and New York, are, in effect, continuing to experiment with either the continuous, comprehensive-planning approach, which places no value on a firm, unified general plan for physical develop-

---

[8] Alfred Bettman, in *City and Regional Planning Papers,* edited by Arthur C. Comey (Cambridge, Mass.: Harvard University Press, 1946), pp. 263 and 264.

ment, or the piecemeal-planning approach, which calls for citywide single-facet plans for obvious needs, such as freeways, rather than first dealing with the basic physical elements that must be covered in the general plan, and in particular the working-and-living-areas element. I believe that it will be simply a matter of time before the comprehensive-planning concept and the piecemeal-planning concept are judged to be less reasonable and less effective than the general-plan concept.[9]

The lessons of practical experience gained by the leading city-planning directors, senior staff members, and consultants who had been directly involved in the post-World War II general-plan programs were brought into focus, crystallized, and expressed in three significant documents that were published in 1950, 1952, and 1955. In 1950, the Housing and Home Finance Agency of the federal government, in carrying out the urban-redevelopment provisions of the Housing Act of 1949, found it necessary to issue a formal policy statement presenting an express definition of the general plan. In 1952 the Board of Governors of the American Institute of Planners approved, by official action, the final draft of an educational booklet entitled "City Planning and Urban Development," which was published that year by the United States Chamber of Commerce, that included a definition of the general plan. And in 1955, the California Legislature approved an amendment to the City and County Planning Enabling Act, replacing the 25-year-old provisions of the Act which had originally been taken from the Standard Act, and which had failed to explain in a logical manner the meaning of the general-plan concept, with an explicit definition of the essential physical elements that must be dealt with in the general plan. The amendment had been proposed by the Legislative Committee of the California Chapter of the American Institute of Planners with the approval of the officers and executive committee of the Chapter. At the time this action was taken, the membership of the California Chapter constituted more than one-fourth of the membership of the entire Institute.

The general-plan definitions included in each of these three documents are identical on three important points. They all reaffirm the Olmsted-Bettman idea that the scope of the general plan should be limited to questions of physical development; they all express agreement with the idea that

[9] A great deal would be gained by everyone from a thorough study and documentation of the full implications of governing a large city with the aid of a well-financed city-planning program that *does not* call for the preparation of a general plan for physical development that can be understood and controlled by the elected leaders of the community.

every general plan must deal with certain essential physical elements, including a working-and-living-areas element, a community-facilities element, and a circulation element; and they all attempt to make the point that the detailed zoning plan of a community must not be confused with the general, long-range proposals set forth in the general plan itself. The consensus expressed by the agreement on these three points represented, in my opinion, a major forward step in the development of the city-planning profession in the United States. Some of the most confusing contradictions that had characterized the practice of the profession during the 1930's and 1940's were faced and resolved by the men who participated in the reformulation and restatement of the general-plan concept that was made necessary by the preparation of each of these documents.

However, while the area of agreement on the technical questions of subject matter, essential physical elements to be dealt with, and the distinction between the zoning plan and the general plan is constantly growing and becoming consolidated, the significance of the change in the basic uses of the general plan, from a technical guide to be used by a supposedly nonpolitical commission to a statement of public policy intended to be used by the city council in governing the physical development of the community, has not been generally recognized. In an effort to clarify the nature of the general plan, therefore, we now turn to an exploration of the uses of the general plan as determined by the needs of its primary client—the municipal legislative body.

III

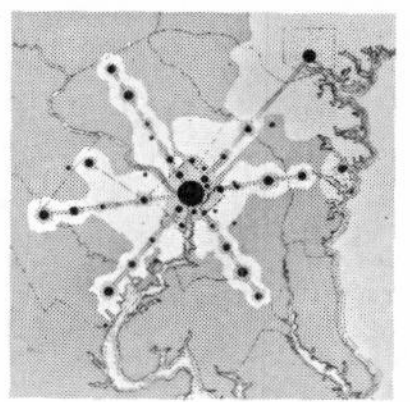

THE LEGISLATIVE USES OF THE GENERAL PLAN

THE USES of the general plan cannot be dealt with in the abstract; they must be related to the particular persons whose needs the plan must serve. Accordingly, this chapter is subdivided into five sections in which the primary *legislative* uses of the plan are considered in detail.

While it is recognized that the general plan will also serve important needs of others—the chief executive, the city-planning commission, the director of city planning, the heads of city departments, other government agencies, the public, and the courts—the needs of the municipal legislature are judged to be paramount. If a conflict should arise between the different needs to be accommodated, it should be resolved in favor of the needs of the municipal legislative body. The needs of the city council must be met first, and after that the needs of the others should be met in the best way possible. If this thesis prevails, we will see the evolutionary development of a new group of supplementary control instruments aimed at meeting the primary needs of the other users of the plan that will enable these users to play their respective roles with ever-greater effectiveness in the collective work of improving the physical environment of our cities.

The legislative uses of the general plan as they are described in this chapter recognize the partnership of the city council and the chief executive in both formulation and implementation of policy. The chief executive uses the general plan in the same way as does the city council. However, the chief executive also has other, more detailed duties than the council in matters of physical development. If the general plan is prepared primarily as an instrument of the executive, rather than as an instrument of the council, the plan necessarily will have a different focus and will be a different kind of document.

The primary legislative uses of the general plan presented here are based upon the premises and beliefs stated in Chapter I. Although no general information is available that gives any indication of how many city councils in the United States operate in the manner described here, city councils will sooner or later find it necessary to have a general plan and to make use of it in the regular performance of their legislative work.

The attempt to clarify and describe the legislative uses of the general plan should not be thought of as an attempt to classify or pigeonhole the activities of the city council in any forced or unnatural way. The following primary legislative uses are not mutually exclusive. The uses do not fall into neat compartments. They are interdependent and overlapping, and at times they operate simultaneously. What is described in this chapter, as comprehensively as possible, are the five most important legislative uses of the general plan for the physical development of a community.

POLICY DETERMINATION

The general plan is first and foremost an instrument through which the city council considers, debates, and finally agrees upon a coherent, unified set of general, long-range policies for the physical development of a community. The general plan should be designed, therefore, to facilitate the work of the councilmen as they attempt to focus their attention on the community's major development problems and opportunities. Plan preparation enables the members of the council to back away from their preoccupation with pressing day-to-day issues and clarify their ideas as to the kind of community they want to create as a result of their many specific decisions.

Since the city council must govern the physical development of the community, the council must develop a group of policies and a general physical design for the community. It is not possible to govern a city without a plan of some sort. A city council unaware of the general-plan concept develops and uses policies that are implicit and unwritten. Unstated policies, which include a scheme for the future physical development of the community, are used to control physical development. Such policies may be understood by all members of the council, or they may exist in the minds of and be apparent only to the dominant members of the council. The general plan brings such implicit policies into the open. It assures that these policies are determined through democratic processes. It puts these policies on record and fixes responsibility for them on the council. In time, the general-plan policy-determination process results in improved policies which lead to major citywide physical improvements.

Policy determination covers everything from the realization that a policy is needed to the final selection of a specific policy. Usually the early steps in the process are taken by the council's advisors—the chief executive, the director of city planning, and the city-planning commission—but the final steps are taken by the council itself.

Since the final policy decision will be made by the council, it is essential that the plan be prepared in a manner that enables the members of the council to be familiar with it and at ease with it. Just as councilmen learned how to control the unified annual budget, and in so doing learned to deal openly and confidently with such major controversial issues as salaries, capital improvements, new programs and positions, and the tax rate, they will learn how to control and use the general plan for physical development.

It is a mistake to underestimate the interest of councilmen in city planning. They are very familiar with the community and soon learn that most of their actions as council members involve questions of physical development. In common with any group of persons, however, every council usually includes some individuals who have not developed the habit of thought that enables them to see the need for any general policy. In matters of physical development, such persons usually can be educated to understand that they must discipline their decisions. They learn that it is to their advantage to acknowledge the need for a plan and to make a plan with their fellow council members, or to dissent from the majority view on the basis of a definite alternative set of policies.

Policy determination should include the consideration and evaluation of the major alternatives that are open to the community, culminating in the council's decision to adopt one of the alternatives as its firm policy. Thorough study of alternatives is not always necessary or possible in conducting everyday municipal affairs, but a thorough study is definitely feasible and desirable in determining the important policies which comprise a general plan.

The council's advisors should present to the council alternatives and indicate the consequences that they judge are most likely to result from pursuing each alternative. In contemporary practice, the presentation of alternatives by city planners is not done often enough. Too many professionals make their own selection of an alternative and present it to the council as a single firm recommendation. City planners should make recommendations, but they should also point out other available choices. If the profession does not anticipate this important need, it will learn about it from the rough demands made by reform groups and the leaders of forceful political minorities.

The alternatives chosen by the city council go into the general plan as statements of adopted policy. It is also desirable to have a record in the general-plan document of the major alternatives that were considered and rejected, along with the reasons for their rejection. When conditions change, these alternatives will have to be reconsidered. They probably will be revived for reconsideration when a different political bloc takes control of the city council.

The general plan's usefulness in policy determination operates at several points in time, specifically during: (1) preparation, consideration, and initial adoption of the general plan; (2) annual review and amendment of the plan; (3) major reconsideration of the entire plan every ten years; and (4) consideration of day-to-day physical-development matters which call for review of general, long-range policies. This day-to-day aspect of the policy-determination use is continuous. It means that the plan is being used constantly by the city council and that, from time to time, it will be necessary to amend the plan during the year between the annual review and amendment sessions.

Determination of the initial policies that go into the plan is the most important stage in this time sequence. When the plan is first adopted, it should represent as accurately as possible the policies of the city council. If this representation is successful, the legislators will be committed to the plan. They will be ready to move forward in carrying out the policies of the plan. They will be familiar with the major development issues confronting their community and they will recognize that despite whatever controversies were precipitated during the preparation of the plan, it is no longer possible to govern without an explicit statement of their physical-development policies.

To achieve the degree of familiarity, confidence, and commitment required by members of the council, there should be an extended period of debate and education between the first presentation of the general plan in its tentative form and final adoption by the council in revised form. During this period the council should study the proposed plan thoroughly, devote work sessions to it, and conduct formal hearings on it. During this period the proposed plan should be distributed to the citizens and to all private, civic, and governmental groups and agencies active in community affairs. Before the council can act, it needs to learn the reactions of its constituents to the proposed policies. The general-plan document must be designed with this need in mind. If the official statement of the proposed plan is not available to or cannot be understood by the citizens and the leaders of the informal governing groups of the community, the debate will be crippled. The council will learn, to its discomfort, that its general plan deals with controversial issues in a politically dangerous and irresponsible manner. When this happens, the council usually, and quite properly, holds the director of city planning responsible.

Council adoption of the general plan should not be recommended if it appears that the action will be no more than a perfunctory formality or gesture. Once the council learns to state and debate its community-development policies openly, however, it will need to adopt the general plan as a formal expression of its unified policy. Only a formal expression of adoption can make clear to the community that the plan does in fact represent the policies of the council.

As conditions in the community change and new problems come to the forefront, the city council will have to alter some of its long-range policies on physical development. Subjects dealt with inadequately in the original version of the plan will require fuller treatment. New information that becomes available will, in certain cases, call for revisions in the plan. It is inevitable that the original plan will contain mistakes which will need correction as time goes by. Some policies of the plan will prove to be unworkable or unrealistic. City planners are limited in their ability to predict the future, and some of their forecasts will turn out to be wrong. The 1950 Washington, D.C., general plan is an excellent illustration of this point. Within a few years after the completion of this plan, there was a tremendous, unexpected increase in population (the 1980 estimate was passed before 1960), racial desegregation of schools was required, and the enactment of the interstate highway program made possible highway construction on a scale and at a rate that was not anticipated in the plan.

Although membership of the city council will change periodically, the general plan should express as accurately as possible the policies of the current council. Freshmen councilmen sooner or later will become aware of the policy agreements worked out by their predecessors; they will be required to act as soon as they take office on proposals that will either implement or go counter to the policies of the general plan. When there is a major political turnover in the council, the new dominant group will find a way to shape and express its own key policies. The general plan should be designed, as a legislative policy-control instrument, to facilitate a political turnover in the council; if the plan hinders the exercise of legitimate power, it will be, and indeed should be, ignored.

Annual review and amendment is a formal procedure that is designed to encourage the council to keep the plan up to date. It requires the council to look over the plan once a year and decide whether any of the long-range policies should be modified in light of physical-development activities during the past year. It also serves to refresh the memories of the councilmen on the provisions of the plan and to inform any newcomers on the council as to the plan's contents. Properly done, the annual review and amendment procedure helps place the principal controversial issues of the preceding year in perspective and encourages the leaders of the council to set their sights on the major steps to be taken during the coming year to carry out the plan.

The annual review and amendment procedure should take place just prior to the yearly reformulation by the council of its capital-improvements program. A major portion of every municipal budget is concerned with capital improvements, and since the general plan is designed to serve as the council's policy guide on all major questions of physical development, the city council will, once the annual review and amendment procedure is understood, find it extremely valuable to review the plan once each year several weeks prior to the time when the councilmen must act on the budget. Such a review procedure brings about a natural focus on questions of physical-development policy by members of the city council shortly before they must make decisions on questions of financial policy concerning the allocation of funds for capital improvements. This timing of the annual review places the general plan in a challenging, practical context. It compels the director of city planning, the city-planning commission, and the chief executive to resummarize, restate, and reclarify the main ideas of the plan. Annual review compels the council to reassert its authority in an area that clearly involves questions of basic policy and that always involves significant controversies and conflicting ideas with which the council, sooner or later, must deal.

Before the idea of annual review and amendment of the plan by the council became crystallized in my mind in 1953, I had no effective answer to the argument that council adoption of the plan results in a policy statement that dates quickly, and hence becomes an actual detriment to those working to bring about improvements in the physical environment. Experience in Berkeley since 1955 has demonstrated that the annual review and amendment procedure does work and that it gradually builds up the confidence of the members of the council and the city-planning commission in their ability, as nonprofessionals, to exercise the control necessary if the main proposals of the plan are to be carried out. Although annual review and amendment now is generally accepted as an obvious and commonsense idea, this was not the case just a few short years ago.

At least every ten years there should be a thorough reconsideration of the entire general plan. This effort should be comparable to that undertaken at the time of the original preparation of the plan. Much staff study will be required and all the background data and forecasts must be brought up to date. Again, there should be a lengthy period of community debate and education before the revised plan is finally acted upon by the council.

This thorough reconsideration is needed because the changes occurring over a long period will not be merely the sum of the changes from year to year. Some long-range trends are not discernible in the issues which arise from day to day, or even at annual review time. Annual amendments to the plan reflect rather specific current issues. From time to time, the city planners and citizen policy-makers must step back from, re-examine, and recreate their basic physical-development policies.

In addition to annual and decennial reviews of the general plan, amendments should be made at any time the council deems appropriate. When a major physical-development issue comes before the council for decision, members of the council must study and restate the general-plan policies that apply to the issue at hand and retrace the thinking that led to the policies. If the policies are reaffirmed, no change in the general plan is needed, but if they are changed, then the general plan should be amended.

This process of restating general-plan policies that apply to the issue at hand results in the frequent testing of plan policies in the heat of legislative debate. As a result, the policies of the plan are upheld, or they are modified. The councilmen, the city-planning commissioners, and the director of city planning cannot anticipate all the implications of the policies and proposals inherent in the general plan at the time the plan is adopted. This inability to anticipate is unavoidable. Later, when it is clear that certain policies of the plan are producing results that were not anticipated or desired, these policies should be changed. In such cases, the council should amend the plan as soon as is possible through normal legislative procedures.

The policy-determination use of the plan operates simultaneously with the policy-effectuation use, described in the next section of this chapter. In addition to the major issues that may lead to general-plan amendments during the year, there always will be a substantial number of specific issues that are not of major importance that must be acted upon every day by the council. Viewed together over a period of time, the total effect of the day-to-day actions on such matters is very important. In minor matters the council will consistently attempt to carry out its general plan, or its actions, viewed over a period of time, will reveal support for a different set of policies than those set forth in the plan or for no coherent set of policies at all.

It is admittedly difficult to draw the line between too many and too few amendments. This is a question which must be answered according to the individual circumstances of each case. If a general plan truly represents the policies of the council, and the councilmen understand it and, as a consequence, are committed to it, then they will not propose many important amendments. Councilmen should realize that the amendability of the general plan is intended to facilitate their direct, unhampered control of the plan. They should understand that the amendment procedures must not be abused, that the general plan must not be in a constant state of flux. The plan, to be useful to the council, must have a substantial degree of permanence and continuity; if policies continually change, then little progress will be made toward achieving any of them. The plan should not be merely a reflection of all current council decisions, some of which are bound to be expedient; rather, the great majority of council decisions on physical-development matters should reflect the long-range policies expressed in the plan.

Responsibility for making the general plan usable as a legislative policy-determination and policy-control instrument clearly rests with the city-planning director. If he makes sure that the original plan embodies the thinking of the council and maintains a determined effort, with the support of the chief executive and the city-planning commission, to teach the councilmen how to use the plan, then he will enjoy the satisfaction of working with a reasonably firm plan that provides the basis for a constructive community-improvement program.

The policy-determination use of the general plan as described in the preceding pages defines the need for a statement of council policy that successfully brings into focus the major physical-development problems and opportunities of the community and sets forth a unified group of basic policies and a general physical design for the community that the council can use in governing the affairs of the community. The policy-determination use highlights the unavoidable responsibility of the city council to make basic policies and to see that its policies are carried out. For the city-planning profession it means that awareness of the policy aspects of plan-making work must be greatly increased. The policy-determination use emphasizes the need for developing a way of thinking and a method of documentation that distinguishes between the policies and the physical-design proposals of the plan, and between the different levels of policy inherent in the nature of the general plan that must be clarified so that the council can make the plan its own and use it intelligently.

POLICY EFFECTUATION

Most city councils meet regularly every week. The agendas for these meetings require action by the council on a wide variety of specific projects, policies, and laws that are directly concerned with the physical development of the city. The general plan enables the council to make its decisions on these matters on the basis of a clearly stated, unified set of general, long-range policies which have been carefully thought out and adopted. Thus, current issues are viewed against a clear picture of what the council itself has decided is the most desirable scheme for the future physical development of the community. The general plan serves as a practical working guide to the councilmen in making everyday decisions.

This use of the general plan by members of the council in the performance of their policy-effectuation work frequently and naturally leads to a new round of debate that is concerned directly with the policy-determination use. When a specific proposal comes before the council for decision, the pertinent portions of the general plan are reviewed and restated. In most cases, recommendations for action by the council will be in accord with the policies of the plan, and the council decision will be made without the need for debate. Frequently, however, the proposal will bring out the need to alter certain of the council's long-range policies, a clear indication that the plan should be amended. To prevent confusion between the two uses, it should be emphasized that policy determination leads to decisions on general, long-range policies, while policy effectuation leads to decisions on specific proposals and issues requiring definite and immediate action. Also, the policy-effectuation use of the general plan is concerned directly and solely with the use of the plan by the council in effectuating its own policies through its day-to-day decisions. Others in city government also effectuate the council's policies, but these activities do not fall within the categories of legislative uses of the general plan.

The policy-effectuation use of the plan is of critical importance. It is in the exercise or lack of exercise of the policy-effectuation use that most general plans succeed or fail. To be effective, the general plan must be brought to bear on all physical-development decisions made by the city council. The existence of an adopted general plan is without meaning or significance unless it is actually used by the city council.

The Legislative Uses of the General Plan

In its use of the general plan as a guide to policy effectuation, the council needs the assistance of its advisors—especially the city-planning commission, the director of city planning, and the chief executive. The council also needs the views of other commissions and department heads as it moves to implement its plan. Once the general plan has been adopted, the city-planning commission and director of city planning should be specifically charged by the council with the duty of studying every current development proposal to judge its relationship to the general plan. Such a procedure of regular, automatic referral calls for a report and recommendation by the city-planning commission on all physical development matters that come before the city council for its decision. If a matter is important enough to require action by the city council, it is important enough to require a report from the city-planning commission.

Basically, however, the general plan, and not the city-planning commission, should guide the city council. This is the inevitable consequence of recognition of the superior role of the council. Once the role of the council is accepted, and after the need for an official statement of council development policy is acknowledged, it is then necessary to guard against rigidity in the application of the plan on one hand and expedient compromise and destructive amendments on the other hand. Acceptance of the council's role and the council's use of the plan in policy effectuation should lead to a new and much closer relationship between the council and the city-planning commission than existed prior to adoption and conscious use of the plan.

The general idea of referral is sometimes taken to mean referral only to the city-planning director and his staff and not to the city-planning commission. Formal action by the city-planning commission is essential. Experience has demonstrated that inevitably situations develop in which administrative officials bring pressure to bear on the city-planning director if he alone is required to determine whether or not specific projects are in accord with the general plan. The planning commission, since it is directly responsible to the council and not subordinate to any administrative officer, is in a far better position to handle such pressures and to assure the council that it will receive the full range of advice that it needs in order to act wisely on controversial issues.

The types of specific physical-development matters which require action during the normal course of council business can be divided into two categories: (1) those measures which are designed to carry out the general plan and give it legislative effect and (2) other matters which routinely require council approval and should be viewed in the context of the general plan. Generally speaking, the first category includes matters which come up only once or at very infrequent intervals, while in the second category are matters which continually arise in the ordinary conduct of council business.

Examples of the first category are the citywide zoning ordinance, subdivision regulations, the annual capital-improvements program, plans for urban-renewal project areas, and detailed development plans for specific districts or precincts and for citywide physical facilities, such as the park system or the circulation system.

The detailed plans in the first category are instruments devised by agencies of the city government to enable the council to effectuate its policies, to carry out its general plan for physical development. Although for many years the relationship between detailed effectuation measures and the general plan was obscured—very largely because the need for such measures is more apparent than the need for a general plan—once a council has adopted a plan it will continue to adjust its way of dealing with physical-development issues until it works out a justifiable relationship between policy and effectuation. Measures that fall into the first category are usually drawn up by the city-planning staff, considered and acted upon by the city-planning commission after review by the particular departments concerned and in most, but not all, cases by the chief executive, and are then forwarded to the city council for final action. There is no question of referral for these matters, since they almost always originate in the city-planning department. Consequently, there is no question concerning the nature of these measures as policy-effectuation devices. The fact that they exist, that they are essential, and that they must be coordinated with one another and must point in some definite direction insofar as the future physical development of the community is concerned illustrates the reality both of the need for a general plan and the need for a procedure that will enable the council to grasp readily the relationship between major physical-development measures and its own long-range general plan.

Examples of the second category include rezoning cases, use-permit and variance appeals, subdivision plans, street closings, park-development plans, specific street plans and similar public-works department projects, transit-route proposals, and school, fire-station, library, and similar public-building projects. Also included in the second category are a wide variety of other matters which the council must act upon that affect the physical development of the community, such as decisions concerning diagonal versus parallel parking, overhead wires versus underground installations, and traffic signals and traffic regulations of all kinds.

The items in the second category constitute the day-to-day business of city planning and, to a very large extent, of city government. Usually they do not originate in the city-planning department, but are the result of proposals developed by private citizens and builders, other departments in city hall, or other public agencies. Some of these proposals normally are considered by the city-planning staff and the city-planning commission prior to submission to the council, but some are not and do require referral by the council.

Clearly the general plan should serve as a guide to council action on the detailed physical-development and control measures in the first category. The general plan provides the context for such measures, and the city-planning staff should rely on the plan in preparing them. These detailed instruments are very significant in city planning, and the general plan must be used in their preparation.

It is not clear whether the general plan is the proper guide to decisions on the day-to-day matters falling in the second category. If the decision is large in scale and importance, then the council should rely on the general plan. This would be true of the location of a freeway interchange or the rezoning of a sizable area. But if the decision is minor, such as the location of a fire station on a specific lot or the rezoning of one piece of property on the boundary of a neighborhood shopping district, the general plan, because of its generality, may not be much help to the members of the council.

The general plan will not provide the answers to all the small questions which come before the council. It is not supposed to; if the general plan were to be made into a detailed development plan it could not play its primary role in policy determination; it is not intended to be either an exact zoning map for all private property or a detailed blueprint for the development of all public property. As a consequence, the general plan will seem to be ambiguous if the council searches in it for a "yes" or "no" answer to certain kinds of detailed questions. Use of the general plan in such cases enables advocates on both sides of the issue to interpret the plan as supporting their position.

The remedy for this inadequacy is the detailed physical-development plan, which is based on the general plan and attempts to deal with specific development questions. If the council has adopted a physical-development plan for the area under consideration, then that plan will usually provide the "yes" or "no" answer for which the council is looking. In general, all of the control instruments mentioned in the first category are intended to mediate between the general plan and detailed development questions.

Despite the "general" character of the plan, the council should look at the general plan before ruling on specific proposals, even the minor and detailed ones. The general plan will give the council an idea of how the particular neighborhood dealt with in a specific proposal fits into the city-wide scheme. The general plan provides a longer look into the future than does a development plan. The general plan may bring out possible future problems and conflicts which the councilmen, if they fail to look at the plan, might overlook in their necessary concentration on specific issues and the need for immediate decisions.

The successful use of the general plan in policy effectuation is difficult to achieve. It requires patience and realism on the part of the director of city planning and the members of the council. It must be acknowledged that a substantial proportion of the citizens who become councilmen are not accustomed to using policy guides, and they may forget or ignore the general plan until they have learned from experience why a general policy is needed.

The policy-effectuation use of the general plan is the most tangible and practical use to the councilmen. In a way, it focuses on the present, rather than the future. It helps the council to make specific decisions *now*. It helps the council to make better current decisions by placing proposals for specific action in the context of a comprehensive, long-range scheme for the future physical development of the community.

COMMUNICATION

Through the general plan, the city council presents a clear picture of its long-range, general policies on community development to all other persons concerned with development. These persons include the city-planning commission and staff, the chief executive, other municipal departments, other governmental agencies, private developers, civic organizations, the general public, and the courts.

The general plan communicates to these persons the policies which the council has adopted. The council is on the "sending" end. Once the general plan is adopted and published, the councilmen themselves are not as actively engaged in communication as they are in policy effectuation; the general-plan document communicates for them.

The communication process is of greatest value to those on the "receiving" end. The general plan enables public and private interests engaged in physical development to anticipate decisions of the council. The people involved can relate specific projects to the general plan at the time they study projects and before the projects are submitted to the council for approval. City officials can use the plan as a guide to administrative decisions which do not require council confirmation.

Charles Haar has written that the general plan serves property interests as a prophecy of public reaction:

> The master plan is at the very minimum an intelligent prophecy as to the probable reaction of the local governmental authorities to a given proposal for development. Notice is thereby served on parties (public as well as private, it should be noted) dealing in decisions affecting urban conditions as to the probable outcome of their proposals, where these are dependent upon planning approval, or even where less direct but often more important sanction of needed public cooperation is involved. . . . In the light of the master plan, the private land owner may shape his own plans in the plastic stage when they have not yet crystallized; collision with the public interest can in some instances be deflected. Hence, the inclusion of the public interest in programs of local development may be effected without controversy.[1]

Haar's comments point out that as an instrument of communication the general plan acts as a positive force. It persuades private developers and suggests development projects to them. There are many physical-development proposals which never require council action—for example, the inauguration of a land use which conforms to the zoning ordinance. In such cases, the general plan in effect acts on behalf of the council by communicating its policies. Many important private decisions, which the council members never know about in any direct way, are made to carry out the plan as a result of publication of the plan by the council.

Although the councilmen may not be personally involved when the general plan is used to communicate council policy, the communication use is of tremendous benefit to them. It saves the council time by screening out many proposals which conflict with the council's policies as stated in the plan. To the extent that the plan is persuasive and self-fulfilling, it carries out the council's policies.

The plan is the basis for many programs and activities of the administrative staff which are aimed at effectuating the council's policies. The

---

[1] Charles H. Haar, "The Master Plan: An Impermanent Constitution," *Law and Contemporary Problems,* Vol. 20, No. 3 (Summer, 1955), p. 363.

city-planning staff, for example, prepares revisions of the zoning ordinance based upon policies which are expressed in the working-and-living-areas section of the general plan. This is an illustration of the communication use. In deciding whether to approve the proposed revision of the zoning ordinance or to make changes in it, the councilmen refer back to the general plan. This "referring back" is the policy-effectuation use in operation.

The general plan is not an infallible "predictor" of the council's actions. Some people will make the mistake of interpreting the plan as being more specific than does the council. The council may amend any part of the plan at any time, so there is never a guarantee that the council will sustain the plan in all of its particulars.

This is as it should be. No one should accept the plan as final and immutable. Everyone has the opportunity of pressing proposals before the council and trying to persuade the council to change the plan. This, in effect, reopens policy determination. Thus the communication use also produces a feedback which may result in revision of the policies originally stated in the plan.

The success of the communication use depends upon widespread distribution of the general plan. For this reason, the general plan should be published and made available free of charge. The general-plan document should be written and designed in a manner that will be both understandable and interesting to the average citizen. (The contents and organization of the general-plan document are discussed in detail in Chapter V.)

The general-plan document should include an explanation that the document is presenting *the* plan adopted by the city council as the official statement of the council's long-range, general policies, and that this is *the* plan used by the councilmen at every meeting in acting on physical-development proposals and issues.

The communication use is severely hampered if there is confusion as to what is the official plan of the city. If the council, city-planning commission, city-planning staff, and the chief executive all have their own plans, there will be confusion. If the plan is changed drastically from month to month, there will be confusion. If the plan is presented in a series of separate reports issued at different times, there will be confusion. If the plan consists of only one set of maps on the walls of the city-planning department office, there will be confusion.

To serve the communication use successfully, it is important that there is one official plan, that it is reasonably stable, that it is complete and self-contained in one document, and that it is readily available to the public. Council adoption of the general plan is the prerequisite to these requirements. The results of experience in Berkeley on these points were summarized by me in 1958 in a statement to newly elected California councilmen:

> . . . only recently have we had city planning commissions and city councils giving serious attention to the vitally important need for effective communication between the citizens and the officials of local government. In Berkeley, these qualities of the general plan have been interpreted to mean that the plan must be described in a single document that is prepared in such a way that it can be readily understood by every interested citizen and is available to every citizen who requests it. It has seemed to us that in no other way can we really succeed in making it possible for the interested citizen to consider at one time all of the related elements of policy and design that are involved in the plan.[2]

The necessity for communication requires that while the general plan must be suited primarily to the needs of the city council, it also must be suited to the needs of those to whom the council must communicate its policies if the policies are to be understood and carried out. Experience will help us find a way to satisfy the different users of the plan, although there always will be some unavoidable difficulties caused by the different needs of the various users. As long as the general plan is consciously limited to general, long-range policies, then the same kind of document should satisfy the primary needs of all the users of the plan.

A plan that has no meaning for the citizens or is in conflict with their views will not receive public support. Such a plan cannot be effective in influencing development. Conscientious, sustained effort to improve the general-plan document to serve the communication use is the only possible course of action open to the council and its advisors and staff in the context of the ideas developed in this book. Such efforts will result in far broader and far more effective citizen participation in plan-making. Such efforts also will result in frequent and desirable controversy on major physical-development issues, open and constructive debate, and sustained improvement of programs for the community.

CONVEYANCE OF ADVICE

The general plan enables the members of the legislative body to receive

[2] T. J. Kent, Jr., "City Planning: A Legislative Policy-Making Job," in *Proceedings, 6th Biennial Institute of Mayors and City Councilmen* (Berkeley, Calif.: League of California Cities, 1958), San Diego, June 5–6, 1958.

the counsel of its advisors in a coherent, unified form which assists them in determining and effectuating general, long-range development policies. The principal advisors involved are the city-planning director, the city-planning commission, and the chief executive.

The general plan is the major instrument by which the city-planning staff and the commission present their findings and recommendations to the city council. Through the plan, the professional planners and the citizen commissioners call attention to the development problems facing the community and propose solutions to the problems. Through the plan, they make an assessment of the present conditions in the community and suggest what the future might be like. The plan enables them to offer their advice in a studied, comprehensive form, rather than on a piecemeal, expediency basis.

It is true that the clear expression of the council's policies is more important to the general plan than is technical merit. The plan, however, should have technical merit. If it does not, the commission will not be able to fulfill its advisory role. The council's policies should reflect reliance on the professional city-planning staff. A statement of development policies which disregards what city planning has to offer is likely to be unsound.

The advisory use of the general plan encompasses much more than just research. It also includes initiating and advocating proposals which will have varying mixtures of factual information and scientific knowledge, professional judgments, and political and social value judgments. The advisory use also signifies the need for leadership on the part of the advisors in guiding and educating the members of the city council.

It has been argued that the city-planning staff is really the group which formulates the general plan, and therefore it is really the staff's plan. The premise is correct, but the conclusion is not. City planners do contribute most of the thought and effort that go into the initial preparation of a general plan. Usually the first complete preliminary version of a plan represents primarily the thinking of the professional staff. However, as the preliminary plan goes through the long period of study and discussion leading to council adoption, the plan increasingly is shaped as the council wants it and becomes less and less the staff's plan. Only after the plan is adopted by the council is it possible for the council's advisors to give advice of the sort that the council needs in a context of policies determined by the council.

The advisory use of the general plan operates when the council specifically requests information and recommendations on special items, when the city planners advance proposals or point out problems on their own initiative, and when the routine procedures of municipal government, such as regular referral, call for reports and recommendations to the city council on questions of physical development. The general plan makes it easier for the council to comprehend the long-range, citywide context in which all specific proposals are set. The plan makes it easier for the advisors to put across their recommendations.

The advisory use of the plan is a continuing process. It leads everyone concerned to a far more critical knowledge and awareness of the plan than is possible if the advisory use were not continuous, not only as the plan is used as a definite framework within which current proposals can be judged, but as a group of policies that constantly must be reconsidered and reaffirmed or modified as they are used. The advisory use operates in this way formally whenever the commission and staff advise the council on proposed amendments. The use of the plan by the staff as required by the advisory use exposes conflicts and weak spots in the plan which the staff can discover in its day-to-day work. Once the director of city planning fully accepts this use of the plan, he will learn the advantages of the regular annual review and amendment procedure and the necessity for the supplementary procedure that enables the council to amend the plan at any time between the scheduled review periods. The advisory use requires the professional staff to keep the plan up to date and to constantly reexamine their own professional judgments.

The advisory use is an important concomitant of both policy determination and policy effectuation. The advisory use complements the communication use. The city council is on the sending end of the communication use, and the city-planning commission and staff are on the receiving end. The opposite movement is true of the advisory use. In the communication use, the council transmits its policies to the city planners. In the advisory use, the city planners develop ideas to implement the council's policies, react to these policies, and, when necessary, suggest new policies.

The advisory use highlights the significant role of the city planner as a professional, a role which tends to be obscured by the other uses of the the plan. Experience has shown that the proper functioning of a general plan is virtually impossible without the constant counsel of a professional city planner. No municipal legislative body is sufficiently equipped or educated to carry out its responsibility for governing the comprehensive physical development of its area without professional assistance. In emphasizing the role of policy in defining the uses of the general plan, it must be stated that it is detrimental to the work of the council if procedures are not devised to assure proper recognition of the importance of technical and professional knowledge. Every policy should have a firm basis in technical fact and professional judgment.

The council is responsible for policy and the city planner is responsible for technical and professional support. It is the job of the city planner to make sure that the council bases its physical-development policies on accurate factual knowledge and sound professional judgment. He must attempt to convince the councilmen of the applicability and merits of his findings and recommendations. This requires that he present his advice to the council in a form which the council can readily comprehend. He must learn to express the complexities and nuances of city planning in terms which the layman can grasp.

Realistically, it must be recognized that the city-planning director will not always be successful in this task. But he should also openly acknowledge that frequently he will not be able to determine which course of action is clearly correct solely on the basis of professional principles and standards. There will be occasions when members of the city council will devise better answers to particular city-planning problems before them than those recommended by the city-planning director. The city planner should not expect the councilmen to agree with him all the time. He must believe, however, that councilmen attempt to work out reasonable, impartial decisions all the time, and that they attempt to understand and act on behalf of the general public interest all the time. However, in a democracy, the final judge of the merit of legislative decisions is not the city planner, but the citizens through their elected representatives.

The advice of the city planner has been referred to as being "technical and professional." By this is meant that city planning is not a scientific discipline. The recommendations of city planners are based not only on facts, but also on personal experience, conviction, and understanding accumulated during years of practice and testing, both as professionals and as individual citizens in our society. Political judgments also are almost invariably involved in the formulation and timing of recommendations.

The relative contributions of the council's advisors to the different parts of the general-plan document are indicated in the following table. The figures are meant to be suggestive, and not definitive. Actually, the council is responsible for everything in the plan.

AUTHORSHIP OF PARTS OF THE GENERAL-PLAN DOCUMENT *

	Percentage by	
	Advisors	*Council*
Background material	100	0
Forecasts	90	10
Assumptions	80	20
Assessment of present conditions and problems	70	30
Community goals and major policies	10	90
Summary of the general plan	20	80
Proposals (including the unified general physical design)	50	50
Rejected alternatives	50	50
Standards and principles	60	40
Methods for carrying out the plan	70	30

* Based on an illustration in *The Functions of the Urban General Plan* (Masters Thesis) by Alan Black, University of California, Berkeley, 1960.

The advisory use of the general plan is most apparent in the background and statistical material on geography, population, the local economy, existing land use, and physical conditions. The advisory use is evident in the forecasts and assumptions on which the plan is based and is reflected in the general assessment of present conditions and problems in the community.

Ideally, the staff has little to do with the community goals expressed in the plan. The bulk of the plan, the proposals embodying technical-political judgments, should represent joint efforts by advisors and council. This includes the general physical design which integrates the council's physical-development policies and proposals and brings out the significant design decisions, including their relationships to one another and to the city site.

It is important to emphasize that the city-planning commission and staff are more than merely passive advisors to the council. They offer ideas, they initiate proposals, they point out problems, they actively attempt to influence the council. This is as it should be, and is one reason why there is an administrative branch of government to help the municipal legislative branch in governing.

But, the final tribunal for the city planners' proposals is the city council. It is up to the city council to accept, modify, or reject the recommendations it receives from its advisors. The city planners must convince the councilmen sufficiently so that they will make the proposals their own, and will adopt them and see that they are carried out.

There are always some professional men in government who look upon the city council as an obstacle to overcome. They believe the public administrator should manipulate the councilmen. They want him to protect and to promote the public interest by mobilizing the informal governing groups and the leaders of the private power structure of the community to bring pressure on the councilmen. In recent years this concept of municipal government has been practiced by some city managers and has been advocated by some political theorists. Also, some city-planning directors see manipulation of the council as part of the role they should play.

Such tactics contravene the democratic political process. It is the role of the public administrator—including the professional city planner—to inform, enlighten, advise, and serve the city council, not to blindfold it. It is the responsibility of the professional city planner to try to guide and educate the municipal legislative body, since many councilmen do not understand their proper role until someone explains it to them. The advisory activities of the city planner must be conducted openly and with a sense of respect for the powers that rightfully inhere in the city council.

There are cases in which a city council or a city-planning commission exerts excessive dominance over a city-planning staff. The staff's activities in such cases are usually restricted and confined to housekeeping duties. Such a situation is demoralizing to the staff and obviously will damage the city-planning work of the council. But the answer is not found in private political activities. A middle ground must be found between the two extremes. This is especially true if the advisory use of the general plan is to be effective.

The following remarks of Hyman G. Rickover apply to the professional city planner:

> Service ceases to be professional if it has in any way been dictated by the client or employer. The role of the professional man in society is to lend his special knowledge, his well-trained intellect, and his dispassionate habit of visualizing problems in terms of fundamental principles to whatever specific task is entrusted to him. Professional independence is not a special privilege but rather an inner necessity for the true professional man, and a safeguard for his employers and the general public. Without it, he negates everything that makes him a professional person and becomes at best a routine technician or hired hand, at worst a hack.[3]

---

[3] Hyman G. Rickover, *Education and Freedom* (New York: E. P. Dutton and Co., 1959), pp. 64–65.

It is possible to conceive of a recurring cycle of the four general-plan uses discussed so far. The general-plan process starts with the advisory use —the staff and commission prepare and submit to the council a preliminary version of the plan. Next comes the policy-determination use—the council debates the preliminary version and adopts a final version. Then the stream divides into two branches, one leading to the policy-effectuation use and the other to the communication use. In policy effectuation, the plan is used by the council to carry out its own policies; in communication, the plan is used by others to carry out the council's policies. Both streams converge back on the advisory use when the staff realizes the need for certain changes in the plan. The staff and commission propose amendments to the council, and the cycle starts over again.

Such a picture simplifies reality, in which there are many other interchanges between uses of the plan and many other people involved. There is feedback directly from policy effectuation to policy determination when specific matters before the councilmen spur them to change their policies. There is feedback directly from communication to policy determination when citizens persuade the councilmen to alter their policies. And the advisory use bears directly on policy effectuation when the staff and commission help the council to take action on specific issues.

The simplified recurring-cycle description of how the general plan is actually used, however, does highlight the four basic uses defined thus far. It also clarifies the close interdependence of the four uses and the need for distinguishing each use from the others.

EDUCATION

The general plan helps to educate the councilmen and everyone who is involved with it or who reads it as to the conditions, problems, and opportunities of their community. It arouses the interest of people, awakens them to the possibilities of the future, offers them factual information on the present status of the city and probable future trends, informs them about the operations of their local government in matters of physical development, and stimulates them to be critical of city-planning ideas.

While the education use of the plan is closely allied to the communication use, it is much broader. The general-plan document does more than just communicate the council's adopted policies. It provides the context in which citizens can take the measure of the council's policies. It offers a wide range of essential background information which will be interesting and useful to many people who initially will not be directly concerned with the plan itself. The general plan stimulates people to think about their city and its future. It is an extremely valuable tool in making possible effective, responsible citizen participation in local self-government.

Education does not have any special section in the plan document, nor does it have any special place in the procedures of adopting and using the plan. It goes on all the time and pervades the whole general-plan process. The education use is not isolated from the other four legislative uses of the plan, but rather is inextricably interwoven with each of them.

The councilmen are the major recipients of the educational impact of the general plan. In considering, debating, and finally agreeing on a plan, the councilmen are educated. Newly elected councilmen are educated as a result of the annual review of the plan. All members of the council learn how to view the physical city as a whole as they use the plan to help them reach decisions at their regular meetings. The plan also helps councilmen to appreciate the practical, powerful influence of big ideas and high standards. In receiving the advice of the city-planning commission and staff and in conducting public hearings which involve the plan, councilmen are constantly made aware of the ways in which others interpret their plan.

One of the major facets of the educational use of the plan is that it makes it possible for councilmen to become informed as to the reactions and opinions of their constituents in the quiet periods between controversies and the formal council meetings at which decisions must be made. Wide distribution of the plan document will bring responses from civic and business organizations, newspapers, individual citizens, and even school children. Communication between councilmen and voters always needs to be improved. The general plan inevitably will spur thoughtful consideration of the city's future and will lead to an increase in communication between the citizens and their elected representatives. In doing this, the plan focuses attention on fundamental questions, rather than on trivia or the type of emotional issue which tends to become dominant in any controversy if the participants have not had an opportunity to educate themselves prior to the debate.

The council contributes to as well as benefits from the education use of the plan. The attention and support the council gives to the plan attract attention to it. The council's financial backing of plan preparation and publication is an essential prerequisite. Council adoption and implementation of the plan lend prestige to it. The knowledge that the plan represents the council's policies commands respect for it.

The period of plan preparation has tremendous educational value for the people most involved—the city-planning commission and the city-planning director and his staff. Realistically, it may not be possible to involve the councilmen and the chief executive at the time the plan is initially prepared to the extent that they eventually will become involved with the plan after it has been adopted by the council and the councilmen and the chief executive learn that they can no longer operate without a public plan. But also speaking realistically, every plan that has been adopted by a council has been understood by the citizen members of the city-planning commission. They will educate the members of the council if the councilmen have difficulty doing so themselves.

Public response to initial presentation of the general plan can be expected to be less intense than it should be, considering the issues of vital importance to the welfare of the community that are dealt with in the plan. But here again, once the city-planning commission has educated itself sufficiently to bring about adoption of the plan by the council, the educational impact of the plan will inevitably make itself felt as a result of the subsequent, unavoidable controversies before the council that will involve the plan.

The publication and wide distribution of the general-plan document is the culmination of the education use. The principal recipient is the general public. The educational benefits of the plan document continue indefinitely and are constantly broadened as subsequent editions are published and distributed.

Charles Haar attaches great importance to the education use of the plan, and has said the plan is "a device for stimulating public interest and responsibility." He writes:

> What the previous categories of the values served by the master plan may very well add up to is simply this: the chief purpose of the master plan is that of mutual education. In the process of making a master plan, the planner may learn which issues are the relevant ones so far as the people are concerned, what terms are meaningful to them, and which alternatives make sense as they view them. This education of the planning board and staff is crucial for any plan to survive. Concomitantly, mustering public interest and participation in city planning is one of the most serious problems faced by the profession: preparing the plan can be an effective channel of communication. It is generally understood that today full use must be made of the democratic process to achieve understanding and acceptance by the people who are affected by planning, and who must undertake the responsibility of enacting and maintaining it.[4]

[4] Haar, "The Master Plan: An Impermanent Constitution," p. 359.

If the educational use of the plan is to be effective, the general-plan document must succeed in bringing about a clear understanding of the need for maintaining a distinction between general, long-range policies and the action programs designed to implement them. There is a natural and powerful tendency to move from general policy-making to specific projects and regulations. City planners and the general-plan document must constantly reiterate the fact that the general, long-range policies that together comprise the plan will become confused if attempts are made to include in the general plan short-range, detailed development plans.

Once a general plan has been adopted, it will start in motion efforts to implement its major policies and proposals. As these are successfully carried out, new issues will be dealt with by the plan. There will be a constant resetting of sights, a constant re-evaluation of standards and of the quality of the proposals in the plan. Without a continuous and effective educational effort to explain why the general plan must remain general, the entire process of city planning will become distorted and the primary and vitally important continuing social need to which city planning is a response will once again be neglected.

The most critical test of the general plan in its performance as an educational agent is the degree to which it commands the respect of newly elected councilmen. If the context out of which the policies of the plan have been shaped is clearly presented, is obviously concerned with the major background factors that must be taken into account if the plan is to be understood, and is fairly presented, then the plan itself will have a fair chance of being considered, approved, and supported by the new councilmen. But if the document does not deal with these factors in an open and educational manner, there will be no common ground for judging the adopted policies in relation to the major rejected alternatives. If the general plan is to serve the council, the presentation and description in the plan document of the context, including the rejected major alternatives, should be acceptable as fair to all members of the council, even to those who disagree with the plan as finally adopted.

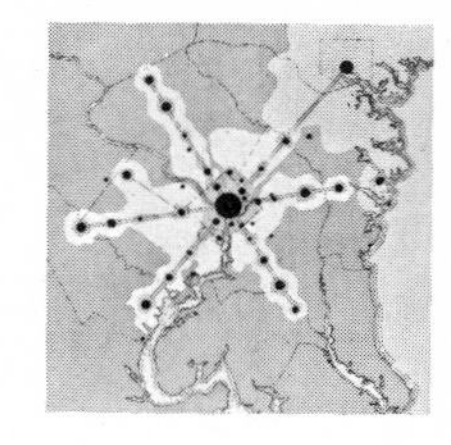

IV

CHARACTERISTICS OF THE GENERAL PLAN

In the following pages an attempt is made to identify and consider in detail the most important characteristics of the general plan which are implied by its legislative uses. By *characteristic,* I mean a significant quality or property that the general plan should possess. The list of characteristics also serves as a recapitulation of the discussion of uses, since it summarizes many of the key points made throughout the preceding chapter.

The following discussion of characteristics essential to the general plan carries the exposition down to a more concrete level. The general-plan characteristics provide the basis for evaluating actual general plans and enable the reader to judge for himself whether or not the general-plan concept presented in this book meets his own tests of reality. The plan characteristics also can be used as a checklist by a city planner about to launch preparation of a general plan.

The characteristics apply to both the general-plan process and the official plan document. They are rooted in the plan uses; a different set of uses would undoubtedly require a different set of characteristics.

Ten characteristics are identified. The first five concern primarily the subject matter of the plan; the five remaining characteristics relate the plan to the orderly and desirable procedures of representative, democratic, municipal self-government in the United States. They will be considered in the sequence indicated in the following outline:

Subject-Matter Characteristics

The General Plan—

(1) Should Focus on Physical Development
(2) Should Be Long-Range
(3) Should Be Comprehensive
(4) Should Be General, and Should Remain General
(5) Should Clearly Relate the Major Physical-Design Proposals to the Basic Policies of the Plan

Characteristics Relating to Governmental Procedures

The General Plan—

(6) Should Be in a Form Suitable for Public Debate
(7) Should Be Identified as the City Council's Plan
(8) Should Be Available and Understandable to the Public
(9) Should Be Designed to Capitalize on Its Educational Potential
(10) Should Be Amendable

SUBJECT-MATTER CHARACTERISTICS

(1) The General Plan Should Focus on Physical Development

The reasons for this subject-matter limitation were stated in Chapter II. As discussed there, during the 1930's and again in the early post-World War II period the influence of social scientists and central-management advocates compelled a re-examination of the scope of the general plan. With the rapid increase in the number of university teaching and research programs in the field of city planning in recent years and the new surge of interest in executive management and coordination techniques, this subject-matter limitation is being questioned once again. It seems necessary, therefore, to retrace the reasons for judging that the physical-development focus of the general plan is a reasonable and a permanent quality that the plan should have.

When the problems created by the rapid, haphazard development of our cities after the Civil War became acute, the need for enlarging the scope of the design professions that had been concerned with the detailed physical elements of the urban environment—buildings, streets, and parks—was gradually recognized, and in the United States the profession we now know as city planning emerged. The scope of the city-planning profession was initially, and consciously, limited to questions dealing primarily with the physical development of urban communities. This is what the clients

THE URBAN GENERAL PLAN

A. USES

1. POLICY DETERMINATION: Enables the city council to consider and agree (a) upon a definite set of policies that will be used to govern the future physical development of the community, and (b) upon a general physical design for the city site showing how the policies are to be carried out.

2. POLICY EFFECTUATION: Enables the city council to view every specific project upon which it must act against a definite framework of desirable long-range development for the entire community.

3. COMMUNICATION: Enables the city council to convey its long-range physical development policy to the citizens and to leaders and executives of government, civic, and business organizations; enables constructive debate and stimulates political action.

4. CONVEYANCE OF ADVICE: Enables the city council to receive recommendations concerning physical-development matters from the city-planning commission and other advisors in a coherent, unified form.

5. EDUCATION: Enables the members of the city council to educate themselves and others concerning the physical-development problems and opportunities of the community and the relationship of these problems and opportunities to the social and economic issues involved.

B. CHARACTERISTICS

If the General Plan is to serve the five uses defined above, it must have the following ten characteristics:

SUBJECT-MATTER CHARACTERISTICS

1. G.P. should focus on physical development.
2. G.P. should be long-range.
3. G.P. should be comprehensive.
4. G.P. should be general, and should remain general.
5. G.P. should clearly relate the major physical-design proposals to the basic policies of the Plan.

CHARACTERISTICS RELATING TO GOVERNMENTAL PROCEDURES

6. G.P. should be in a form suitable for public debate.
7. G.P. should be identified as the city council's plan.
8. G.P. should be available and understandable to the public.
9. G.P. should be designed to capitalize on its educational potential.
10. G.P. should be amendable.

C. ORGANIZATION

THE URBAN GENERAL PLAN

INTRODUCTION: Reasons for G.P.; roles of council, CPC, citizens; historical background and context of G.P.

SUMMARY OF G.P.: Unified statement including (a) basic policies, (b) major proposals, and (c) one schematic drawing of the physical design.

BASIC POLICIES

1. CONTEXT OF THE G.P.: Historical background; geographical and physical factors; social and economic factors; major issues, problems, and opportunities. (facts, trends, assumptions, forecasts)
2. SOCIAL OBJECTIVES AND URBAN PHYSICAL-STRUCTURE CONCEPTS: Value judgments concerning social objectives; professional judgments concerning major physical-structure concepts adopted as basis for G.P.
3. BASIC POLICIES OF THE G.P.: Discussion of the basic policies that the general physical design is intended to implement.

GENERAL PHYSICAL DESIGN

Description of plan proposals in relation to large-scale G.P. drawing and citywide drawings of:

1. Working-and-living-areas section.
2. Community-facilities section.
3. Civic-design section.
4. Circulation section.
5. Utilities section.

These drawings must remain general. They are needed because single G.P. drawing is too complex to enable each element to be clearly seen.

(Plus regional, functional, and district drawings that are needed to explain G.P.)

This diagram also suggests the contents of the official G.P. and publication as a single document.

Continuing Studies Based on G.P. that Suggest G.P. Improvements and Formal Amendments

Studies of basic policies and of all social and economic factors that control policies, objectives, assumptions, principles, and standards.

- Up-to-Date Record of Suggested Revisions of Major Development Policies.

Detailed Development Studies

Individual-District Development Studies for Working and Living Areas

- General Physical Design
  - C.B.D. → Indust. Dist. → Etc.
  - Res. Dist. → Res. Dist. → Etc.

Citywide Studies of Individual Functional Elements

- General Physical Design
  - Living and Working → Civic Design → Separate Com Facilities → Separate Utilities
  - Transit → Traffic Ways → Railroads → Etc.

Combined Citywide Studies of 5 Sections of General Physical Design

- Combined Studies on One Drawing
  - Up-to-Date Record of Suggested Revisions of General Physical Design

—at that time the legislative bodies of our cities—unmistakably defined as the subject matter of the field.

With the spread of the council-manager form of government and the consequent application of the central-management idea during the last twenty years, some city-planning commissions were assigned tasks wholly outside the field of city planning as traditionally defined. Because they had been able to build up permanent staffs that included analysts and research workers, they were asked to conduct surveys of unemployment, to work out detailed financial plans, and to collect and analyze information dealing with social and economic problems of many kinds. The theory implicit in this new and different role of the city-planning agency is that city planning provides a jumping-off place for planning of all kinds. That the application of this theory has led to confusion and uncertainty concerning the scope of the general plan is completely understandable. It also has made it necessary for the city-planning profession to re-examine its field of endeavor and to restate its definition of the scope of the general plan.

The point of view adopted in this book, which calls for the general plan to focus on problems of physical development, may be restated as follows: Since there is a demonstrated need for a general physical-development plan that the municipal legislative body can use as a guide, and since the task of preparing and maintaining such a plan requires a special staff engaged continuously in the work of general physical planning, the agency responsible for this task must not be required to perform additional tasks in ways that will disrupt its work or confuse its primary mission. This does not mean that a new and carefully defined set of duties may not be given to the city-planning commission by the city council. It does mean, however, that if this is done, it must be done in a way that avoids misunderstandings as to the clearly defined focus of the general plan on problems of physical development and as to the primary role of the city-planning commission in performing its general physical-planning function. Only by avoiding misunderstandings and by a reasonable and workable division of labor can the general physical-planning task, along with all of the other important kinds of planning that must be done in governing a city, be successfully carried out.[1]

---

[1] An interesting solution to this problem is included in the *Report of the British Royal Commission on Local Government in Greater London, 1957–60.* The model metropolitan government proposed in the Report would have an "Intelligence Agency," in addition to a general physical-development plan-making agency.

Financial and social problems that must be dealt with by municipal governments can be more intelligently handled, I believe, by city councils with long-range financial plans and long-range plans focusing on complex social problems, such as those caused by residential racial segregation. In Berkeley we are cautiously attempting to strengthen "planning" efforts in these subject-matter areas. But it is inconceivable that the city council would ever assign the professional staff work on financial and social planning to the same office that is attempting to do the complex, always controversial job of physical-development planning simply because the city-planning office has the term "planning" in its title.

There are obvious relationships between every kind of planning activity. But planning, in the broadest sense, is not a "professional" activity and can only be performed by those who must do such planning—city councils and boards of directors—on the basis of separate plans developed by groups having special competence in a particular field. City planning as traditionally defined is such a field. Experience has shown that coordination of physical development is a practical necessity, that a general plan that focuses on physical development can be understood by the city council, and that the general plan has gained increasing recognition as an important policy instrument needed by the city council in carrying out its over-all responsibility to promote and protect the general welfare of the community. Therefore, while acknowledging the fact that a long-range, comprehensive, general plan for the physical development of a community must take into account basic social and economic factors, it is considered essential that its major policies and proposals be consciously limited and dealt with in such a way that they can be plainly identified by the council as being concerned primarily with questions of physical development.

(2) The General Plan Should Be Long-Range

Since the earliest days of the American city-planning movement the terms *long-range, comprehensive,* and *general* have been used by city planners to describe to citizens and city councilmen the nature of the general plan. *Long-range* has always meant, in simplest terms, that the plan should be forward-looking, that it should attempt to provide for the future needs of the community insofar as it is possible to make reasonable judgments as to what these needs will be. *Comprehensive* has meant that the plan should encompass all the significant physical elements of the urban environment, that the plan should be related to regional-development trends, and that the plan should recognize and take into account important social and economic factors. And the term *general* has meant that the plan should not involve questions of detail, but should attempt to define the main outlines of desirable future development by showing the general location, character, and extent of the major physical elements of the community and the significant relationships between these elements.

To anyone not familiar with contemporary city-planning practice, the reasonableness of these brief definitions may seem apparent. However, since 1940, during the first period in our history when we prepared and used general plans on a continuing basis as a result of the establishment of permanent, well-organized city-planning staffs throughout the country, these three basic general-plan characteristics have been interpreted so loosely and in such contradictory ways that their essential meanings have almost been lost. There are, for example, general-plan documents that are intended to be *long-range* and yet include proposals that are clearly of only immediate and short-range significance, such as relatively minor adjustments in the existing zoning ordinance. There are general-plan documents in which the meaning of *comprehensive* is extended to justify the inclusion of a financial program as well as a physical plan, and there are documents in which the meaning of the term *general* is ignored by including exactly described specific sites for certain relatively unimportant physical elements of the community. If the city-planning profession is to continue to serve the basic social needs that brought it into being, the logic and meaning of the original definitions of *long-range, comprehensive,* and *general* must be re-examined and modified, reaffirmed, or completely recast by each new generation.

Long-range for most communities means at least a twenty-year time scale for the general plan; but only careful study of all the factors involved and informed judgments concerning the controlling factors can establish the most reasonable time period to be covered by the general plan for a particular community.

In most cases the time scale of the plan is determined by a combination of the population and economic forecasts and the predictability and stability of the subject matter relevant to each major physical element dealt with in the general plan. For example, if conditions are such that a reasonably firm population forecast can be made for a twenty-year period, then the portion of the plan concerned with residential areas should be designed either to accommodate or to limit, as determined by the basic policies of the plan, the predicted population in accordance with desirable standards of residential density. And once this portion of the plan is blocked out, the essential key has been provided for planning those community facilities and utilities that are directly related to residential population densities, such as schools, parks, playgrounds, circulation facilities, fire stations, and the water-supply and sewage-disposal systems. Likewise, the location and extent of needed commercial areas that are directly dependent on residential density, such as neighborhood and district shopping centers, must be determined to a great extent by the basic proposals expressed in the residential-areas section of the plan. Since residential areas and their related uses occupy far more land than any other major physical element of the urban community, the time scale used in planning for future residential needs usually becomes the dominant time scale of the plan as a whole.

The factors that must be dealt with in developing reasonable forecasts of the economic activities of a community are more variable and more complex than those involved in making population forecasts. Technological changes are continuously making possible, and forcing, adjustments in ways of doing business and in methods of industrial production. And these changes result in organizational changes, which affect physical facilities, that in many cases can be reasonably anticipated for only short periods of time. But the primary locations of industrial and business activities which are dependent to a very large extent on obvious geographic features, such as deep water and flat land, are also dependent on the location of the residential districts that house the working population, and on those urban facilities, such as the water-supply and transportation systems, that must be designed to accommodate the residential and the industrial and commercial areas of the community. Thus the time scale for the development of the industrial and central-business-district areas dealt with in the living-and-working-areas section of the general plan is closely related to and in many cases is dependent on the time scale of the population forecast.

To a certain extent the opposite is also true—the residential-area time scale is held down by the shorter ranges of the industrial- and business-activities forecasts. For even if national and regional conditions affecting population growth for a particular community made it possible for planners to look ahead more than twenty to thirty years with reasonable certainty, the rate of change created by modern technology affecting the location of industries and businesses is so great today that it would not be reasonable to plan ahead more than twenty to thirty years for those physical elements of the urban community that are not automatically tied to a longer time period.

There are certain important features of the plan that must be based on judgments concerning the future that involve time periods much longer than two or three decades. Some features, such as the costly water-supply, sewage-disposal, and drainage systems, must be based on definite design features intended, hopefully, to accommodate all needs for periods of as long as fifty years or more. Others, such as large park and greenbelt proposals, should be based on a time perspective of indefinite length, but one that extends far beyond the dominant time scale of the plan. The inclusion of such proposals in the general plan should be dictated by the logic of the particular situation. In most cases they will have to be included to indicate why the more easily planned for physical elements of the community, such as elementary schools, are placed in the locations assigned them by the general plan.

As described above, *long-range* means that the general plan usually will have a dominant time scale of twenty to thirty years. The general plan may refer to a specific target date, but this is merely a useful guide for coordinating certain forecasts and should not be taken too seriously. It is not even necessary that the plan have a specific target date, since parts of the plan must have time scales differing from any arbitrary target date. The general plan is not supposed to be a picture of an end-state at some particular year, but rather a statement of end-directions which are continually adjusted as time passes.

Perhaps the most important point to emphasize in attempting to spell out and clarify the meaning of *long-range* is that the plan should not confuse needs that are immediate and pressing, but in the long view are relatively unimportant, with the presentation of a clear statement of the major requirements that must be provided for to promote desirable physical development over a period of several decades. Thus, although the plan must include, in an appropriate general context, projects of vital importance to be carried out in the near future, it must be successful in relating such projects, which attract attention because they are aimed at solving current problems, to the larger scheme of long-range growth and development. The plan must specify distant objectives so that the community can make sustained progress in one direction.

(3) The General Plan Should Be Comprehensive

Comprehensive, as defined by city-planning practice, has three specific meanings: (1) It means that the general plan should deal with *all* of the essential physical elements of the urban environment within the boundaries of the city; (2) it means that the general plan should take into account the development trends in the larger geographic setting within which every city is situated; and (3) it means that the general plan should be consciously related to the social and economic forces that it proposes to accommodate and that are themselves bound to be affected by the scheme for physical development expressed in the plan. *Comprehensive* means, in other words, that a general plan for physical development, in order to be a logical, reasonable, and useful plan, must recognize and define its relationships with all significant factors, physical and nonphysical, local and regional, that affect the physical growth and development of the community.

Before the need for community control over the use of all privately owned urban property was generally recognized about fifty years ago, it was not uncommon for city-planning reports to be published that did not describe the basic judgments that had been made concerning the future development of the privately owned commercial, industrial, and residential areas of the city upon which the plan for related public facilities was based. Such reports gave the impression that a general plan could be prepared without taking into account the basic privately owned physical elements of the community. However, even before the constitutionality of zoning was finally established in 1927, some of the leaders of the profession had demonstrated the logical necessity of making proposals for the commercial, industrial, and residential areas of the city, regardless of the lack of direct public control over the private property affected, in order to provide a rational basis for determining the general location, character, and extent of those publicly owned physical elements dealt with in the general plan for which the community as a whole was directly responsible. Today, this meaning of *comprehensive* as applied to the scope of the plan is taken for granted.

It is obvious from the foregoing discussion of the basic elements of the physical environment that must be considered in a general plan that the plan must cover the entire city, not just one or two districts. Although this meaning of *comprehensive* is also unquestioned today, early city-planning reports frequently failed to make this clear because of the emphasis given to particular districts that were already publicly identified as problem areas, such as slum neighborhoods or waterfront districts. Today, the need for defining the relationships between special problem areas and the remainder of the city is fully recognized. In the 1949 Housing Act, Congress offered to assist communities in their efforts to redevelop blighted areas, but only after each community had prepared a general plan showing how the proposed redevelopment projects would fit into the future development of the city as a whole.

Comprehensive is sometimes used in contemporary city-planning reports in the description of a single functional element, such as the street-and-highway system. In this instance *comprehensive* should mean simply that the proposals in the plan for the street-and-highway system have been related to all other significant factors that affect or are affected by the proposals. *Comprehensive* should not be used in such a way as to give the impression that a "comprehensive street-and-highway plan" constitutes, by itself, a comprehensive general plan for the city. Unfortunately, it is not uncommon to see the term *comprehensive* misused in this way even today.

Two additional relatively common misinterpretations of the meaning of *comprehensive* as applied to the physical scope of the general plan should be noted. One is the suggestion that the general plan, in order to be *comprehensive,* must be complete in the sense that it must deal with *every* physical element, regardless of its significance as part of a plan that must be long-range and general. And the other is the suggestion that the plan must eventually become a detailed blueprint. These misinterpretations conflict directly with the primary legislative uses of the plan, since they unavoidably tend to confuse policies of major and minor importance with one another, and questions of detail with proposals that are of a general nature and of a much broader significance. The need for completeness and for detail in planning for the effective improvement of the urban environment can be provided for in other ways.

Every responsible effort to prepare a general plan for the physical development of the territory within the boundaries of one city has recognized the fact that development trends in both the immediately adjacent urbanized territory and the larger geographic region must be studied and taken into account if the general plan for the individual community is to be a reasonable plan. This requirement means, in effect, that the urban-general-plan concept recognizes that eventually there must be a regional general plan, and is an expression of the second meaning of *comprehensive* as applied to the urban general plan.

There are some excellent examples of the way in which the logical steps involved in the preparation of a general plan for a specific municipality lead to recognition of the need for defining regional relationships and to the preparation of a regional plan. The Cincinnati metropolitan-area general plan, completed in 1948, is an outstanding example. Guided by an able city-planning commission and a well-informed city council, Cincinnati financed the preparation of a metropolitanwide general plan under the direction of a voluntary joint commission representing all of the local governments in the area in order to provide the most reasonable regional framework within which to develop a general plan for its own territory.

Sooner or later local and state legislative bodies will recognize, either as a result of the force of events or enlightened political leadership, the need for regional planning and for some form of regional government, and it will then be possible for the general plans for each local urban community and for the larger geographic regions to be determined on a more comprehensive and a more logical basis than is possible at the present time. In the intervening period, the essential quality of geographic regional comprehensiveness required of urban general plans will lead to voluntary, cooperative, educational regional-planning efforts in many locales. And in every instance involving an urban general plan it will lead to conscious recognition of the regional setting and an open statement of the regional assumptions upon which the plan is based.[2]

The one remaining quality associated with the characteristic of "compresiveness" that must be considered has to do with the way in which a physical plan is related to social and economic factors. As defined in this study, and as emphasized and explained in the discussion of the fifth characteristic of the general plan, this quality of comprehensiveness means simply that there must be an open recognition at every stage of plan preparation and use that a plan for physical development is an expression of the social and economic objectives of the community as determined by the city council. It must not be interpreted to mean that the city-planning commission and staff in carrying out their general physical-planning responsibilities should also assume responsibility for social and economic planning. As previously stated, I believe that our municipal governments will continue to foster and to maintain several general planning activities, each one focusing on a subject-matter area of major importance. Each such activity should be characterized by continuing efforts on the part of those responsible to understand and state the basic social and economic objectives of the community that have special significance for their work.

In recent years, an increasing number of city-planning programs have produced plans, such as the *Berkeley Master Plan,* that illustrate, however crudely, the meaning of the quality of comprehensiveness called for here. They attempt to state openly the judgments made concerning the most significant

[2] The general plan for the metropolitan San Francisco Bay Area published in 1956 by the Bay Area Rapid Transit Commission could not have been completed in the time available if most of the city and county governments in the Bay Area had not already completed their general plans and considered their metropolitan socio-economic functions. For a proposed metropolitan regional plan-making agency and limited-function metropolitan government based on the evolutionary approach suggested here, see my essay "City and Regional Planning in the Metropolitan San Francisco Bay Area," Institute of Governmental Studies, University of California, Berkeley, 1963.

nonphysical factors upon which the physical plan is based, they place directly in the hands of the council the task of setting the social and economic objectives which the physical plan seeks to accomplish, and, by an open statement of their limitations, they foster recognition by the city council of the need for a more effective system of social, economic, and physical planning than we now have.

(4) The General Plan Should Be General, and Should Remain General

If it is to be effective in its primary policy-determination uses, the general plan must focus on the main issues and the "big ideas." The plan document should not include any details that will tend to obscure or distract attention from the major policies and the major physical-design proposals. The plan is intended only to provide a general picture of the locations and sizes of the major physical elements of the urban community and to indicate the desirable relationships between them. The plan is a schematic guide, and not a map or a blueprint. Above all, the general plan must be distinguished from those specific and detailed documents which are intended to implement it, such as the zoning ordinance, subdivision regulations, development plans, and the capital-improvements priority and financing programs.

The characteristic of generalness is troublesome, and admittedly it cannot be maintained invariably. The plan cannot be so general that it is vague, as some plans are; its general physical-design proposals must be clear and firm so that there will be no question as to what the council's policies signify. Every general plan is a mixture of the general and the specific, and it is necessary usually to explore specific proposals before reaching decisions on general policies. When a city council is considering a general plan, sometimes it is required to express general policies and proposals in specific terms in order to satisfy some of the citizens. When this is necessary, the plan document should include an explanation of the reasons for being specific and should restate the general policy that is expressed by the decision.

There are many illustrations that could be used to show how difficult it is to achieve, and to retain, the quality of generalness that is required by the continuing policy-determination use of the plan. The tendency to seek support for the plan primarily on practical grounds, which is most compelling when the plan has just been completed, usually results in efforts to translate the plan into cost estimates and time schedules. For example, the authors of the Philadelphia long-range physical-development plan, when the plan was first presented to the public in 1960, consciously chose to emphasize in the plan document's Introduction that they had conceived of the plan as a "blueprint for the Philadelphia of tomorrow." They called attention to the detailed studies that had been made of the financial implications of the plan and described these implications in a separate section of the plan document presenting estimates of the funds that would be needed to construct the capital improvements called for by the plan. In the third chapter, "Costs and Strategy," of the document the authors state:

. . . In order to carry out all the proposals outlined in this Plan, it will be necessary for government as a whole to make capital investments of some $3,482,839,000 in Philadelphia . . .

At the present rate of $25,000,000 per year, it will take approximately 37 years to accomplish the tax-supported projects implied by the Comprehensive Plan . . . However, if the rate increases as fast as Philadelphia's total personal income is expected to increase, then all tax-supported projects can be accomplished in 28 years . . .

These statements give the reader the impression that the plan has been worked out in detail and that the main emphasis, now that the plan has been completed, should shift from policy determination to policy effectuation. The need to distinguish between the work of policy determination and the work of policy effectuation seems elemental in considering the needs of the members of the municipal governing body; the same needs exist for the citizen members of the city-planning commission. Since both policy determination and policy effectuation are of continuing importance, and especially since the latter is, and will always remain, so dependent on the former, it seems essential to consciously avoid doing what the authors of the Philadelphia plan have done. This point is well stated in the introductory chapter of "A Guide to the Cambridge [England] Plan," published in 1956:

. . . it is meaningless to talk of the "cost" of a plan in money terms. Plan or no plan, money will go on being spent on development, and with no plan—or a bad plan—much of it would be wasted. The Cambridge Plan does not seek to prescribe how much development of one kind or another ought to be undertaken; it simply tries to estimate how much development of one kind or another will in any case take place in Cambridge during the next twenty years, and indicates the forms in which the planners think it would yield the best value for the money.

. . . a plan is not a blueprint or a working drawing, but a statement of policy. Its submission by the planning authority (the local legislative body) and its approval by the Minister do not necessarily imply a final decision that the proposals it contains shall be carried out. They mean that, as far as can be seen at the time, the developments proposed appear to the authority and the Minister to represent the best use of the resources likely to be available, and that the authority and the Minister will accordingly do what they can to promote such developments . . . unless and until it becomes apparent that the public interest demands an amendment of the plan . . .

I believe that the overriding necessity on the part of the councilmen to understand the main ideas of the plan, in order to justify to themselves and their constituents the controversial decisions which they inevitably will have to make and by which they inevitably will either implement or ignore the plan, will spur the councilmen to become more and more insistent on their demands that the city-planning commission and the director of city planning express accurately, in language and drawings that everyone can understand, just what the "main ideas" of the plan actually are. Most professionals tend to underrate and misunderstand the importance of the quality of generalness that the plan must achieve and maintain. It is a quality upon which most councilmen will sooner or later insist.

(5) The General Plan Should Clearly Relate The Major Physical-Design Proposals to the Basic Policies of the Plan

Every plan for the physical development of a community is an expression of value judgments. Value judgments must be made when the primary community objectives are determined and when assumptions are made concerning governmental, economic, social, and physical factors. They are also expressed in the city-planning principles and standards used to shape general physical-design proposals. To clarify the subordinate relationship of physical-design proposals to policies, and to bring about, insofar as it is possible to do so, a full awareness and recognition of the nontechnical value judgments upon which the plan is based, it is essential to give special and continuing attention to the relationship between physical-design proposals and basic policies in the official general-plan document.

This requirement presents a major challenge to the city planner, for knowledge about the interrelation between socioeconomic factors and the physical environment is largely intuitive and speculative. In most cases it is not possible to know with any certainty what physical-design measures should be taken to bring about a given social or economic objective, or what social and economic consequences will result from a given physical-design proposal. Therefore, the city council and the city-planning commission, rather than professional city planners, should make the final value judgments upon which the plan is based. The general-plan characteristic identified here is intended to facilitate this, and to guard against the danger of having basic value judgments made solely by the city-planning director and the members of the professional staff.

The open relationship between policies and physical-design proposals which is specified here is recognized by many experienced city planners as desirable. It is, however, very difficult to achieve. To illustrate the difficulties and to clarify what is meant by "basic policies," the Berkeley official general-plan document will be used as an example.

The major physical-design proposals of the *Berkeley Master Plan* can be understood without too much difficulty. The document contains as an integral feature a drawing of the citywide physical-design proposals which is titled "Master Plan for Berkeley," and there is a twelve-point Summary that is presented as a separate chapter. The Summary is preceded by chapters titled "Introduction," "Background," "Assumptions," and "Objectives" that attempt to place the Summary in its proper context. This explains why the Summary itself does not include a statement of the broad objectives of the *Plan;* they are presented in the chapter directly preceding the Summary.

If, in preparing the *Berkeley Master Plan,* an attempt had been made to determine and set forth the "basic policies" of the *Plan,* the eleven judgments described in the "Assumptions" chapter and the five general objectives stated in the "Objectives" chapter would have been reduced in number and stated in different terms. Since this was not done, what is called the "Summary of the Master Plan" focuses almost entirely on the design proposals of the *Plan*. For reference purposes, the "Assumptions," "Objectives," and "Summary" chapters of the document, together with the general-plan drawing, are reproduced in full on the following pages.

The first two points of the Summary, although cast in physical terms, are concerned with questions of basic policy. The first recommendation of the *Plan* calls for "the allocation of the existing area of Berkeley among . . . four basic uses (residential, commercial, industrial, and the University of California) in such a way as to achieve a balanced community, with each part of the City devoted to its most suitable purpose."

The second recommendation of the *Plan* "sets a limit of 180,000 persons for Berkeley—this being the maximum number of persons which the City Planning Commission believes may be accommodated in Berkeley without damage to the existing predominantly open character of the City . . ."

Of the remaining ten points in the Summary, nine are directly concerned with the general physical-design proposals and, when studied together with the general-plan drawing, give a reasonably complete, outline picture of the main physical elements and features dealt with in the section of the *Plan* on physical-design proposals. The one exception is simply a procedural recommendation, calling for continuing coordination by the University of California and Berkeley of their long-range development plans.

It will be noted that the major physical-design proposals concerning the University, which is the dominant physical element in Berkeley, are not summarized, and that neither of the two basic policies that are included in the Summary refer in any way to the role that Berkeley is to play in the metropolitan Bay Area. These issues were faced when the *Plan* was prepared. Their omission from the Summary is explained partly by the evolutionary way in which every plan must be developed and clarified. It is very difficult to summarize a general plan accurately until after it has been completed and used. Ten years of experience in using the *Berkeley Master Plan,* in its preliminary and final form, has helped to determine and to clarify the most important (*Text continued on page* 112.)

MAJOR POLICIES AND PROPOSALS OF THE *BERKELEY MASTER PLAN*

CHAPTER III. ASSUMPTIONS

Future plans must be based upon research, forecasts, and assumptions. Carefully formulated assumptions are necessary when more precise data are not available, or when time has not permitted sufficient research and study to determine precisely how present trends will develop or the exact nature of future needs and desires. The Planning Commission believes that the assumptions which underlie the Master Plan should be clearly stated as a part of this report. Each citizen may then interpret and evaluate the Plan in the light of the stated assumptions. In the future, when new and unexpected developments occur, the Plan can be more readily revised when it is understood why certain proposals were made and how they should be changed in respect to new data or new conditions.

Berkeley is a part of the large metropolitan area surrounding the San Francisco Bay. As part of this metropolitan area, Berkeley's future is influenced to a great extent by developments throughout the entire region. For this reason, the assumptions for the Master Plan are developed for the San Francisco Bay Area as a whole as well as more particularly for Berkeley.

In addition to these more specific assumptions there are some general assumptions implied in any planning process. Any event such as a major change in our form of government or economy, a large-scale disaster, or an all-out war would have unpredictable effects, possibly nullifying the best prepared plans. Therefore, we must assume that such catastrophic changes will not occur.

1. A regional planning agency will be established to coordinate the planning activities in the Bay Area. The proposals in our Master Plan are assumed to be based upon principles similar to those which will guide the regional planning agency.

2. The population will continue to grow due to the strategic location and desirable living conditions of the Bay Area and the economic development of the West. The

* population of the nine Bay COUNTIES WILL INCREASE FROM 3,638,322 PEOPLE IN 1960, TO 4,788,000 IN 1970, TO 5,890,000 IN 1980.

3. Residential development will continue to spread over the Berkeley hills and all the more accessible and buildable portions of the Bay Area, as a result of the continued growth in population.

4. With the growth of the region, Oakland and Berkeley will become increasingly important parts of the urban core during the next twenty-five years. Countering this trend will be a continued decentralization of commerce and industry throughout the region.

5. An area-wide circulation network will be constructed between all major cities from San Jose to Santa Rosa and will include both freeways and rapid transit lines. The circulation network will incorporate at least two more crossings of San Francisco Bay. A centrally located airport will be constructed on the presently submerged lands of the East Bay Area. Planned port expansion will be carried out in Oakland and Richmond.

6. Recreation facilities will be further developed with emphasis on the conservation and development of natural bayshore, mountain, and ocean-beach recreation resources throughout the nine-county area.

7. There will be continuing development of the submerged lands bordering San Francisco Bay.

Assumptions Concerning Berkeley, 1960–1980

1. Berkeley will be a major city in its own right and at the same time it will retain a satellite relationship to San Francisco and Oakland, thus performing a dual function in the core of the metropolitan area.

2. There will be a high volume of traffic between Berkeley and San Francisco, Oakland, Richmond, and the interior of Contra Costa County. Traffic routes of the East Bay which traverse Berkeley will carry increasingly heavy volumes of traffic.

3. Enrollment on the Berkeley Campus of the University of California will rise to + about 27,500 as state population increases. Academic policies will emphasize graduate and research activities.

4. Development of the submerged land west of Berkeley's present waterfront will become economically feasible within the next twenty-five years.

CHAPTER IV. OBJECTIVES

The Master Plan is a comprehensive and coordinated guide for the future development of the community, including both private and public activity. Implicit in this statement is the necessity for general public agreement on the kind of community we wish to achieve. Without such agreement on objectives, it will obviously be impossible to develop and carry into effect a comprehensive and coordinated plan.

For the past several years the Planning Commission has been studying the City of Berkeley and consulting with its citizens in order to formulate a set of general goals or objectives which will represent the needs and desires of a majority of the people of

---

* Text printed in capitals was amended as a result of the Berkeley City Council Resolution #38563-NS of September 19, 1961.

+ Text printed in capitals was amended as a result of the Berkeley City Council Resolution #38563-NS of September 19, 1961. [In this case, the footnote refers to the figure 27,500.]

Berkeley, and which will at the same time be physically, economically, and politically possible of achievement.

These broad objectives of the Master Plan are stated here in order that each citizen may decide for himself how well the Planning Commission has realized the potentialities of the Community and interpreted the aspirations of the people. The objectives are as follows:

1. *To preserve the unique character of Berkeley which has grown out of its unparalleled physical setting and its generally harmonious development.* Conservation of the physical and social values that characterize Berkeley can only be accomplished by facing squarely the problems of growth and change. Berkeley cannot retain its character and charm by retiring into the past.

2. *To reach a balance between the number of families in Berkeley and the space we have to live in.* Optimum living and working conditions cannot be attained when there is either overcrowding or underdevelopment.

3. *To establish a pattern of land uses which will promote the highest degree of health, safety, efficiency, and well-being for all segments of the community.* There should be a smooth-working relationship between lands used for residence, commerce, industry, and the University.

4. *To develop a circulation system—both highways and mass transit—which will provide for the safe and convenient movement of people and goods within Berkeley and other parts of the region.* Such a system must be designed so that the trafficways will serve rather than interfere with and destroy the industrial, commercial, and particularly the residential areas of the community.

5. *To secure for Berkeley her rightful place in the long-range development of the San Francisco Bay Area.* Berkeley should receive a just proportion of the economic and population growth of the region. At the same time, Berkeley should strive to preserve her unique position as a residential city and educational center. Berkeley should work with her neighbor cities for the sound development of the entire Bay Area.

CHAPTER V. SUMMARY OF THE MASTER PLAN

This summary is a word picture of Berkeley as our community can develop during the next twenty-five years when the fundamental recommendations for its future development, as set forth in the Master Plan are accepted and carried out by the citizens of Berkeley.

These major recommendations, broadly stated in this chapter, are developed in greater detail in the following sections of this report and illustrated on the Master Plan Map.

1. The Master Plan is based upon the finding that there are four essential uses of land in Berkeley. These are: (a) residential land use with the accompanying schools, parks, churches, etc.; (b) commercial land use; (c) industrial land use; and (d) the University of California. The Plan proposes the allocation of the existing area of Berkeley among these four basic uses in such a way as to achieve a balanced community, with each part of the City devoted to its most suitable purpose. (Land Use Section, pages 25 through 60a.)

2. Because of its limited land area the City of Berkeley cannot be permitted to grow indefinitely without serious overcrowding and a resulting deterioration in living conditions. The Master Plan sets a limit of 180,000 persons (exclusive of residential areas in the waterfront development) for Berkeley—this being the maximum number of persons which the Planning Commission believes may be accommodated in Berkeley

without damage to the existing predominantly open residential character of the City. The Master Plan provides for the distribution of population in Berkeley in planned residential areas, varying from low-density single-family areas to high-density apartment-house areas. (Population Section, page 23; Residential Areas Division, and pages 26 through 36.)

3. The Master Plan defines within the residential areas of Berkeley a series of residential neighborhoods, each of which will be of a proper size to support essential residential services such as schools, churches, and shopping centers, and each of which will, insofar as is possible, be kept free of large volumes of through traffic and other disturbing influences. (The Neighborhood Plan, pages 34 and 36.)

4. The Master Plan recommends the improvement and enhancement of the Berkeley Central District in order to better serve the community. The District is concentrated within the boundaries of Grove Street, Oxford Street, Hearst Avenue, and Durant Avenue. The Master Plan calls for improvements in off-street parking, pedestrian circulation, the number and quality of business establishments, and the physical appearance of the area. (Commercial Areas, pages 37 through 48; Central District, pages 41 to 44.)

5. The Master Plan groups the business establishments of Berkeley in conveniently located commercial centers, each of which will fit into one of the following four categories: The Central District, commercial service districts, community shopping centers, and local shopping centers. (Central District, pages 41 to 44; Commercial Service Districts, pages 44 and 45; Community Shopping Centers, pages 46 and 47; Neighborhood Shopping Centers, pages 47 and 48.)

6. The Master Plan provides for a limited and selective industrial expansion in Berkeley, exclusive of the waterfront development. The Plan provides for the establishment of a firm and logical boundary between industrial and residential areas in West Berkeley. Solution of this longstanding boundary problem will: (a) stabilize the two residential neighborhoods in West Berkeley, and provide security which will lead to new investment and rehabilitation of residential properties; (b) encourage sound industrial development free from the interference which results from scattered dwellings within the industrial district. (Industrial Area, pages 49 through 53.)

7. The Master Plan recognizes the interdependent roles of the City of Berkeley and the University of California, and calls for the continuing coordination of long-range plans in order that the University and the City may each continue to benefit from the presence of the other. (The University of California Division, pages 55 through 60a.)

8. The Master Plan proposes that Berkeley's trafficways be improved to a standard adequate to handle anticipated traffic volumes for the next twenty-five years. The most important trafficway plans are as follows:

a. Improvement of the Sacramento Street thoroughfare in order to provide a connection at the north into Colusa Avenue and San Pablo Avenue.
b. Widening of Grove Street between Berkeley Way and The Alameda.
c. Provision of a new access road to the Berkeley hill area by way of La Loma Avenue, Glendale Avenue, and Campus Drive.
* d. EXTENSION OF THE SHATTUCK SECONDARY THOROUGHFARE THROUGH TO SOLANO AVENUE TO PROVIDE A DIRECT CONNECTION BETWEEN THE SOLANO SHOPPING CENTER AND CENTRAL BERKELEY.

---

* Text printed in capitals was amended as a result of Berkeley City Council Resolution #37160-NS of January 27, 1959.

e. Development of Dwight Way and Haste Street as one-way streets from Piedmont Avenue to Grove Street, and widening of Dwight Way west of Grove Street.

f. Opening and widening of Cedar Street between Sacramento and Chestnut Streets in order to provide a trafficway from the Eastshore highway to the Berkeley hill residential neighborhoods. (Circulation Section, pages 61 and 62; Trafficways Division, pages 63 through 80.)

9. The Master Plan proposes that everything possible be done to increase transit patronage. To further this goal, the Master Plan recommends provision of an adequate local transit system with service within approximately one-fourth mile of each Berkeley residence, where topography permits, and the development of an integrated, regional rapid transit facility linking Berkeley to all parts of the Bay Area. (Circulation Section, pages 61 and 62; Transit Division, pages 81 through 84.)

10. The Master Plan recommends that present and future school facilities be carefully studied in the light of the anticipated growth and distribution of population and the pattern of Berkeley neighborhoods provided by this Plan. The Planning Commission believes that school grounds should be increased in size in order that they can better serve their educational as well as their recreational and community-center functions, and that the responsibility for this enlargement should rest jointly with the City of Berkeley and the Unified School District. (Public Facilities and Services Section, page 85; Schools Division, pages 87 through 90.)

11. The Master Plan adopts the policy of increasing Berkeley's park and recreation areas in order to meet the needs of present and anticipated future population. Preservation and development of existing streams and canyons and provision of hiking trails and viewpoints are particularly recommended. (Public Facilities and Services Section, page 85; Recreation Division, pages 91 through 96.)

12. The Master Plan outlines the development of Berkeley's submerged waterfront lands for a balanced combination of uses including residence, commerce, industry, and recreation. Careful attention must be given to the appearance of the area both from within and as seen from the Berkeley hills. Industrial development must be carefully regulated to prevent creation of dust, smoke, odors, or unsightly establishments. (Waterfront Section, pages 97 through 102.)

Elements of the Plan

The following pages will describe and discuss the Master Plan which has been prepared to achieve the stated objectives. The Plan will be presented in four sections:

1. The LAND USE SECTION considers the needs of the City for lands to be used for residence, commerce, industry, and the University of California.

2. The CIRCULATION SECTION considers the safe, efficient, and convenient movement of people and goods throughout Berkeley and between Berkeley and other parts of the Metropolitan Area.

3. The PUBLIC FACILITIES AND SERVICES SECTION considers the proposals necessary for the functioning of a modern community. Included in this section of the Master Plan are the problems of public utilities, schools, and recreation.

4. The WATERFRONT SECTION establishes broad policy for the future filling and development of Berkeley's submerged lands.

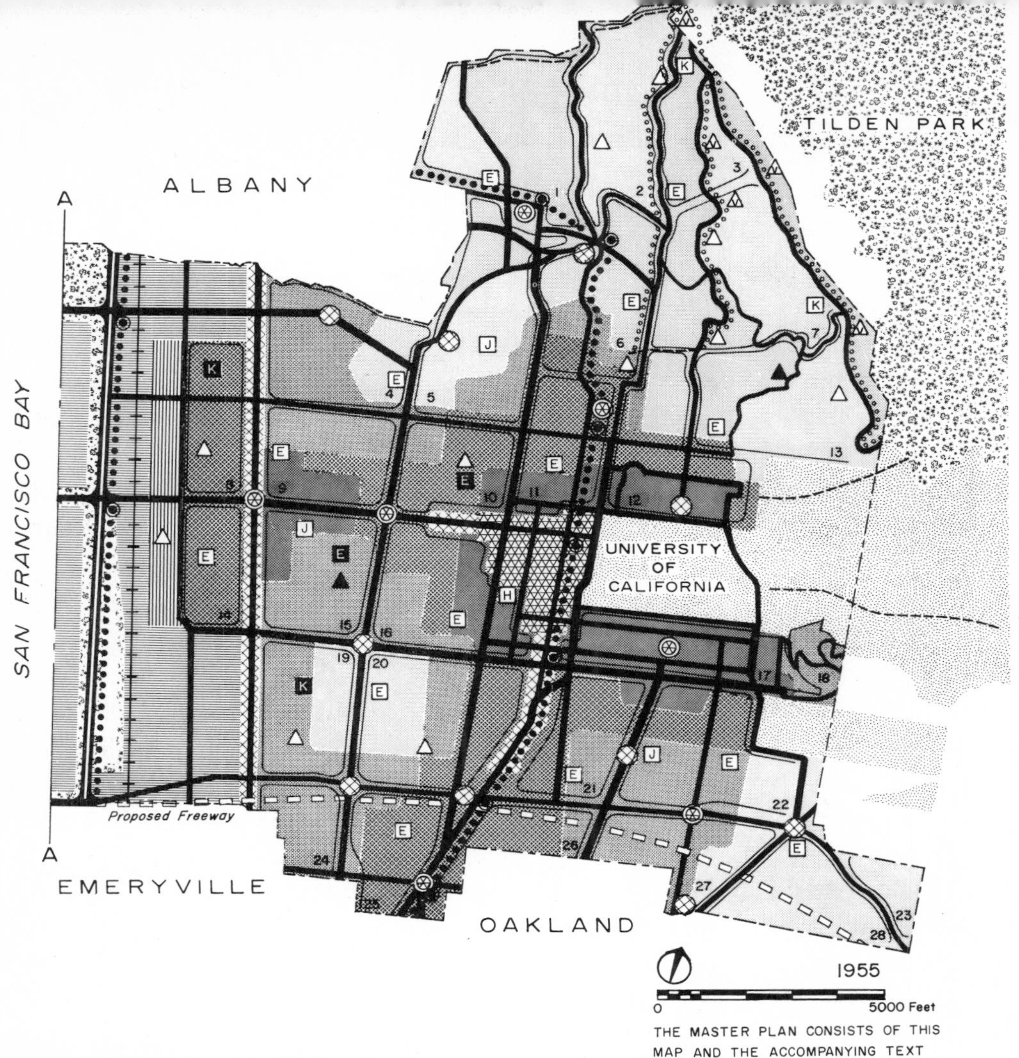

BERKELEY MASTER PLAN

(Note: That portion of the plan drawing showing schematic proposals for the development of the tidelands west of line A-A has been deleted.)

RESIDENTIAL AREAS

NET RESIDENTIAL DENSITY

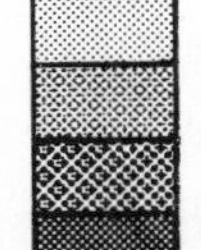

0-30 Persons Per Acre
30-50 Persons Per Acre
50-80 Persons Per Acre
80-150 Persons Per Acre
6 Neighborhood Boundary and Number

COMMERCIAL AND INDUSTRIAL AREAS

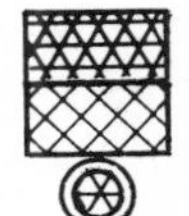

Central District
Commercial Service District
Community Shopping Center
Neighborhood Shopping Center

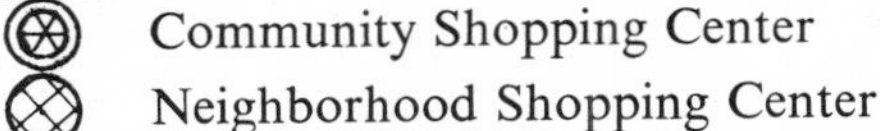

Special Industrial District
Industrial District

PUBLIC SCHOOLS

Existing
Proposed
K Kindergarten-Primary
E Elementary
J Junior High
H Senior High

RECREATION AREAS

Existing
Proposed
Viewpoint
Scenic Drive
Trail

CIRCULATION SYSTEM

Freeway
Major Thoroughfare
Secondary Thoroughfare
Feeder Street
Rapid Transit Route
Rapid Transit Station

issues, as well as the ability of the governing groups in the community to deal with these issues openly.

Experience with the *Berkeley Master Plan* has demonstrated to me repeatedly that there should be, as an integral part of the official document, a single, unified summary that presents (1) the basic policies of the plan, (2) the major physical-design proposals of the plan, and (3) a schematic drawing picturing the citywide physical-design proposals of the plan. If the summary does not attract attention to the basic policies of the plan, recommendations intended to implement the physical-design proposals that should be measured against the basic policies tend, unnecessarily, to be considered and argued about as though they are the kind of recommendations on which compromises—in many cases damaging—can readily be made.

Major policies and physical-design proposals are implemented not only by decisions on projects and regulations that will obviously affect the entire city. They are also implemented or not implemented, to a far greater degree than is generally recognized, as a result of the several decisions made every week by the city council on what may seem to be relatively minor matters. This decision-making context requires that emphasis be given to the fact that the physical-design proposals are dependent on the basic policies of the plan. If this can be done, the nontechnical, intuitive, subjective nature of the basic policies will have to be recognized. Once this has happened, the municipal legislative body will realize that it must and is able to take control of the general plan.

On the basis of more than a decade of direct experience in the capacity of a user of the *Berkeley Master Plan,* as a citizen commissioner from 1948 to 1957 and as a city councilman from 1957 to 1963, I believe that if the distinction between the basic policies and the major physical-design proposals of the plan is made in the summary of the general plan, and is made successfully, without unduly complicating the summary, the value judgments that are implicit in every physical-design proposal will be much more readily understood by everyone concerned.

The restatement of the *Berkeley Master Plan* Summary presented on pages 114–115 illustrates specifically what is meant by "basic policies" and shows the practicality of the unified, three-part summary suggested here. It must be remembered that in actual practice the summary would be one section of the official general-plan document. Hence, it is assumed that the reader is already familiar with the local and regional geographic setting, historical background, existing conditions, and major development issues, as well as the major assumptions and forecasts that have been made concerning the economic, social, and physical factors with which the plan deals.

The five basic policies of the *Plan,* as I have restated them, include many important assumptions, secondary policies, and other judgments concerning social values, economic trends, and questions of feasibility. The ten major physical-design proposals as restated also have many value judgments embedded in the city-planning principles and standards mentioned that may seem to be taken for granted.

I believe that the kind of all-inclusive, rough groupings I have made here in an effort to pin down the "main ideas" of the *Plan* are essential, however, to make clear the most important value judgments upon which the *Plan* is based. Differences on fundamental issues will have to be clarified if these judgments are openly talked about. Eventually, a consensus among those directly responsible will be reached on fundamental values, and on the secondary judgments that will be needed to translate these values into the kind of physical-design proposals for the city that are most likely to reflect the agreed upon values.

For example, the policy I have termed "Metropolitan Opportunities" leads to a commitment to support the Bay Area regional rapid-transit plan. This physical-design proposal is an expression, to me, of the following basic social, economic, and professional city-planning judgments: Our society values the dignity of the individual; we believe that the individual should be as free as possible to develop his unique abilities and personality as he sees fit; we believe that by increasing real incomes, individuals will have more freedom and real opportunities to shape their lives as they wish.

The value judgments stated above, which can be challenged most readily only if they are openly stated, lead to the following assumptions that express a secondary group of judgments: The physical concentration of people in cities increases the production of ideas, goods, and services; this increase in productivity, which makes possible rising real incomes, is a direct result of the division of labor and the resultant development of specialized skills and abilities; the largest effective urban labor supply, therefore, will create the most productive urban concentration. Enterprises of all sorts will be fostered by great cities, production will increase, incomes will rise, freedom of individual development will be enhanced.

These judgments form the basis for the following professional city-planning judgments: Most distinctly urban enterprises are more productive if they are concentrated in the central districts of cities; to foster this physical

UNIFIED SUMMARY OF THE BERKELEY GENERAL PLAN

This three-part restatement of the summary of the Berkeley General Plan for physical development is intended to be an integral part of the official general-plan document.

1. BASIC POLICIES

1. BERKELEY—A UNIVERSITY-RESIDENTIAL COMMUNITY: The Plan proposes that Berkeley should continue to emphasize its specialized social and economic functions in the metropolitan San Francisco Bay Area as an educational-residential city. This policy is of fundamental importance to the Plan. It means that industrial and high-density-apartment developments, although of importance to Berkeley, are to be subordinated and limited.
2. UNIVERSITY DEVELOPMENT: The Plan proposes to accomodate, but at the same time to influence, the growth and development of the University. The physical size of the campus must be limited if the unique character of the City, which is vital to the life and work of the University, is to be preserved and enhanced.
3. POPULATION LIMIT: The Plan proposes to protect and renew low-density residential neighborhoods in all parts of the city. This policy, combined with an increase in the high-density apartment house areas surrounding the campus and the central business district, means that the population of Berkeley, which was 120,000 in 1950, will not be permitted to exceed 180,000. The Plan encourages other cities in the Bay Area to provide the additional high-density districts that will be needed, just as the University plans to encourage new campuses elsewhere by limiting the Berkeley campus to 27,500 students before 1970 (an increase of 7,500 over 1950).
4. METROPOLITAN OPPORTUNITIES: The Plan proposes that Berkeley help to develop a unified metropolitan region in order to make a wide range of jobs and cultural opportunities accessible to Berkeleyans, and, in turn, to enable the University and Berkeley businesses to draw upon and be accessible to Bay Area citizens. This policy will, it is believed, enable Berkeley to share in a more productive Bay Area, higher family incomes, and greater individual choice and freedom. The physical expression of this policy calls for major concentrated business, cultural, and employment centers in San Francisco and Oakland, to which Berkeley will be linked by a regional rapid-transit system. This policy also is supported by recognition of the need for a metropolitan regional plan and a limited-function metropolitan government.
5. BERKELEY'S "UNIQUE" CHARACTER: The Plan, basically, represents an attempt to respect the special qualities that have resulted from the City's historical development as an educational-residential community. This policy, although admittedly difficult to define, is the basis for the most important proposals of the Plan. The dominating role and cosmopolitan atmosphere of the University, the tree-covered hill districts, the influence of the City's large group of San Francisco commuters, the exceptionally high quality of the residential areas on the flatlands for families of moderate incomes, and the magnificent physical site facing San Francisco, the Bay, and the Golden Gate—all of these have contributed to what is known throughout California and the world of universities as Berkeley's unique character. In its attempts to appreciate and strengthen these qualities, while at the same time attempting to provide for growth and for those changes that are judged to be necessary and desirable, the Plan represents a cautious, positive approach.

2. GENERAL-PLAN DIAGRAM

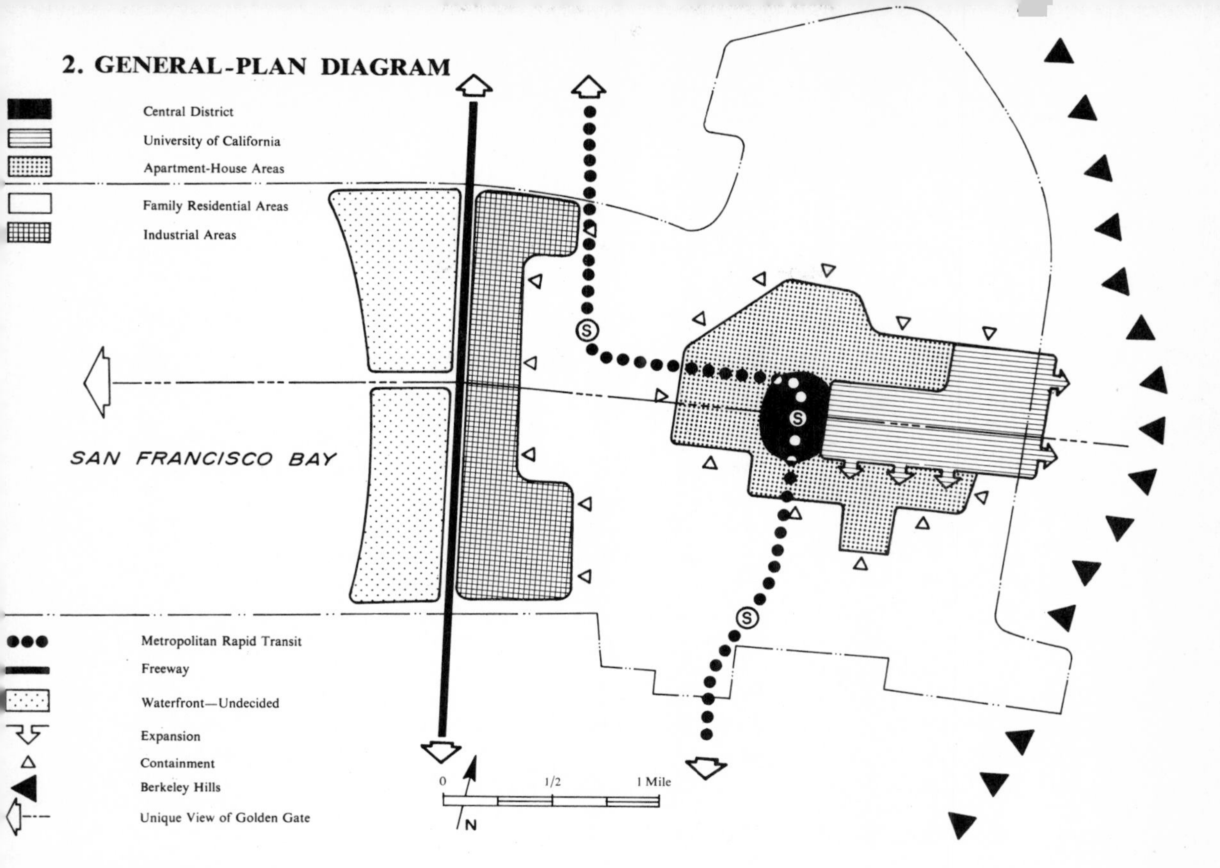

3. MAJOR PROPOSALS

1. UNIVERSITY: Physical expansion to the south and into the hills; firm boundaries determined. Campus shopping districts protected.
2. FAMILY RESIDENTIAL AREAS: Neighborhoods in all parts of the City to be enhanced and renewed. Plan requires rezoning of 8,000 lots from high to low density. Population of 800,000 possible under 1920 zoning ordinance.
3. CENTRAL DISTRICT: Compact central business district. Mainline metro transit station in center. Expansion of office, cultural, and retail activities to be encouraged.
4. APARTMENT-HOUSE AREAS: Fifty per cent increase in present population to be accomodated mainly in a ring around the central business district and the University. New zoning district required. High standards specified.
5. INDUSTRIAL DISTRICTS: Limited expansion of selected University-related industries.
6. SHOPPING CENTERS: Seven district and ten neighborhood shopping centers to be strengthened. Gadual elimination of strip zoning and most existing strip development.
7. SCHOOLS AND PARKS: Five district recreation centers proposed. Schools, playgrounds, and parks to be developed jointly. Higher standards recommended; major expansion required.
8. TRANSIT: Metro Bay Area rapid-transit system assumed; three Berkeley stations planned; underground construction recommended. Radical improvement in local public transit service called for.
9. TRAFFICWAYS: City linked to regional freeway network; one state freeway opposed. Primary and secondary street system for most of City; narrow feeder streets to serve hills. University-City parking problems unresolved.
10. WATERFRONT AREA: Tentative proposal calls for 2,000-acre development. Final decisions require further design studies.

concentration and at the same time make possible the largest possible labor supply for the enterprises to draw upon, a peak-hour system of daily transportation is required that will permit large areas in the metropolitan region to be devoted to residential uses, and, relatively speaking, small areas to be devoted to the economic and cultural activities that benefit from concentration.

Finally, a third level of judgments, also primarily professional, leads to the physical-design proposal: Present and foreseeable transportation technology indicates that a system of grade-separated rail rapid transit will provide the most advantageous, most efficient, least costly physical system needed to create the kind of metropolis that has been judged to be desirable for the encouragement of rising production, rising incomes, and individual values. The suggested principal alternative system, based on the automobile, was considered and rejected because it was judged that the physical problems of the automobile caused by the facilities necessary to provide approaches to, storage at, and circulation within compact central districts are insurmountable if the objective is to enlarge the central-district concentrations and the effective daily metropolitanwide pool of specialized skills and abilities.

I realize that the chain of reasoning I have attempted to describe here may seem far-fetched to many readers as a set of propositions that have relevancy to city planning. But to me, every general plan unavoidably involves the making of physical-design proposals that will affect the way of life of the community concerned. This is illustrated just as well, I hope, by the other four basic policies of the *Berkeley Master Plan*. The decisions (1) to attempt to strengthen the educational-residential role of Berkeley, (2) to attempt to control the physical size of the University campus, (3) to attempt to maintain a limit on the future population holding capacity of Berkeley, and (4) to move cautiously on all matters that might adversely affect the things that are judged to have made Berkeley "unique" will, if implemented—as they have been for ten years—shape Berkeley life in a definite way. If the professional city planners state their basic policy decisions to themselves and others as clearly as possible—regardless of how elemental or dull or mundane or ridiculous or dangerous they may seem—they will sooner or later learn how to inform themselves as well as the councilmen and citizenry as to most of the underlying value judgments with which, as a practicing profession, they will always be required to deal.

I believe that the kind of intellectual effort suggested here is as important in preparing a general plan for a small summer-resort community, such as the town of Inverness forty miles north of San Francisco, as it is for the great metropolis of London and the municipal governments of the large specialized cities, such as San Francisco and Berkeley, that make up every metropolitan region.

Many other value judgments of seemingly lesser importance that are expressed in the five policies and ten physical-design proposals of the *Berkeley Master Plan* could be used to emphasize the point made here. The neighborhood concept, the organization of commercial, industrial, and residential activities into separate areas, the idea of a "balanced" community, the notion of combined school and recreation centers, the idea that low-density residential areas will assure a good environment for family life, the idea that strip commercial development is uneconomical, the idea that concentration of economic activities is beneficial to the community—these all should be "confessed," in my opinion, in some thoughtful way in the official general-plan document. Every underlying idea that has a significant influence on the physical plan, even if it has been observed and described and is considered to be in reality a "law" of social behavior, should be stated in the official plan document.

If the general plan is not conceived and presented in such a way as to invite the conscious making of its final key physical-design proposals by the elected representatives of the community and the citizen members of the city-planning commission, the members of the city-planning staff will find themselves making these proposals as a matter of practical necessity. That this is wrong when done consciously is plain if the political philosophy of representative self-government is accepted. When done unconsciously by the professional staff, it is not only an expression of the immaturity of the city-planning profession, it inevitably will create situations that will be damaging to both the profession and the community.

Another important reason for requiring the general plan to present a clear statement relating the basic policies of the plan to its major physical-design proposals is primarily technical. A large proportion of city planners will always tend to think of their work in technical terms. This is natural since only a relatively few members of each city-planning staff will be concerned continuously at the level of the commission and council with questions of basic policy. It is extremely important, therefore, for the city-planning commission and the director of city planning to maintain effective control over the work of the city-planning staff and over all aspects of the city-planning program. Unless this is done it is possible that the physical-design proposals of the plan as developed by the staff may give too much weight to problems that are obviously important, but that are, relatively, of lesser importance than problems that are not so easily seen and identified. For example, a general plan for the central city of a large metropolitan area that gives primary emphasis to freeway and off-street parking problems as compared with the need for radical improvements in the rapid-transit system may entirely overlook basic objectives and basic policies. Generally speaking, if the role of the central city has been carefully considered and if the broad social and economic objectives of the metropolitan community as a whole have been defined, the general plan normally would give priority to those elements of the circulation system most needed to enable the economic and cultural elements in the central district to prosper—or, in other words, priority would be given to the daily transportation needs of the mass of the people, rather than to improvements concerned mainly with the circulation needs of persons using private automobiles. If no effective metropolitan rapid-transit system exists at the time the general plan is initially prepared, and if agencies do exist for building freeways, the apparently important problems posed by automobile congestion are likely to get far more attention than they deserve and far more than they would receive if the policy-design relationships suggested here were consciously stated and understood.

The general-plan characteristic that the relationships between the basic policies of the plan and its major physical-design proposals should be clearly stated provides a device that tends, almost automatically if properly used, to keep the physical-design proposals of the plan focused on the major social and economic needs and objectives of the community. Viewed in this light, the statement embodying this plan characteristic is a technical city-planning instrument of primary importance in the task of preparing and maintaining a general plan.

A third reason for focusing attention on the social and economic implications of the general physical-design proposals in the general plan is the positive one of making possible maximum community support for the plan. Only a small number of the general plans published since the war have the quality of openness that has been suggested in this discussion. Far too few professional city planners realize how quickly most legislators and civic leaders discover for themselves the important ways in which the life of the community will be affected by the proposed scheme of physical organization called for in the general plan. If these community leaders learn that the city-planning commission and its staff are also alive to the central objectives of community life, they will become much more interested than they had been in the past in the work of the city-planning commission and in the policies and physical-design proposals of the general plan. They will look upon the general plan as an immediately useful guide for decisions and action on issues that are of fundamental importance. Things will start to happen much more rapidly than might have been expected. This is more likely to be true if a careful procedure, involving a broad cross-section of the governing groups of the community, is followed with regard to the formulation and annual reconsideration of the community objectives and basic policies as expressed in the major physical-design proposals of the general plan.

CHARACTERISTICS RELATING TO GOVERNMENTAL PROCEDURES

(6) The General Plan Should Be in a Form Suitable for Public Debate

This requirement is dictated by the fact that the two primary general-plan uses—policy determination and policy effectuation—are performed by an elected legislative body. Such bodies, according to tradition and political philosophy, are supposed to act on important questions of policy only after a thorough and public debate. In carrying out such debates, experience has demonstrated that under a democratic form of government it is essential to have formulated as soon as possible a clear official statement of the proposition under consideration that is recognized as such by all groups and individuals participating in the debate. Prior to its initial adoption, the general plan as prepared in preliminary form by the city-planning commission should serve as such a statement. It should, therefore, be designed to serve both as a means of focusing the initial public debate on the basic policies and physical-design proposals for community development recommended in the preliminary plan and as the basis for the official legislative document that will finally be adopted. Once the plan is adopted, it should be maintained in a form that will enable it to serve as the official statement of legislative policy that will be used by the council and citizens as they debate and make judgments concerning all subsequent issues affecting the physical development of the community.

The requirement that the general plan be presented in a form that will serve the needs of public debate imposes some very definite limitations on the method of plan presentation. It affects the content and organization of the official general-plan document. It also is the basic "procedural" requirement upon which depends the validity of the remaining four suggested general-plan characteristics.

If the general plan is to serve as an effective aid to the kind of continuous public debate we are considering, I believe that it must be presented to the council and the citizens in its entirety—as a unified and complete statement—and that the plan document must also include a presentation of the context of facts and judgments from which the plan itself was developed and without which the logic of the plan cannot be understood. It also means that the plan document must include a unified summary that focuses the debate on the basic policies, the major physical-design proposals, and the schematic drawing picturing the citywide physical-design proposals of the plan.

A significant number of the major city-planning programs established since 1940 still do not recognize these requirements. Whether or not these programs will continue to receive the support they have been given thus far if their professional leaders do not submit to the legislative body for approval a unified statement of the basic policies and major physical-design proposals that are embodied in the technically sound general plans that they have prepared, together with the background information and interpretations that explain the plan, only time will tell. But if the ideas defined in this book prove to be correct, eventually they will be required to do so.

The requirement that the general plan must be organized in a form suitable for public debate means that it must be submitted to the council and the community as a single document that can be reproduced and made widely available. In other words, it must be treated in the same manner as all other important and controversial legislation. This means that the essential drawings and maps must be designed as integral parts of a written report. It also means that for reasons of expense, as well as of relevancy, much of the data obtained from surveys, together with other kinds of detailed background information, must be separated from the general-plan document itself and made available in the form of supplementary reports. This does not mean, however, that only the conclusions and recommendations should be presented in the final document.

The questions that must be asked repeatedly in preparing and maintaining the general plan in a form suitable for meaningful public debate are: What account of our reasoning, what basic factual data, what amount of historical background information, and what description of current problems and of major alternatives considered and rejected are essential for an accurate understanding of the proposed general physical design recommended in the plan and of the community objectives and basic policies that are expressed in the design? Some of the answers to these questions have already been indicated. Others are suggested in the following pages. In Chapter V these questions are considered in detail in the discussion of the contents and organization of the plan document that are required by the general-plan uses and characteristics outlined in this book.

It is customary for city councils to have important policy statements upon which they intend to act referred to the city attorney for review as to form prior to final action. Once the general policy nature of the actions the council wishes to take is clear, and once the role of the general-plan document as the basis for public debates preceding council actions is clear, most city attorneys will become very interested in the contents and organization of the general-plan document.

(7) The General Plan Should Be Identified as the City Council's Plan

After the general plan is adopted by the council, it will be used by many individuals in many different capacities. Officers and committee members of civic groups and business firms will study it and their subsequent decisions will be influenced by it; local, state, special-district, and federal officials and their staffs will be guided by it in planning and carrying out their respective programs in the community; and individual citizens—as home owners, investors, owners and operators of small businesses, and in many other capacities—will consider it before making final decisions on plans of their own. It is extremely important, therefore, that the general-plan document express clearly the fact that the basic policies and major proposals for community development described in the document represent the views of the legislative body, rather than of the city-planning commission or the professional city-planning staff. If the general-plan document fails to do this, if it is phrased in unnecessarily technical terms and has only a brief note of transmittal indicating, at most, perfunctory approval by the council, it is bound to foster a misconception of the basic legislative uses of the plan in the minds of most readers. It will also imply incorrect relationships between the professional staff, the city-planning commission, and the city council that inevitably will suggest methods of altering the plan that will result in a weakening of the position of the council on the more controversial proposals that were worked out and agreed upon at the time the plan was initially formulated and adopted.

Undoubtedly the successful development of a general plan that is identified in the minds of the citizens as "the council's general plan" is primarily a result of the procedure followed in the plan-preparation stages, of the manner in which the debate prior to the initial adoption of the plan was conducted by the council, and the way in which the plan is used by the council after adoption. If the councilmen themselves were directly involved in the task of plan formulation, in the consideration of alternative proposals, and in the making of the final compromises and adjustments that represent the key proposals of every general plan, the community will know this and will know that the plan as finally adopted will have a major influence on future community development. The community will understand that the plan can be changed only by legislative action. The form of the official document, however, can help or hinder expression of the fact that it represents legislative policy.

Most of the official general-plan documents published since the war illustrate principally what not to do. The publication of the general plan in book form, with elaborate color plates and an unusual typographic layout, although expressive of the seriousness with which the municipal government views its responsibility for guiding the future development of the community, cannot help but suggest that a general plan is something that is highly technical and complex, is very costly to prepare, and requires a major, concerted effort that can be undertaken only once every generation. Likewise, an oversimplified, popularized presentation with slick drawings and eye-catching cartoons is also inappropriate. What is needed is a relatively simple, straightforward document—one that is plainly a working instrument designed to be used in the normal operations of municipal government. If it is to be used by individual councilmen during the regular meetings of the council, it must not be large and cumbersome, it must not include unnecessary, detailed survey data, and it must contain, as an integral part of the text, the exact, sometimes awkward, language that was drafted by the council itself to define the policies finally agreed upon when the plan was adopted.

Once the council learns from experience how to use the plan effectively, the official resolution of adoption should be reshaped gradually to express accurately why the plan is needed by the council, how the council uses it, and where in the document the citizen reader will find the key decisions of policy and design summarized in language for which the council members assume direct responsibility. Although other features of the document, such as the title page and the letter of transmittal, can be helpful in identifying the council as the author of the plan, the resolution of adoption has great advantages for this purpose. It is a familiar way for councils to act, and it is an action that requires direct participation by every member of the council. Its value should be appreciated and its advantages should be fully exploited.

The dominant position of the council in local government, its direct responsibility to the citizens, and its tremendous influence in community development require that the plan be the council's plan. These realities sooner or later make themselves felt and continually press us to improve the general-plan document as an accurate expression of the thinking of the council that leaves no one in doubt as to council's role as its principal author.

(8) The General Plan Should Be Available and Understandable to the Public

This characteristic is required by each of the five legislative uses of the general plan, but especially by the communication and education uses. It means that copies of the complete plan document must be readily available to every interested citizen free of charge, and that the organization, language, and drawings used to present and describe the plan must be colloquial—they must make full use of local, familiar terms and ways of thinking and seeing.

If citizens cannot obtain copies of the official plan during the quiet periods between public controversies, the work of the council will be unnecessarily complicated and slowed down. If the document itself, even though available, is uninteresting, incomplete, or unclear, support for the council's policies will be lacking when needed and debate on the major alternatives, which will be required if the adopted policies must be abandoned because of lack of understanding, will not be as constructive as it could be. These lessons of experience dictate the general-plan characteristics of availability and understandability.

The qualities that the official general-plan document must have if it is to meet the requirements of availability and understandability are similar to those imposed by the requirement that the plan be presented in a form suitable for public debate. It has seemed important, however, to give special emphasis to the tremendous advantages that the council will enjoy if the plan, by a conscious and continuing effort, can find its way into the homes and into the minds of the citizens when public debates and controversies do not require that full attention focus on particular questions. Of all the general-plan characteristics, (6) and (8) are the most obvious and, at the same time, the most frequently ignored.

(9) The General Plan Should Be Designed to Capitalize on its Educational Potential

Every year a new group of young people become voters, changes take place in the membership of the council and the city-planning commission, and new leaders in business, civic, and governmental affairs emerge. Most communities, however, are governed by a coalition of formal and informal leadership groups that usually remains in power for a generation or so. There is a tendency on the part of such leaders and their advisors to ignore the need for continuous educational efforts aimed at introducing the newcomers to the basic policies and methods of municipal government. The general-plan characteristic considered here is intended to check this tendency. Properly understood and supported, it encourages stability in government, facilitates sustained progress, and changes fundamentally the methods previously used to govern physical development in a way that will not be opposed by or give unfair advantage to either the incumbent political leaders or their challengers.

If the general plan is to capitalize on its educational potential it must attempt for each new reader to place the basic policies and design proposals of the plan in the context that made the council judge them to be necessary and good; it must anticipate the fact that a large proportion of the citizens tend to be confused by the relationship of the general plan to other related but distinctly different activities of the city-planning commission and the municipal government; and it must, in particular, attempt to inspire and raise the aspirations of everyone, including the members of the council, in matters of civic design and city planning.

Many readers of the general-plan document will not have basic factual knowledge of the geographic setting or of the main stages of historical development of the community. Without such knowledge the plan cannot be understood. It must also be assumed that a large proportion of plan-document readers will be unaware of the judgments made by the council defining the critical major problems which the plan attempts to solve, or of the major alternatives to the policies and proposals of the plan that were considered and rejected. Since widespread critical understanding is required to make the plan useful, the official general-plan document should attempt to inform and educate on these points, and it should continue to do so, year after year. The need to re-educate constantly tends to be forgotten by busy political and professional leaders. No official document of any sort will solve this kind of educational problem by itself; but it seems unwise to remove the plan from its context if it is not necessary to do so. Experience gained in recent years indicates that we can summarize and present such background information effectively in the general-plan document, and that in those communities where this has been done on a continuing basis such summaries have been factors in the gradual development of citywide improvement programs that have received sustained and effective public support.

A special and continuous effort is also necessary to clarify the relationship of the general plan to the other activities of the municipal government that are identified in the minds of the citizens with the work of the city-planning commission. The major effort to re-educate a community to bring about a full comprehension of the major duties of the city-planning commission must precede the development and use of a general plan. No city council will appropriate the funds needed to strengthen the professional staff, without which a really useful general plan cannot be prepared, until its members are convinced that something besides the policies and regulations embodied in zoning and subdivision-control ordinances are needed to enable them to bring about the high quality of over-all urban development that every community desires.

After the councilmen and civic leaders of the community have formed for themselves a clear idea of the essential uses of the general plan, and after the city-planning commission has completed the first draft of the general-plan document describing the basic policies and general physical-design proposals, it will be as necessary as before to clarify the role of the city-planning commission and the uses of the general plan. Regardless of the normal continuing educational efforts of the city-planning commission, many citizens will confuse the proposed general plan with the zoning ordinance and will study the general plan carefully in an attempt to discover specific proposals that will affect them and their properties. It is necessary, therefore, to include in the general-plan document itself a description of the relationship of the general plan to the other major activities for which the city-planning commission is responsible.

It is necessary to recognize and educate others concerning the need for defining a workable relationship to the new scope of the city-planning commission's program that will develop naturally as a result of the adoption and effective use of the general plan. Every city-planning commission that has successfully completed a general plan has seen the major proposals outlined in the plan receive serious consideration, and usually has been assigned new tasks requiring, among other things, the preparation of what are referred to throughout this book as detailed development plans. Studies for such plans, whether they are concerned with large areas of the city or with citywide functional elements, such as the park and recreation system or the public-transit system, lead inevitably to the formulation of specific, detailed project proposals. Proposals of this nature do not belong in the general plan. Indeed such proposals, generally speaking, in most instances should be developed by the operating agency directly concerned. But the fact that the general plan will frequently require adjustments in the final designs of specific projects prepared by the different agencies carrying out projects that are located in the same area of the city seems to call for the active participation of the city-planning commission and its staff in the coordination of the detailed design work that must be done if the area as a whole is to be developed in a way that will make the most of the several separate projects.

As yet we have had relatively little experience with this level of coordination of city-planning work. It marks a new stage in the development of the profession. It may require the formation of a new staff agency closely linked with the chief executive of the city government so that the degree of detailed design and construction coordination required can be carried out effectively. However, for several years city-planning commissions probably will be expected to conduct the detailed design studies needed, and to prepare the nongeneral development plans called for. This will be especially true in the case of areas and citywide facility systems whose emerging problems have been identified primarily as a result of the work of the city-planning commission, such as blighted areas for which redevelopment has been recommended and the need for integration of transit and freeway projects.

It seems apparent, therefore, that if the general plan is to remain a broad policy instrument, and if the city-planning commission is to help rather than hinder the powerful community desire to translate the general plan into the reality of a more beautiful and a more functional city, a continuing effort must be made to define the relationship between the general plan and the detailed development studies and plans for specific areas, special features, and functional elements that will also be needed. To achieve this the city-planning commission must clarify the basis upon which it intends to establish a line of demarcation between what properly should and should not be included in the general plan. Then every opportunity must be taken to explain the reasons for the distinction and the city-planning commission's positive interest in each of the two levels of city-planning work that are involved. As to the effect of this requirement on the organization of the general-plan document itself, little can be said other than that a description of the definition of relationships worked out should be included in the document, and that in the document great caution should be exercised in the use of examples and illustrations to avoid any suggestion that the major physical-design proposals in the general plan are of a detailed, specific nature.

The need for the general plan to capitalize on its educational potential grows out of the confusion of the past and the already visible needs of the future. This plan characteristic must be understood and expressed in the official general-plan document and in the daily activities of the city-planning commission and its staff if the city-planning profession is to help bring into being the new range of civic design work that is so essential and that, sooner or later, will parallel the work of general city planning.

One of the most difficult educational uses of the general plan by the council involves the setting of goals and standards. Everyone agrees that the plan should point toward a better, a more desirable physical environment. But in moving to the center of the municipal-government stage, in becoming an instrument of policy that the council actually uses, the plan cannot avoid entering the real world of compromise. In the early stages of acceptance and use, there is a danger that high standards may be cut down in order to overcome practical arguments. For example, in Berkeley it gradually has become clear to practically every thoughtful civic leader that, even on the basis of very modest standards, the city must attempt during the next decade to double the amount of land devoted to parks and playgrounds. As this policy is implemented, new leaders will emerge and new judgments will be made as to what is desirable; the standards in today's plan inevitably will be raised. The plan, therefore, must be presented in a manner that will encourage the council to raise its standards, to reset its sights, to improve the quality both of the goals it has in mind and the programs intended to move toward the goals.

If the members of the city-planning commission and the council are educated by the director of city planning to understand the educational uses of the plan, ways will be found to achieve this general-plan characteristic. Idealists as well as realists will always be present among the members of the legislative bodies of democratic city governments. The general plan should be an instrument that will be fair and useful to both points of view.

(10) The General Plan Should Be Amendable

This requirement is of paramount importance to the general-plan concept presented in this book. If the legislative body is presented with a general plan in a form that makes it difficult to change, the plan will not be kept up to date and, as a consequence, it will not be used. It is essential, for both technical and political reasons, that the plan be maintained as an expression of the best current judgment of the city council. A general plan that is not amendable should not be adopted by the council.

The policy-determination use of the general plan calls for a plan that recognizes the significant physical-development problems and opportunities facing the community and that enables the city council to frame reasonable policies with regard to these problems and opportunities. Effective policy determination requires that such policies must be firm and definite, but not frozen. It specifies, accordingly, that the general plan must be reviewed once a year, prior to action on the financial policy of the community as expressed in the annual budget. It also calls for a complete review and reconsideration of the entire plan at least once every ten years so that the implications of the accumulated annual revisions can be seen in perspective and major adjustments can be made.

The policy-effectuation use of the general plan also requires a plan that can be kept up to date. If the plan as expressed in the official document is one that cannot be readily amended whenever necessary to take into account the current, changing forces that are affecting the physical development of the community, it will not and should not be used as a guide.

Acceptance of the annual review and amendment procedure prior to initial adoption of the plan enables the council to concentrate its first efforts on the fundamental issues and decisions that must be faced. Knowing that the plan will be regularly reviewed, the council is able to postpone action on less important matters—to sidestep decisions on controversies that are not initially of basic significance to the plan and concerning which additional information and study would be helpful. On the other hand, knowing that the plan will be regularly reviewed, the council will be willing to act on the fundamental questions that must be answered if there is to be any plan at all. In doing so, it invariably will be necessary to act in the face of arguments calling for more study, more information, more debate. Such arguments are no longer valid once a council has decided it must have a publicly stated plan and has understood and committed itself to the annual review and amendment procedure.

The requirement that the plan be amendable enables the council, over a period of time, to constantly broaden the area of community agreement on basic development policy. This requirement invites open reconsideration of alternatives to major decisions and encourages the exploration of side issues and secondary questions that, without agreements of the sort embodied in the adopted general plan, tend to be put off endlessly.

The *Berkeley Master Plan* has been reviewed every year since it was initially adopted in 1955, and several important amendments have been made. Major decisions concerning the location of rapid-transit and freeway routes have been modified, urban-renewal policies and proposals have been added, and the basic objectives, policies, and physical-design proposals of the *Plan* have been reaffirmed. As a result, the *Plan* is familiar to both new and incumbent council members, and it has proven a solid foundation for action programs and for constructive consideration of important controversial issues. It is an imperfect plan, and some of its most important policies and proposals were, in effect, ignored by the council for several years after it was initially adopted. The annual amendment procedure has made it a better plan and it also has, slowly but surely, enabled the council to face up to the implications of its most important and most controversial policies and proposals.

The general-plan attributes that are indicated by the requirement of amendability are similar to those suggested by the previously considered requirements that the general plan be in a form suitable for public debate and that it express the thinking of the city council. It must be simply and clearly organized, described, and indexed, and it must bring into focus the basic policies and design proposals that form the core of the plan. It must be designed to facilitate the annual review and amendment procedure —to invite the making of every change that the council considers, in its judgment, to be necessary.

Strong arguments have been made to support the view that it is not realistic to expect the city council, for one reason or another, to keep the general plan up to date. These arguments emphasize the technical complexity of the general plan and the need for "flexibility." In effect, these arguments lead to the conclusion that the top policy-making body of a municipal government must be excluded from all policy-making activities in one of its most important areas of responsibility.

The general-plan concept presented in this book accepts the supremacy of the city council on all key questions of public policy and attempts to define a general plan that will enhance this supremacy and still provide an effective instrument consistent with the technical requirements of general physical planning for community development. The arguments that this is impossible to accomplish must simply be set aside until a creative, sympathetic, and sustained effort has been made to develop the general plan in a form that is expressly suited to the needs of the city council.

V 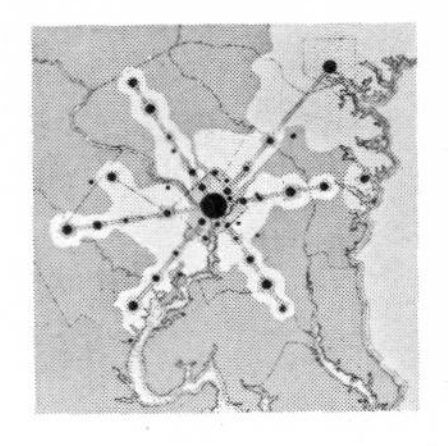

THE GENERAL-PLAN DOCUMENT

THE SUGGESTIONS presented in the following pages are necessarily on a different plane than the ideas described in chapters III and IV. They are suggestive rather than definitive. It will require many more years of widespread local experience before we discover whether the needs of city councils throughout the country will result in a common definition of the contents and organization of the general-plan document. I believe that a common definition of the uses and characteristics of the general plan will emerge and will be beneficial. I am not aware of any significant agreement within the city-planning profession, as yet, on the contents and organization of the general-plan document that is expressive of the uses and characteristics of the general plan, either as I have defined them or as defined by others.

However, certain definite ideas concerning the contents and organization of the general-plan document are suggested by the ten general-plan characteristics based on my conviction that the city council is the primary client of the plan. If these ideas are not recognized and emphasized, the requirements of the federal government may encourage city councilmen to undertake the preparation of general plans that will not be useful to them as local legislators.

Experience in England since the passage of the 1947 Town and Country Planning Act, and in the United States since 1949 when Congress imposed the requirement of a general physical-development plan as a condition for federal financial aid for city planning, provides convincing evidence that we are once again in the midst of a period when higher levels of government will attempt to specify, for their own purposes, what they consider to be the essential uses and characteristics of the general plan and the contents of the official general-plan document. Federal and state governments cannot plan and govern our cities, except during limited periods of extreme emergency. It is physically impossible for them to do so. If they mislead themselves and local governments (or if local governments permit themselves to be misled) into thinking that they can do so, we can anticipate an era of good intentions and disappointing results such as we had during the first period of the New Deal in the 1930's. Because the contents and characteristics of the urban general plan are now actually being defined by federal regulations, everything possible should be done —for the sake of the state and federal programs as well as for the success of local programs—to encourage municipal governments to do their own thinking and make their own decisions on general-plan questions, and to do so, always, on the basis of their own technical and political needs.

The decision of the Town Planning Committee of the City Council of Cambridge, England, in 1956 to publish a booklet entitled "A Guide to the Cambridge Plan" several years after the completion of their development plan illustrates this point. The Cambridge Council found it necessary to have the booklet prepared because the official plan document adopted by the Council, which had to comply with national regulations, was simply not useful locally. On page 1 of the booklet, the author, Mr. Derek Senior, wrote:

> . . . if you are interested in the Plan as a citizen, as a member of the University, or as one of thousands of people all over the world who know and love Cambridge, then *you will find* . . . [the official] documents by themselves of little use. *They will not tell you what the Plan is all about, or explain how one proposal is related to the rest.* . . . even if you had time to . . . [read] all these publications you might well, in the end, find it hard to see the wood for the trees.
>
> In this booklet I have tried to show you the wood as a wood. *Since it is not a statutory document it can concentrate on essentials, both in text and in diagrams.* When you read it you will, I hope, be able to see the Plan in the round, to appreciate the problems which its authors had to solve, and so to reach your own informal and independent judgment as to how well they have discharged their task. [Emphasis added.]

The needs of state and federal governments to understand municipal and metropolitan general plans are legitimate and important. After city councils fully comprehend, for themselves, their own plans, they will see to it that plan documents that make sense are prepared and made available.

IMPLICATIONS OF THE USES AND CHARACTERISTICS OF THE GENERAL PLAN

The implications of the ideas that have been described thus far for the contents and organization of the general-plan document may be summarized as follows: The general plan must be presented in the form of a single document; the document must be designed and written so that it can be published, made available to, and understood by, every interested citizen; the document must be in a form that is amendable. The contents of the document must include a summary of the plan, a description of the plan, and a statement of the context of the plan. The plan itself must focus on physical development; it must be long-range, comprehensive, and general; and it must distinguish between basic policies and major physical-design proposals. Finally, the urban general plan must be the council's plan.

Every city-planning director, staff member, and consultant who has been involved in the preparation and use of a general plan is aware that the implications of the uses and characteristics of the general plan for the contents and organization of the plan document so briefly stated above continue to be the subject of disagreement and debate among the members of the profession who are working in cities where the need for a plan has been recognized. To others, the implications may appear to be questions that are of minor importance. However, if they are not considered seriously and are, in effect, ignored, decisions will be made concerning the contents and organization of the plan document that will adversely affect the usefulness of the plan. As a consequence, the work of the city council as it strives to do a better job of guiding the physical development of the community will be needlessly complicated.

In the following discussion certain of the points I try to make are illustrated particularly well by the general-plan documents published by the cities of Cleveland (1950), Berkeley (1955), and Philadelphia (1960). I mention these specific documents because they are available for comparative study, because they are familiar to students of general-plan theory, and because they are expressions of successful city-planning programs that have become accepted within the municipal government of each city. Each of the documents was prepared with a different client in mind, and each one, consequently, takes a very different form. The Cleveland document is a popular report on the general plan from the city-planning commission to the citizens of Cleveland. The Berkeley document is the official statement of the city council setting forth its long-range physical-development policies. The Philadelphia document is a very thorough, very complete description of the comprehensive physical-development plan for the city; it is officially addressed to the mayor and city council, although I believe its authors have addressed themselves primarily to their professional colleagues in Philadelphia and throughout the country.

Since 1945 hundreds of general-plan documents have been published by municipal governments throughout the United States. In the cities where general plans have been put to use, there no longer is any uncertainty concerning the reasons for and the reasonableness of the physical-development focus of the plan. Nor are there today any serious questions in these cities concerning the essential elements of the physical environment that must be dealt with in the general plan for physical development. There continue to be, however, strong differences of opinion expressed concerning most of the other general-plan characteristics discussed in this book, and, as a consequence, there are important differences as to the desirable contents and organization of the general-plan document.

CONTENTS AND ORGANIZATION OF THE GENERAL-PLAN DOCUMENT

The discussion of the official general-plan document that follows deals with what I believe should be the five principal components of the document:

(1) Introductory Material
(2) Summary of the General Plan
(3) Social Objectives and Urban Physical-Structure Concepts
(4) Description of the General Plan
  (a) Basic Policies and Major Physical-Design Proposals
  (b) The Working-and-Living-Areas Section
  (c) The Community-Facilities Section
  (d) The Civic-Design Section
  (e) The Circulation Section
  (f) The Utilities Section
(5) Conclusion and Appendices

For the purpose of this discussion it is assumed that the public debate preceding the initial adoption of the plan has been completed and that the plan has been adopted, as a legislative document, by the city council.

(1) Introductory Material

Three groups of ideas should be communicated to the reader in the opening pages of the official general-plan document. First, the principal authors, major purposes, and organization of the document must be made clear. Second, the reasons why the municipal government is involved in guiding the physical development of the community and the methods to be used by the city council in carrying out its program must be stated. And third, the existing major physical-development issues and problems that the plan attempts to deal with must be described and presented in their full context, including information on trends, forecasts, and assumptions concerning the social, economic, and physical factors with which the plan deals.

Anyone familiar with the importance and difficulty of establishing a receptive frame of mind on the part of the citizen reader will agree that the way in which the introductory sections of the official general-plan document are handled—both as to content and design—can greatly affect the degree of interest and respect with which the ideas and policies presented in the document are subsequently studied and used.

The cover, title page, and official resolution of adoption, viewed together, should provide the citizen reader and the government official with a clear picture of the key role of the city council as the responsible author of the plan. Most of the general-plan documents completed in the United States since 1945 are represented as being the work of the city-planning commission and its professional staff or consultant. Even in the relatively few instances where general plans have been adopted by the municipal legislative body, the council is not usually clearly identified as being responsible for the plan. If the general-plan uses as defined in this study are accepted, it will be necessary in reality to subordinate the role of the city-planning commission and its staff to the primary role of the council, and to express this relationship in the opening pages of the general-plan document so that the citizen reader, in formulating and expressing his critical judgments of the plan, will address himself directly to the members of the city council, as well as to the members of the city-planning commission and the professional staff.

The major purposes of the general plan and the specific ways in which it will be used by the council can be summarized effectively. This should be done in the opening pages of the document. The experiences of an increasing number of California cities suggest, as I have already indicated, that the official council resolution of adoption is one practical means of doing this. It not only is an authoritative statement, but the fact that it must be formally acted upon by the council enables the director of city planning, with the help of the city-planning commission and the chief executive, to restate and clarify the legislative uses of the plan in the minds of the council members at least once each year when the plan is formally reviewed, as illustrated by the Berkeley resolutions of adoption and review.

BERKELEY CITY COUNCIL
MASTER PLAN ADOPTION RESOLUTION

April 12, 1955

RESOLUTION NO. 35,073 N.S. ADOPTING THE BERKELEY MASTER PLAN, PROVIDING FOR THE ANNUAL REVIEW THEREOF, AND PROVIDING FOR THE INTEGRATION OF THE CAPITAL IMPROVEMENT PROGRAM AND THE PHYSICAL DEVELOPMENT OF THE CITY THEREWITH.

BE IT RESOLVED by the Council of the City of Berkeley as follows:

WHEREAS, the Planning Commission of the City of Berkeley after careful study and after two public hearings has recommended to this council a master plan for the City of Berkeley; and

WHEREAS, this Council has carefully considered the master plan and has held a public hearing thereon and finds that said plan constitutes a suitable, logical, and timely plan for the future development of the City of Berkeley over the ensuing twenty-five years.

NOW, THEREFORE, Be it Resolved, that the document consisting of text, maps, and charts, entitled "Berkeley Master Plan" and dated 1955, is hereby adopted as the Master Plan of the City of Berkeley in accordance with Section 1 [of] Ordinance No. 3403 N.S.

RESOLVED, FURTHER, that in order that the Master Plan shall at all times be current with the needs of the City of Berkeley, and shall represent the best thinking of the Council, Planning Commission, and boards, commissions, and departments of the City in the light of changing conditions, the Planning Commission shall annually review the Master Plan and recommend to the Council extensions, changes, or additions to the Plan which the Commission considers necessary. Should the Commission find that no changes are necessary, this finding shall be reported to the Council. This review procedure should be timed so that any necessary amendments to the Master Plan may be adopted by the Council prior to the commencement of the formulation of the Capital Improvement Program.

RESOLVED, FURTHER, that the Master Plan shall be the guide for the Capital Improvement Program insofar as said Capital Improvement Program affects the physical development of the City. The Planning Commission shall submit an annual report to the Council regarding the Capital Improvement Program, which shall review each project for its conformity to the Master Plan; review the program as a whole in order to suggest any improvement in economy or efficiency which might be affected through the combining of various projects; and suggest any needed improvements which do not appear in the program.

RESOLVED, FURTHER, that all matters affecting the physical development of the City shall be submitted to the Planning Commission for a report to the City Council as to conformity to the Master Plan. Such report shall be made to the Council within thirty (30) days after presentation of the matter to the Planning Commission, provided that said time may be extended by the Council. If said report is not submitted to the Council within said thirty (30) day period, or any extension thereof, the matter shall be deemed approved by said Planning Commission.

Dated April 12, 1955

Adopted by the Council of the City of Berkeley by the following vote:

Ayes: Councilmen BECKLEY, HARRIS, HINTON, MARTIN, PARCE, PETTITT, RICHARDS, THOMAS and President CROSS

Noes: None

Absent: None

LAURANCE L. CROSS
Mayor and President of the Council

Attest: RUTH C. KEMP
City Clerk and Clerk of the Council

BERKELEY CITY COUNCIL
MASTER PLAN 6TH YEAR REVIEW RESOLUTION

January 2, 1962

RESOLUTION NO. 38,705 N.S. REAFFIRMING THE OBJECTIVES, POLICIES, AND PROPOSALS OF THE BERKELEY MASTER PLAN

AND INSTRUCTING THE CITY PLANNING COMMISSION TO CONTINUE TO STUDY AND RECOMMEND IMPROVEMENTS.

BE IT RESOLVED by the Council of the City of Berkeley as follows:

WHEREAS, the Berkeley Master Plan was adopted by the City Council in 1955 as a suitable, logical, and timely plan for the future development of the City of Berkeley; and

WHEREAS, the Planning Commission and the City Council have reviewed the Master Plan on an annual basis and have attempted to keep the Master Plan current with the best thinking on the future needs of the City; and

WHEREAS, the Planning Commission has completed the Sixth Annual Review of the Master Plan in consultation with citizens of the City, and the City Council has restudied the basic objectives, policies, and proposals of the Master Plan as well as progress made toward achieving these objectives; and

WHEREAS, several Master Plan amendments are being considered by the Planning Commission and the City Council and the Sixth Annual Review resulted in identification of additional areas for study leading to further amendments.

NOW, THEREFORE, Be it Resolved that the basic objectives, policies, and principles of the Berkeley Master Plan are hereby reaffirmed; and that the Master Plan constitutes a suitable, logical, and timely plan for future development of the City of Berkeley.

FURTHER RESOLVED, that the amendments now under consideration and the additional areas for study, as indicated in the Sixth Annual Review, will be reviewed and recommendations for improvements and modifications to the Master Plan will be made as necessary.

Dated January 2, 1962

Adopted by the Council of the City of Berkeley by the following vote:

Ayes: Councilmen BROWN, DEBONIS, HARRIS, KENT, MAY, SWEENEY, THOMAS and President HUTCHISON

Noes: None

Absent: Councilman BECKLEY

CLAUDE B. HUTCHISON
Mayor and President of the Council

Attest: NAOMI E. HESS
City Clerk and Clerk of the Council

If a community and its city council have reached the stage of political maturity at which the actual majority leader of the council is identified as such, it would be beneficial to augment the resolution of adoption with a personal letter of transmittal to the citizens from the leader of the council. One of the principal aims of such a letter should be to inspire the citizen reader so that he will appreciate both the opportunities for improving his community as set forth in the plan and the vital necessity of developing a personal sense of responsibility on his own part for judging the plan and acting to see that it is implemented. The introductory statement in the 1943 general plan for the metropolitan county of London by Lord Latham, the parliamentary leader of the council majority, on behalf of the entire legislative body, is a superb example of what should be an essential feature of the official general-plan document. Lord Latham's statement follows below:

This is a plan for London. A plan for one of the greatest cities the world has ever known; for the capital of an Empire; for the meeting place of a commonwealth of Nations. Those who study the Plan may be critical, they cannot be indifferent.

Our London has much that is lovely and gracious. I do not know that any city can rival its parks and gardens, its squares and terraces. But year by year as the nineteenth and twentieth centuries grew more and more absorbed in first gaining and then holding material prosperity, these graces were over-laid, and a tide of mean, ugly, unplanned building rose in every London borough and flooded outward over the fields of Middlesex, Surrey, Essex, Kent.

Athens was the glory of Greece, Rome the great capital of a great Empire, a magnet to all travellers. Paris holds the hearts of civilised people all over the world. Russia is passionately proud of Moscow and Leningrad; but the name we have for London is the Great Wen.

It need not have been so. Had our seventeenth century forefathers had the faith to follow Wren, not just the history of London, but perhaps the history of the world might have been different. For the effect of their surroundings on a people is incalculable. It is a part of their education.

Faith, however, was wanting. It must not be wanting again—no more in our civic, than in our national, life. We can have the London we want; the London that people will come from the four corners of the world to see; if only we determine that we will have it; and that no weakness or indifference shall prevent it.

We shall need, and I am sure we shall have, the cordial co-operation of other authorities, including the City of London Corporation, who are preparing a plan for the area under their control; we shall need greatly enlarged statutory powers; we shall need labour, materials and finance, but above all we shall need faith and firmness of purpose. This is the challenge.

There are great technical difficulties in the planning and replanning of London; but they are surmountable. I believe that the authors of this Plan have shown us the way to surmount many of them. Nor have they set us an impossible task. They have not forgotten that a town is a living growth; they have not forgotten that people must continue to live and work in London, and that as soon as the war is over there will be urgent housing and other problems which will rank high in the order of priorities. They have shown themselves practical visionaries. Their proposals are bold and far-reaching, but also flexible, because in their humility they are acutely aware of the limits of human foresight. The Plan provides for short-term needs and long-term possibilities, in order that urgent things may be so done that they form part of the whole conception, even if it may have to be modified as the future unfolds. In this most difficult field of period planning the authors have, I think, successfully found a balance between the known and the unknown. We owe them a deep debt of gratitude. They have done their best to ease our task—the task of faith. But it remains a task. Sir William Beveridge has talked of giants in the path of social security. There are giants too in the path of city planning. There are conflicting interests, private rights, an outworn and different scale of values, and lack of vision.

But just as we can move mountains when our liberties are threatened and we have to fight for our lives, so can we when the future of our London is at stake. If only we will. The economics are difficult, the timing is difficult, the moral, intellectual and physical effort is difficult. I do not believe, I do not think that any one of us really believes, that any of these difficulties is unsurmountable. But let there be no mistake. A new London cannot be built out of mere wishing. No bold plan can be carried out unless Parliament clothes us with ample powers and resources. As the opportunity is inspiring, so is the task immense.

The war has given us a great opportunity, and by the bitter destruction of many acres of buildings it has made easier the realisation of some of our dreams. The authors of the London Plan have, I believe, taken every advantage of the destruction which the enemies of freedom have wrought.

The fate of London in the post-war years will be one of the signs by which posterity will judge us, and by which it is right that they should judge us. We need and seek the constructive thought and criticism of all who have a contribution to make, for they can help greatly in the final formulation of policy. As I write, the Plan has not yet been submitted to the Council, and only when we have before us the considered views of all concerned will the Council be able to decide on the principles and projects of the Plan.

I do, therefore, most earnestly commend this Plan to the people of London and, indeed, to all people of goodwill everywhere, for their thought, for their criticism, but, above all, for their enthusiasm, not necessarily for the particular projects in the Plan, but for the faith it embodies and the hope it inspires. There is a long road to travel before London can become the city she ought to be. Most of us cannot expect to see more than the beginnings. But if we do not make these beginnings, if we do not set our feet on the right road, we shall have missed one of the great moments of history, and we shall have shown ourselves unworthy of our victory.

Therefore, let us begin now.

If the fact that the council actually has a leader—as every legislative body must and does—is not acknowledged as yet by the formal governing habits of the community, the document should not include a letter of transmittal. Personal statements by the chairman of the city-planning commission, or by the mayor or city manager, will confuse the reader as to who the responsible authors of the plan really are, and can be expected to cause the council as a whole, and its dominant members in particular, to become less directly involved than they should and otherwise would become.

The table of contents, if properly designed, can provide a clear picture of the scheme of organization used and can emphasize to the reader the importance of giving careful attention to the essential introductory and background material before the summary and description of the plan are considered. This is obvious to those members of the city-planning profession who have had sustained, successful experience in the preparation, presentation, and use of a general plan. But if one were to judge the profession as a whole on the basis of the general-plan documents that have been published, it would be evident that the value of a carefully designed table of contents has not been widely appreciated. Some of the best general plans prepared in recent years have been presented initially in documents that contained no tables of contents at all.

Examples of actual tables of contents are shown on pages 144 and 145. The headings of the first six sections of the Philadelphia plan document illustrate particularly well the importance of preceding the description of the plan with a presentation of the context within which the plan has been developed. The Chico document also illustrates an excellent solution. The Berkeley example is pedantic, but it is complete; the Philadelphia and Cleveland documents, it will be observed, contain no summaries of the major policies and proposals of their plans.

The second major group of ideas that must be presented in the introductory pages of the official general-plan document is concerned with the reasons for the city-planning program of the municipal government and the methods used by the council in carrying out this continuing program.

This section of the document should sketch the historical background of the need for community control over the physical growth and development of the community and should enable the reader to appreciate the significance of the efforts of earlier generations to provide for the needs of the future. It should present a simple and accurate description of the official, formal duties of the city-planning commission, of the relationship of the city-planning commission to the council, and of the uses and characteristics of the general plan. Finally, it should include a description of the ways in which citizens can participate in the community task of policy formulation and in the continuing work of building the city in accordance with the policies finally agreed upon and defined in the general plan.

No brief statement of general-plan uses, such as that presented in the resolution of adoption, will provide a sufficiently clear understanding of the major purposes and uses of the plan. Nor will it enable the reader to appreciate fully the practical utility of the plan. The legislative uses of the plan must be spelled out in detail in the general-plan document, and the different roles of the city council, the city-planning commission, and the independent citizen and civic and business groups in making use of the plan must be clearly described. Once this has been done, the nature of the plan that has been developed to serve these uses should be defined. Our society is predominantly pragmatic and problem-solving, and it is never safe to assume that citizens will readily agree that long-range, comprehensive, and general policies are actually needed or of practical value.

The way in which the presentation of the plan itself has been organized also should be described in the introductory pages. Every community will have its own unique combination of local conditions, attitudes, and development problems that will require special attention and emphasis. The relationship of the sections of the plan dealing with these matters to the more or less standard sections should be explained so that those proposals which are noncontroversial and which may be taken for granted, but which are of fundamental importance to the basic scheme, are recognized and given proper consideration when the more controversial features of the plan are being studied.

The third and last group of ideas that should be presented in the introductory section of the document in order to set the stage for consideration of the basic policies and major design proposals of the plan is concerned with the substantive context of the plan. The introduction of the Philadelphia document, on page ix, contains the following explanation of the importance of the context:

Clear understanding of the Plan's objectives calls first for a careful analysis of the conditions under which it must operate. To make this possible through a presentation of matters in their logical order, the chapters that follow deal first with the historical developments which brought about present conditions; the nature of the City's people, and estimates of the size and composition of the population of the City and Region in the future.

The strategy which this Plan proposes to carry out in meeting these problems . . . [is] followed by a discussion of the technical concepts of planning which serve as a framework for the entire program. What occupies the balance of the report is a chapter-by-chapter demonstration of the way it will be applied to the different segments of Philadelphia's community activity.

The ideas and information needed so that the plan can be seen in its proper context include (a) *History:* An outline of the main stages of the historical development of the city and region; (b) *Geography:* A description of the geographic setting of the city, its environs, and the larger region of which it is a part, including a discussion of the natural resources and other geographic factors that are of significance to the city; (c) *Population and Economic Base:* A statement of current facts and conditions and of future trends, forecasts, and assumptions concerning the population and economy of the city and region; (d) *Physical Factors:* A statement of current facts and conditions and of future trends, forecasts, and assumptions concerning the use of land and the physical environment and facilities of the city and region; and (e) *Major Physical-Development Issues:* A summary statement of what are judged to be the critical physical-development problems and opportunities facing the community. The judgments expressed concerning these issues will explain the special attention given later in the document to the most controversial proposals of the plan. The fact that the physical-development plan about to be described is an expression of value judgments concerning many nonphysical factors, and that, of necessity, this will always be true, should be emphasized. The Philadelphia plan document makes this point on page ix:

Any plan such as this is prepared by fallible people in a fallible society. It is important to be explicit at the outset about the terms within which this Plan has been prepared.

Major parts of it are based upon careful statistical analyses and projections. Other parts, of necessity, are the product of judgments made in the field of human values—values which cannot be measured statistically, but which, as factors influencing final decisions, are just as important as the measurable ones. The value judgments employed here are set forth as explicitly as possible, but public officials and citizens who study this Plan should be aware that explicitness is not always possible.

Although many of the successful general plans developed in the post-war period have been presented in documents that included, in one form or another, the introductory material outlined here, the leaders of some of the most outstanding programs have recently been suggesting that the plan document now should be stripped of everything but the summary and a brief description of the main sections of the plan. I believe this would be a mistake. As explained in the discussions of general-plan uses and characteristics, the need to educate and re-educate is a continuing one. Policies dealing with controversial issues cannot be understood out of context. What one generation of leaders has learned to take for granted should not have to be rediscovered by accident by the next generation.

(2) Summary of the General Plan

From a technical point of view, the process of plan preparation is not complete until the basic policies and major physical-design proposals as finally integrated in the plan have been identified and evaluated as a unified, interrelated group of ideas. Likewise, from a political point of view, the task of presenting the plan in a suitable document is not complete until the ways in which the plan should be used are fully understood and until this understanding is expressed in a manner that will satisfy the governmental-procedures characteristics required by the general-plan uses. These requirements, as described in chapters III and IV, specify the need for a summary of the plan and for the presentation of this summary in a written and graphic form that is nontechnical and readily understandable.

In organizing an effective summary of the plan that will meet the needs of the council, it is necessary, first, after distinguishing the policies and proposals of primary importance from those of secondary importance, to reduce the relatively large number of significant proposals and new ideas embodied in every general plan to a group that is of manageable size. Second, there is the problem of integrating the written and graphic presentation of the major policies and proposals of the plan into a single summary. And third, there is the organizational problem of placing and identifying the summary in the general-plan document in such a way that it will be seen and judged in its proper context.

Inevitably, every proposed general plan for the physical development of a community will contain a fairly large number of important new ideas and recommendations. Only after the technical work of plan preparation

BERKELEY MASTER PLAN

TABLE OF CONTENTS

CHICO GENERAL PLAN

CONTENTS

CONTENTS OF THE GENERAL-PLAN DOCUMENT

CLEVELAND GENERAL PLAN

contents

PHILADELPHIA COMPREHENSIVE PLAN

CONTENTS

has been completed will it be possible to identify these proposals in their final context and to determine their importance in relation to one another. When this has been done, the principal ideas of the plan will become clear —whether they are logically classified (a) as *policies*, which express assumptions, goals, principles, and standards, or (b) as *major physical-design proposals*, upon which most of the remaining features of the plan are dependent. The final step that must be taken is to judge which of these ideas and recommendations constitute, as a group, the ten to fifteen most important policies and proposals of the plan, and then to restate them in written and graphic terms that will be understood locally.

The London and Berkeley plans provide good examples of the written portion of the summary that is required. The main ideas of the 1951 official physical-development plan for London prepared by the London County Council are presented in a summary entitled "London: The Next Twenty Years." The first fourteen points are grouped under the heading, "The Main Principles of the Plan." The principles describe the primary social and economic activities that the physical plan provides for, and the key decisions concerning reconstruction and decentralization, the main ideas embodied in the sections of the plan dealing with commercial, industrial, and residential elements, and the controls placed on population growth as a result of the adoption of higher standards for housing and community facilities, particularly schools and playgrounds. The second section of the summary is entitled "The Main Proposals in the Plan." It contains, under seven headings, brief descriptions of the most important physical-design proposals and translates them into quantitative terms, such as acres, miles of roadway, number of schools, and the like.

The Berkeley plan summary, as restated in the preceding chapter on pages 114 and 115, also illustrates the practicality and value of trying to to make the most of the general-plan summary. Neither the Cleveland nor the Philadelphia plan documents include summaries of the London and Berkeley type. The omission of this clarifying effort in each of these otherwise outstanding plans is probably explained by the lack of a demanding client. The city councils in London and Berkeley had to understand and take final action on their respective plans, which was not the case in either Cleveland or Philadelphia.

Any attempt to summarize all of the ideas and proposals that seem to be "significant"—any attempt, in other words, that is aimed at completeness in a literal sense—is bound to result in a statement that is too complex and too lengthy to serve as a summary. If the general plan is to be used effectively, it is essential in organizing the summary to exercise great restraint in order to limit the number of ideas and recommendations to be included, and to avoid the use of too many classifying terms. In doing this, however, care must be taken not to misrepresent by oversimplification. This is admittedly an extremely difficult task. The only alternative method of dealing with this problem that has been used requires the preparation of several summaries of relatively equal importance, one for each major classification of ideas or for each physical element dealt with in the plan. Such alternatives will not meet the needs of the council members or the average citizen reader. It is essential to prepare a single unified summary of the principal policies and proposals embodied in the plan, and to do so without the use of complex groupings and terms. As will be made clear, this does not mean that the dependence of the design proposals on the underlying assumptions, objectives, principles, and standards, and on the basic policies that result from the combination of these factors to provide the basis for the general physical design, should not be plainly spelled out elsewhere in the general-plan document. It does mean that the summary must actually be a summary, and must, therefore, deal in an uncomplicated manner with the major policies and proposals that define the essence of the plan.

Another good example of the value and feasibility of the kind of rough summary being suggested is the ten-point memorandum summarizing the general plan for the Washington, D.C., metropolitan region issued by the late President Kennedy in 1962. The statement, and a schematic drawing of the physical plan it describes, are reproduced on pages 148–149. This written and graphic summary of the plan, when studied in the context of the plan document, *The Nation's Capital: A Plan for the Year 2000,* enables any interested citizen to grasp readily the main ideas of the plan.

As indicated in the preceding chapter, my experience suggests that the ways in which the plan has to be used require a single summary that is composed of three closely related parts: policies, physical-design proposals, and a simple schematic drawing. Authors of city plans have made very little progress in the successful development of this vitally important feature of the general-plan document in the form suggested. Most general plans do include a carefully prepared written summary of their major physical-design proposals, and every year more plan documents are published in which attempts are made to summarize the basic policies that are expressed in the physical design, but almost all published plans still rely on the large-scale general physical-design drawing to serve as the graphic

SUMMARY OF THE GENERAL PLAN FOR WASHINGTON

TEXT OF MEMORANDUM BY JFK ON PLANNING *

Text of 1962 Memorandum by the late President Kennedy summarizing the basic development policies approved by him for the Washington, D.C., metropolitan region.

Because of the importance of the Federal interest in the National Capital Region, I want the greatest possible coordination of planning and action among the Federal agencies in developing plans or making decisions which affect the Region.

Decisions of the Federal Government affect directly and indirectly the location of employment centers, highways, parks, airports, dams, rapid transit, utilities, and public and private housing. These decisions all have a crucial bearing on the future development of the metropolitan area outside as well as within the District of Columbia.

In order that the effect of the Federal Government's activities on the Region will be consistent and directed in a manner which will foster the implementation of modern planning concepts, the following development policies are established as guidelines for the agencies of the executive branch, subject to periodic review.

1. Planning for the Region shall be based on the prospect that regional population will approximate 5 million by the year 2000.

2. The corridor cities concept recommended by the Year 2000 Plan, prepared by the National Capital Planning Commission and the National Capital Regional Planning Council in 1961, shall be supported by agencies of the executive branch as the basic development scheme for the National Capital Region.

3. The success of the corridor cities concept depends on the reservation of substantial areas of open countryside from urban development. It shall be the policy of the executive branch to seek to preserve for the benefit of the National Capital Region strategic open spaces, including existing park, woodland, and scenic resources.

4. It shall be the policy of the executive branch to limit the concentration of Federal employes within Metro-Center, as defined in the Year 2000 Plan, over the next four decades to an increase of approximately 75,000.

5. It shall be the policy of the executive branch that new facilities housing Federal agencies outside Metro-Center shall, to the maximum extent possible, be planned, located, and designed to promote the development of the suburban business districts which will be required to serve the new corridor cities.

6. Planning to meet future transportation requirements for the Region shall assume the need for a coordinated system including both efficient highway and mass transit facilities, and making full use of the advantages of each mode of transportation.

7. It shall be the policy of the executive branch to complete and enhance the Mall complex as a unique monumental setting.

8. It shall be the policy of the executive branch to house new public offices of an operational nature in non-monumental buildings which, through the use of the highest quality of design and strategic siting, will have a dignity and strength to establish their public identity. Within Metro-Center, this policy shall be carried out by locating new nonmonumental Federal buildings in relatively small but strategically situated groups in and adjacent to the Central Business District.

9. It shall be the policy of the executive branch to encourage the development of a system of small urban open spaces throughout the District of Columbia as adjuncts

---

* *Washington Post,* November 28, 1962.

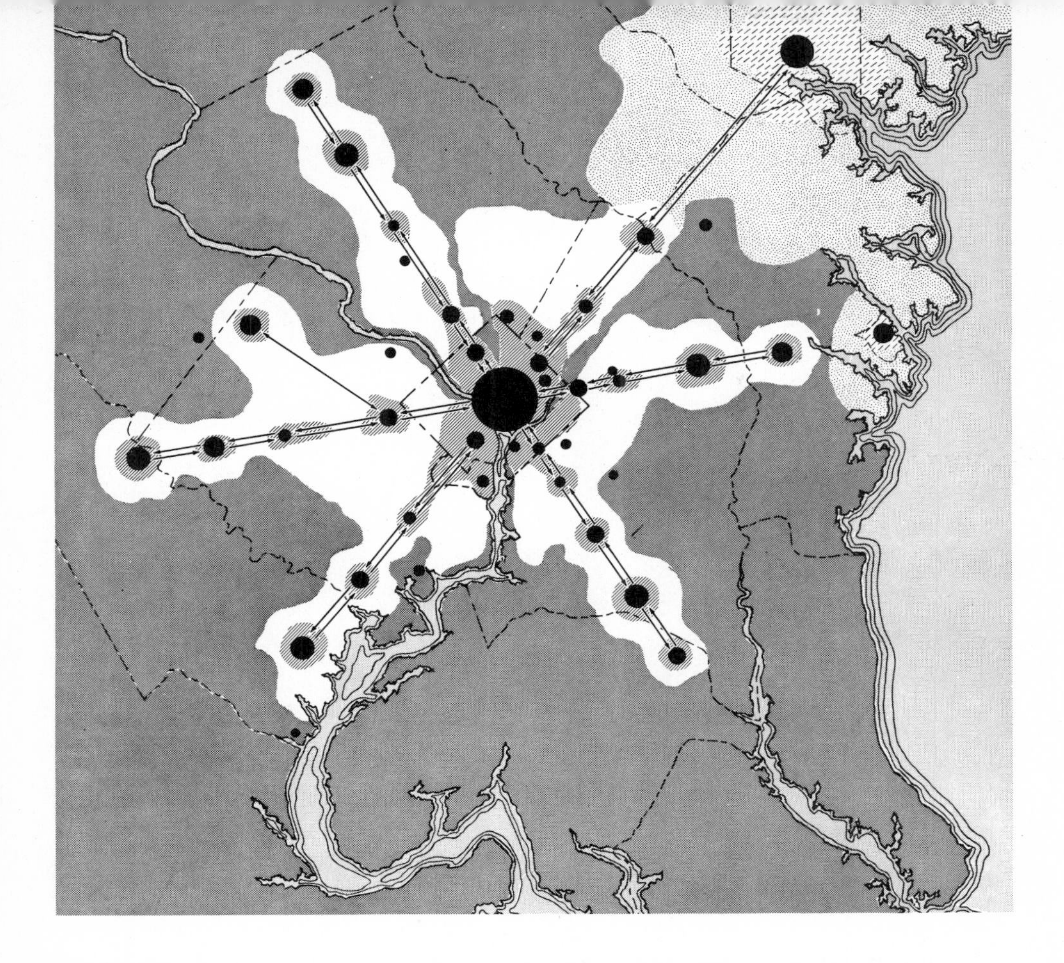

THE WASHINGTON RADIAL CORRIDOR PLAN

New Town Centers

Controlled Open Space

Baltimore and Annapolis

Metro-Center

Main Communication Lines

Source: The Nation's Capital—A Plan for the Year 2000. National Capital Planning Commission and Regional Planning Council, 1961.

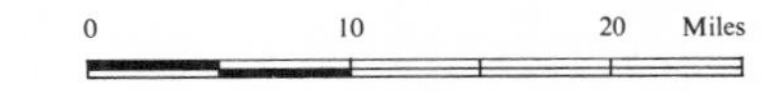

to the development of new Government, institutional, commercial and high-density residential facilities. In addition, a system of important streets and avenues shall be designated for special design coordination and treatment.

10. The executive branch will participate with local governments in the formulation of complementary policies essential to the coordinated development of the Region.

I am requesting each department and agency head concerned to give full consideration to these policies in all activities relating to the planning and development of the National Capital Region, and to work closely with the planning bodies which have responsibilities for the sound and orderly development of the entire area.

portion of the summary. The general-plan concept as defined here calls for a much simpler and much more schematic summary drawing, and for a conscious integration of this drawing with the written portion of the summary. The professional staff members engaged in the preparation of the general plan for Oakland, California, found it useful to prepare a schematic drawing of the plan as an integral feature of the summary. The unified summary of the Oakland general plan is shown on pages 152–153. In Oakland, the city council is the general-plan client, and they adopted the plan in 1959.

The fact that there are very few good examples as yet of the kind of schematic general-plan summary drawing that I am suggesting is understandable. The task of preparing technically sound general plans absorbed most of our time and attention during the initial postwar decade. This led first, inevitably, to widespread recognition on the part of city-planning commissioners and professional staff members of their own need for the unified, large-scale general-plan reference drawing, an excellent example of which is the 34⅜-by-24⅝-inch drawing which is folded and enclosed in an envelope at the back of the Cleveland plan document. During the following period, bringing us up to the present day, we have been concentrating on the description, presentation, and use of general plans that were not designed to serve as legislative policy instruments. Hence, we have seen a continued reliance on the comprehensive and complete general-plan drawing as the focal graphic feature of technically sound but overly complex general-plan documents. The general-plan drawing in the Philadelphia document is an excellent illustration of this. In the years ahead, the need for a simplified schematic summary drawing should become clear. If the legislative uses of the general plan as discussed in this book have been correctly understood and defined, ways will be found to solve the graphic-design and communication problems that are involved in the preparation of an effective unified summary, and the summary drawing will become one of the principal features of every general-plan document.

The placing of the summary in the official document requires special attention. The document as a whole must be organized in such a way that the summary can be found easily. At the same time, the dependence of the summary on the introductory material must be made unmistakably clear. One way of meeting these practical requirements is to place the summary at the end of the introductory sections of the document, and to use some simple device, such as pages of a different color from those used in the remainder of the document, so that the reader's attention will be attracted to it and so that he will be able to locate it easily. The special needs of the general-plan document seem to suggest a variation from the rules of common practice with regard to report writing which normally would call for placing the summary either at the end or at the beginning of the document.

(3) Social Objectives and Urban Physical-Structure Concepts

The success of every significant sustained city-planning effort in the past has resulted primarily from the fact that the major physical-design proposals of the general plan used to direct the effort were a reasonably accurate expression of a set of basic policies that recognized the most important needs and desires of the community, regardless of whether or not the policies were explicitly stated in the plan. There are countless examples of proposed plans that have been rejected or ignored because they were not in accord with the social objectives of the community.

The fact that the major physical-design proposals of every general plan are the direct expression of a single, abstract urban physical-structure concept is brought out clearly by the Philadelphia plan. This plan also attempts to clarify the relationships between the dominant physical elements of the environment and social objectives by explaining that the urban physical-structure concept consciously selected for Philadelphia was chosen because it was judged that it would best facilitate the achievement of one assumed major social objective. The Philadelphia document is exceptional because of the open manner in which it has related major physical-design proposals, social objectives, and an urban physical-structure concept to one another. I have no doubt that the qualities of intellectual confidence and professional clarity that the plan expresses explain in no small measure the strong support that has been given to the city-planning program in Philadelphia since the early 1940's by the governmental and civic leaders of this city.

The Philadelphia example illustrates particularly well the value of concentrating the main discussion of these subjects in a separate section of the document. One cannot study the Philadelphia plan even casually without becoming aware, as a result of the distinctive treatment given to it, of the importance of the chapter entitled, "General Concepts," and of the fundamental importance of the objectives and concepts described in the chapter to the actual plan itself. Many of the difficulties caused by discussing such abstract ideas separately, in a single chapter, somewhat apart from the familiar physical features of the city with which the actual general physical-

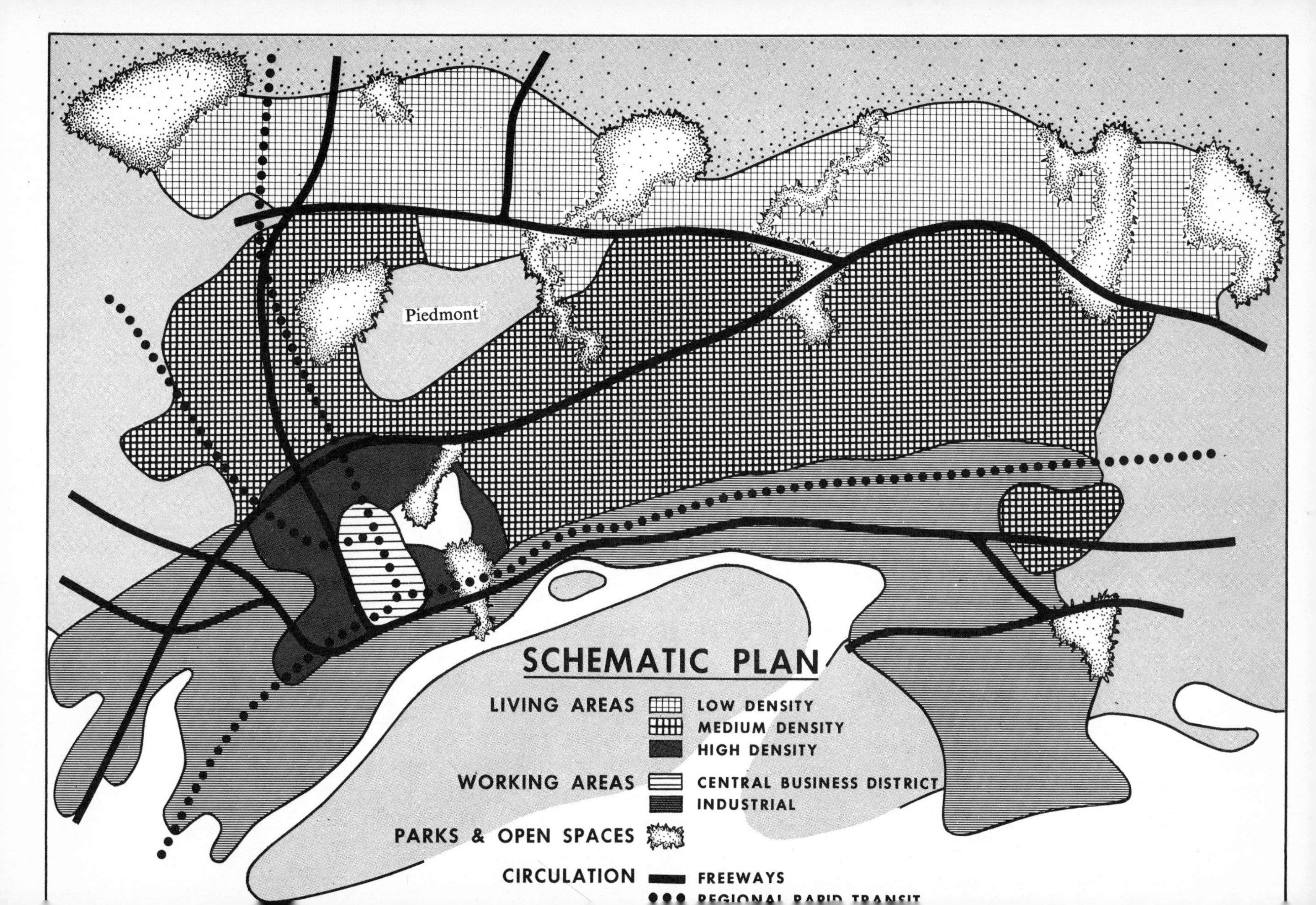
Piedmont
SCHEMATIC PLAN
LIVING AREAS
LOW DENSITY
MEDIUM DENSITY
HIGH DENSITY
WORKING AREAS
CENTRAL BUSINESS DISTRICT
INDUSTRIAL
PARKS & OPEN SPACES
CIRCULATION
FREEWAYS

UNIFIED SUMMARY OF THE *OAKLAND GENERAL PLAN*

SUMMARY

The drawing to the left represents in schematic fashion the pattern of future development proposed in the Oakland General Plan. It illustrates the basic requirements for Oakland's growth as a regional center: a well-developed central business district, an extensive industrial area, and an efficient transportation system for movement by air, water, rail and highway. The schematic plan shows the way in which these functions should be related to the future pattern of residential areas and major recreation facilities.

Because of its size and geographic location, and the historical pattern of relationships to the region that has developed, Oakland performs important regional as well as local functions. These include retail and wholesale distribution, administrative and manufacturing activities—some shared with San Francisco, some Oakland's unique contribution to the region. Just as transcontinental rail and deep-water port and storage facilities are crucial to industrial growth, so too are the regional freeway and rapid transit systems essential for transporting shoppers and workers to the Central Business District and industrial areas. Oakland's growth as a regional center will require maximum exploitation of the city's unique competitive advantages in the region and the Pacific area.

The schematic plan illustrates an important principle of city development: the separation of living areas from working areas. More than two-thirds of the area of the city is planned as living area: neighborhoods of homes together with their schools, parks, churches, shopping centers and other facilities. As the primary areas for the development of wholesome family life and the education of youth, these living areas must be designed for beauty, safety and quiet, and protected against the noise, traffic and confusion found in working areas.

Working areas occupy the remaining third of Oakland's land. These commercial and industrial areas function best if not hampered by residential development in their midst. For this reason, the General Plan delineates major living areas and working areas and draws a boundary between them.

The Central Business District is the commercial, administrative and cultural heart of Oakland. Because its successful functioning depends on a concentration of activities in a limited area, its actual size understates its local and regional significance. Industrial activities—manufacturing, wholesaling and warehousing—occupy the balance of the working area. They are situated on level lands along the Estuary and Bay and are well served by rail, highway, ocean and air transportation. Planning for the expansion of much of the industrial area is the responsibility of the Port of Oakland. Port plans are incorporated in the General Plan and integrated with plans for the rest of the city.

The schematic plan illustrates Oakland's enviable setting: a growing urban area with San Francisco Bay on one side and regional parks and watershed hill lands on the other. Fingers of open land reach into the city from the hills while the Bay has reached into the heart of the city to form Lake Merritt. Preservation of this natural beauty is one of the four goals of the General Plan.

Land allocations for working areas and residential densities in living areas have been based on an expected population of one half million by 1980. With the explosive growth of the Bay Area, it is possible that such an increase—one quarter again Oakland's present population—may be reached before this date. If Oakland wishes to encourage a more rapid population growth, the Plan will be adjusted accordingly.

design proposals deal, will be overcome as more experience is gained. The advantages, as illustrated by the Philadelphia example, are clear.

In the first paragraph of the "General Concepts" chapter of the Philadelphia plan, the major assumed social objective of the plan is stated and what is judged to be the main problem to be solved by the urban physical-structure concept is defined.

> Formerly, cities were built for the protection and enjoyment of a fortunate few—others were left to find what advantages they could in city life and, doubtless, even for these the advantages were considerable. In the present democratic era, however, the only allowable objective is that ALL men be helped to avail themselves of ALL of the opportunities which the city offers and, if possible, to avoid the more harmful effects of city life. For City Planning, which must serve the instinct of the age, this means planning the city in such a way that all people have good access to facilities of all kinds. Here is one of the great technical objectives of contemporary planning and perhaps it will play the same role in giving cities form, which the requirements of military defense, trade and industry have each played at various times in the past.

The remainder of the "General Concepts" chapter in the Philadelphia plan is devoted to an explanation and justification of the urban physical-structure concept that was consciously adopted as the basis of the general plan, and of which the general physical-design proposals of the plan are simply an elaboration. The physical-structure concept chosen is the familiar and controversial one that has been adopted by practically every large European city and by a steadily increasing number of America's major cities—the concept of a main center as the dominant point, surrounded by constellations of lesser centers, with residential communities throughout the entire area accessible to the centers and industrial concentrations at daily peak hours mainly by means of a fixed regional rail rapid-transit system. There is, unfortunately, no simplified, diagrammatic summary drawing of the concept, although the drawing shown on page 155, which appears in the Philadelphia plan document in a subsequent chapter, does this very well except for the omission of the circulation element.

The decision in the Berkeley plan, which recommended support for a regional rapid-transit system for the metropolitan San Francisco Bay Area several years before the system now being built was planned, was based on a similar set of objectives and a similar physical-structure concept, as explained in Chapter IV in the discussion of general-plan characteristics. However, neither the Berkeley nor the Cleveland general-plan documents contain discussions of the sort being suggested here.

PHYSICAL-STRUCTURE CONCEPT OF THE *PHILADELPHIA COMPREHENSIVE PLAN*

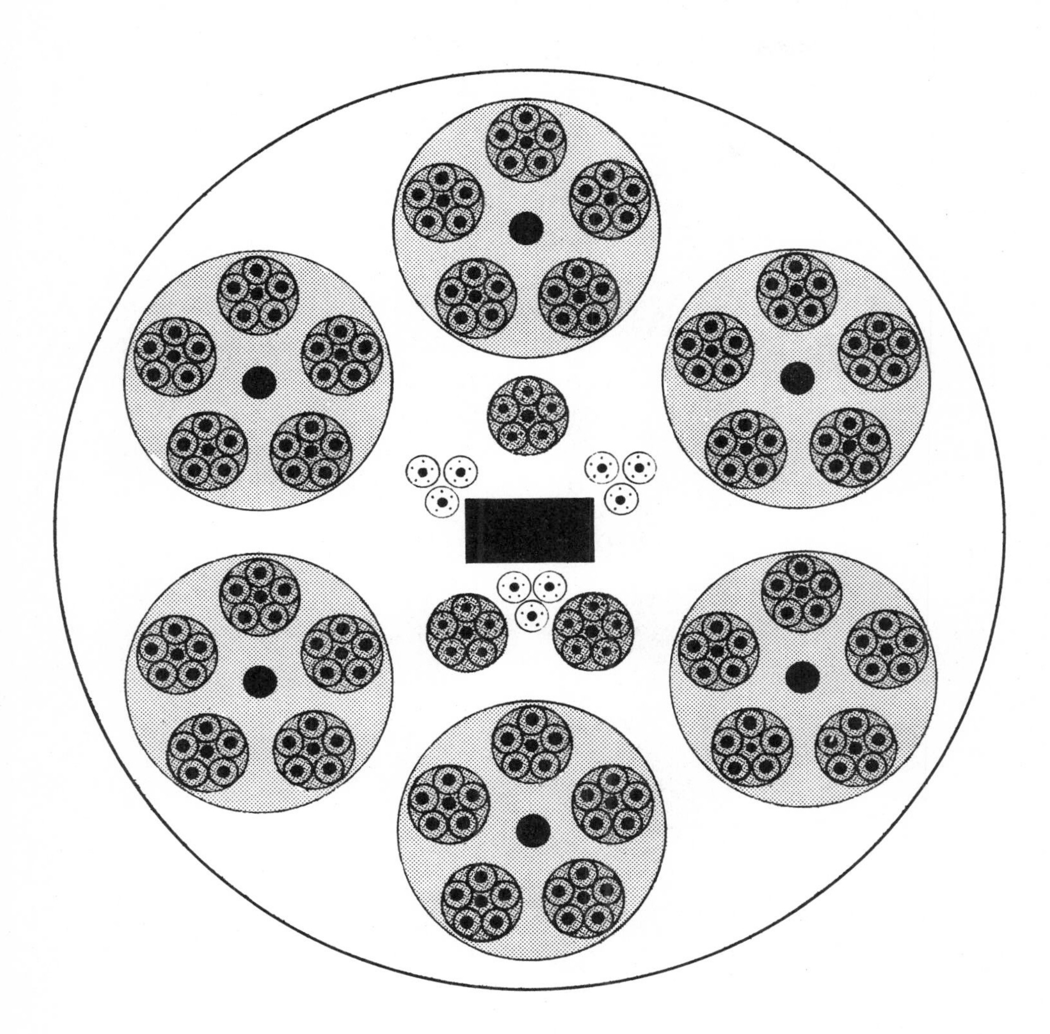

SCHEMATIC FORM OF CITY

This drawing, which appears in the official 1960 *Philadelphia Comprehensive Plan* document in the chapter describing the plan element concerned with business and commercial activities, illustrates superbly the effectiveness of a schematic drawing in simplifying and clarifying the proposed basic structure of a general plan for physical development. Such drawings are used frequently in plan documents for small cities; they are even more necessary, and just as feasible, for very large cities. In the above drawing, the rectangle symbolizes the central business district, and the dots and circles indicate the relationships between this district and locations for commercial activities of a regional, intermediate, local, and convenience nature.

The need to acknowledge and clarify the relationships between the social objectives, the urban physical-structure concept, and the general physical-design proposals of every plan will inevitably be recognized. Major alternatives exist at each of the three levels of ideas. As a result, major controversies also exist at each level. The leaders of the city-planning profession should take the initiative in bringing about open consideration of these issues; if they do not, other professionals surely will. The suggestion that every general-plan document should feature a discussion of these matters is intended to enable the political leaders of our cities to become aware of the far-reaching social and economic implications of general plans for physical development, and to enable them to take control of their city-planning programs, regardless of questions of professional jurisdiction.

(4) Description of the General Plan

For the purpose of technical study as well as for the purpose of public presentation and explanation, the chapter containing the description of the plan should group the sections comprising this portion of the document in accordance with some logical sequence of presentation. Many plan documents still fail to do this. I suggest six sections in the following order:

(a) Basic Policies and Major Physical-Design Proposals
(b) The Working-and-Living-Areas Section
(c) The Community-Facilities Section
(d) The Civic-Design Section
(e) The Circulation Section
(f) The Utilities Section

It should be remembered that in an actual general-plan document the chapter in which the general physical-design proposals are presented *in full* will constitute the main body of the document. Each physical element dealt with in the plan should be described in whatever detail is necessary, in words and drawings, and the proposals in each section should be presented against a background that includes a statement of existing conditions, summaries of significant trends and forecasts, a discussion of the pertinent policies and value judgments, descriptions of the city-planning standards and principles used, and a review of the major alternatives considered before the final policy and design decisions were reached.

Each of the five sections dealing with the physical elements covered by the general physical design, when seen in the plan document, will present explanations of proposals that already have been presented in the unified summary of the plan. Hence, the principal relationships of each major design proposal to the other design proposals, to the site, and to the major policies already have been indicated. However, before they are isolated so that they can be studied and understood more fully, the basic simplicity and unity of the scheme should be emphasized in the manner described in section (a) below.

(a) Basic Policies and Major Physical-Design Proposals. Preceding the description of the physical-design proposals of the plan, those basic policies that have had the most obvious and direct influence on the design as a whole should be restated and the most important and controversial policies should be reiterated. This reiteration should not be a detailed exposition, and it should not be abstract. Statements on the full implications of the policies expressed in the plan will be included in the appropriate sections of the chapter, and the most important social objectives and physical-structure concepts already have been highlighted earlier. But the major physical-design proposals of the plan will be better understood if at the very outset of their full presentation the reader is required to recognize the fundamentally intuitive, nonscientific foundations of social and professional value judgments—the most important of which are termed *basic policies*—upon which the entire plan has had to be worked out. By the time the reader has reached this point in his study of the document he will be aware of the main ideas of the plan; he will be ready to focus his attention on the most important controversial policy issues dealt with by the council in making the plan.

In the *Berkeley Master Plan,* for example, the description of the traditional physical elements of the community that are dealt with in general physical-design proposals is preceded by a one and one-half page statement that emphasizes the fact that the *Plan* is based to a very large extent on the judgment that the predominantly low-density residential character of Berkeley should be maintained throughout the city, if Berkeley is to continue to play its specialized role as a university-residential community in the metropolitan Bay Area, and that this policy leads to density and population-distribution proposals that will limit the number of people who can be permitted to live in Berkeley. Elsewhere in the document it is made plain that the validity of the physical plan, in a practical sense, is completely dependent on the political will of the community, as exercised by the city council, to carry out this policy by a drastic revision of the existing zoning ordinance. The text of the *Berkeley Master Plan* presents these ideas in the following way:

The question of the future population of the City is a problem basic to all four sections of the Master Plan. One of the objectives of the Plan is to "reach a balance between the number of families in Berkeley and the space we have to live in." The number of families which a given area of land will support depends upon the standards the people set for themselves regarding the character and density of residential development, the size and distribution of parks, schools, libraries, and other public facilities, and the amount of land devoted to commerce and industry.

Standards for density and distribution of population set forth in the residential portion of the Master Plan are based on a belief that the great majority of Berkeley citizens wish to retain the generally open and uncrowded character which the City has today. These standards establish an ultimate population for Berkeley (exclusive of the waterfront lands) of 180,000 persons. It should be emphasized that 180,000 is not necessarily the goal toward which the City is aiming, but that this population is the maximum which the area of Berkeley can accommodate with the standards established by the Plan. The ultimate population of Berkeley could become larger than 180,000, but only by accepting more crowding in the residential areas . . . Implementation of the Plan by means of sound zoning regulation will permit the people of Berkeley to control this most important single element affecting the future character of their City.

The general plan for metropolitan Copenhagen affords another example of how to attract attention to the fact that a plan for any urban community, regardless of size, is the expression of a relatively few really basic value judgments and design decisions. In the description of the 1960 plan, published by the Greater Copenhagen Regional Planning Office, the basic policies expressed in the plan are described under the heading "Main Objectives":

The advantages of the large city are, for the individual, the many and varied employment opportunities, wide choice of consumption goods and access to a wide range of cultural, social and entertainment facilities. For commerce and industry the advantages are the presence of a large and highly diversified labour supply, and a large consumer market, together with excellent opportunities for industrial linkage and mutual cooperation.

However, these advantages are only achieved where the various parts of the urban region are in close physical contact, and form an effectively integrated whole . . .

Despite technical improvements in their transport systems, there is in most metropolitan regions at the present day a steady increase in the average length of the "journey-to-work." The proportion of the national product accounted for by transport costs also shows a steady increase, despite a considerable rise in the general level of production. One of the essential aims of planning should be to counteract these tendencies, since they curtail leisure time and restrict the rise in the standard of living. This aim can be achieved in two ways, partly by increasing the speed of the transport services, and partly by limiting the length of the journeys. In the [1950] Finger Plan, this aim was realized by means of consistently concentrating all new developments along the suburban railways. Thus, travelling time was limited by making the fullest possible use of transport services with comparatively high speeds.

Up to the present [support for] the Finger Plan has ensured that the urban region could function as an integrated whole. Wherever one lives in the Finger Plan region, once can reach most of the places of employment within reasonable travelling time. The offices and commercial establishments of the central area, and most of the region's industrial areas, can be reached within 45 minutes. Similarly, there is a wide choice of residential areas within reasonable travelling time of the city center and of the other main centers of employment.

However, if the population of the capital rises to 2½ million [from the present 1½] and the built-up area becomes three times greater than at present, then the urban region will become so large in extent that it will no longer be possible to find a place to live within a reasonable distance of the centers of employment. There will be an unduly long journey to work and unreasonably high travelling expenses.

It should, therefore, be one of the essential aims of planning not only to increase the speed of the transport services, but also to restrict the actual length of the journey to work.

Reduction in travelling distance can only be achieved by making it easier for the individual to find employment, and to satisfy other everyday needs, in that part of the urban region where he lives. If this is to be achieved, there must be decentralization . . . [and] new "city sections" [must be created], which will accommodate entirely new as well as relocated enterprises . . . [They] must be sufficiently large to support . . . [industry, commerce, and cultural and entertainment facilities], and . . . must be so placed as to be easily accessible to all the inhabitants . . .

While this decentralization is taking place, the new "city sections" should be linked up with the existing metropolitan area in such a way that the region functions as an integrated whole, and so that one can reach the city center and the other centers of employment from the new "city sections" as quickly as possible.

MAIN IDEAS OF THE COPENHAGEN GENERAL PLAN

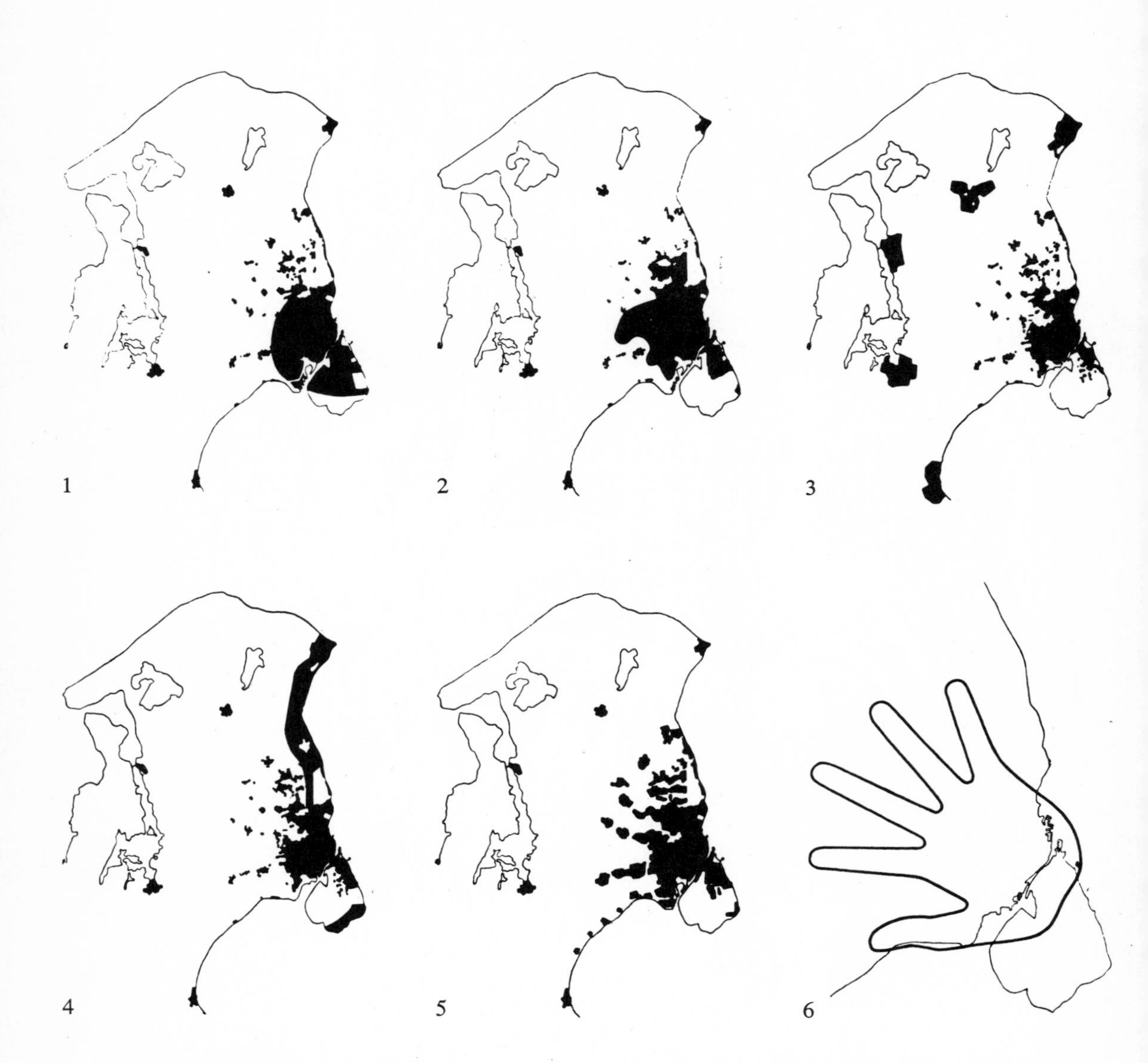

Source: Greater Copenhagen Planning: Status, Steen Eiler Rasmussen, Copenhagen, 1952. (Published by Ejnar Munksgaard, under the auspices of the the Copenhagen Regional Planning Committee.)

Alternatives and Recommended 1948 General Plan: The first five drawings show the major alternative metropolitan physical-structure concepts considered. The sixth drawing clarifies and emphasizes the main ideas embodied in the recommended Plan, number 5. The Plan, which provides for a population of 1,700,000, has been known popularly as the "Finger Plan."

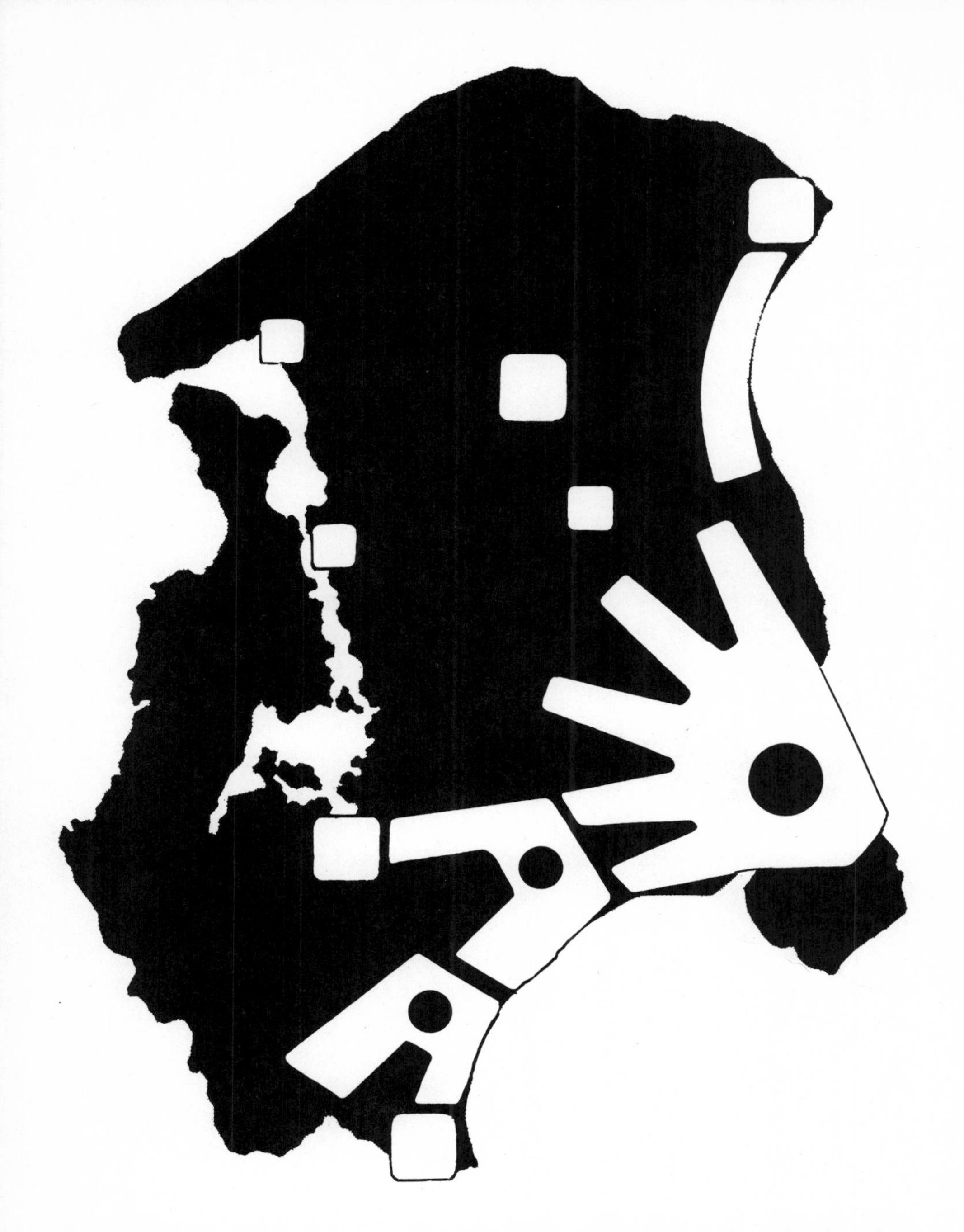

Proposed 1960 Revision of the 1948 General Plan: This simplified drawing shows graphically the main ideas of the revised Plan. It compliments the written summary of the "Main Objectives" of the Plan. The documents presenting the 1960 General Plan and an English translation of the official report contain a number of remarkably effective drawings, both of the general physical design as related to specific features of the site and of the main ideas expressed in the form of diagrams adapted to the site. The area shown above is approximately 30 miles by 50 miles. The revised Plan provides for a population of 2.5 million; the population in 1960 was 1.5 million.

Increasing distances ought therefore to be accompanied by an increase in the speed of travel, so that the time spent in travelling between the new "city sections," and the existing metropolis is kept within reasonable limits. Rapid means of transport—motorways, and railways with widely separated stations—must link together the important points, i.e., they must bring into close contact the centers of the new "city sections" and the center of Copenhagen itself.

The section of the Copenhagen plan document from which the above paragraphs have been excerpted obviously is intended to focus attention on the major metropolitanwide development policies that were judged to be necessary if the assumed social and economic objectives so clearly stated in the first paragraph are to be achieved. Combined with the schematic general-plan drawings shown on pages 160 and 161, this statement leaves the reader in no doubt as to the main ideas of the plan, and illustrates superbly well the kind of discussion that should serve as the final prelude to the full presentation of the physical elements of the community as expressed in major physical-design proposals.

It is also necessary at some point prior to the discussion of the individual physical elements dealt with in the plan to call attention to and to explain the importance of the large-scale general-plan drawing, regardless of its location in the document. The manner in which the different sections of the plan have been integrated into a unified scheme will become more and more apparent to the reader as he considers each set of proposals in sequence. But it will be helpful to him if he realizes at the outset of the chapter that the large-scale general-plan drawing has been prepared especially to show in relatively realistic terms the relationships between the different physical elements and to emphasize both the unity of the citywide general physical-design proposals and the necessary compromises and adjustments that have had to be made in arriving at a workable plan.

Many postwar general-plan documents contain in the chapter describing the plan an opening statement which refers to the large-scale general-plan drawing and emphasizes the unity of the physical elements of the community described in the plan. Very few, however, ever attempt to state openly the most important value judgments and intuitive hunches that have been made concerning what is "desirable" and upon which the most important physical-design proposals are based.

(b) The Working-and-Living-Areas Section. This section deals with the proposed general location, character, and extent of the central business

district and the industrial, residential, and secondary commerical areas of the city. Other uses of land that require significantly large areas or concentrations of activity, such as major parks and universities, must also be dealt with in this section. Residential-area design proposals must indicate the population densities called for, and the local and district residential-area boundaries used in the determination of the density and holding-capacity proposals. The proposals for the industrial areas should be sufficiently described in the explanatory text and on the plan drawings to indicate plainly the character and intensity of industrial development intended. The business- and commercial-district proposals must be described, and whatever special proposals have been decided upon with regard to the central business district should be set forth here. The general location, character, and extent of the primary and secondary shopping centers must be described and related to the residential population-density proposals. Proposals dealing with commercial districts serving special purposes that require relatively large amounts of land, such as automobile sales and service districts, should also be included in this section.

The spatial relationships of the basic economic and social activities indicated here and the land areas and physical facilities proposed to accommodate them should be dealt with first in the presentation of the physical-design proposals of the plan because, taken together, they form the foundation upon which all of the remaining sections of this plan chapter are based. After the special conditions and qualities of the site have been surveyed and analyzed, and after the first tentative conclusions have been formed concerning the degree of permanence of the existing major features of the city, regardless of which design section they will later be assigned to, first-stage decisions must be made concerning the most desirable and feasible future locations of the central business district, the principal industrial districts, and the residential and outlying commercial areas. The major physical systems of community facilities and circulation routes that will be needed to serve the activities located in these areas can then be studied and planned. Experience gained in technical general-plan physical-design work since 1945 in widely different locations and types of cities, and involving professional staff groups representing more than one school of thought on other matters, indicates the validity of the judgment expressed above concerning plan-preparation procedure and sequence of presentation. Indeed, it seems that the judgment is self-evident. But it was not self-evident less than fifteen years ago, and it certainly is not universally accepted within the profession today.

The Cleveland plan document offers the best example of presenting

WORKING-AND-LIVING-AREAS
ELEMENTS OF THE GENERAL PLAN

(From *Cleveland Today . . . Tomorrow: The General Plan of Cleveland,* 1950, pages 8–9.)

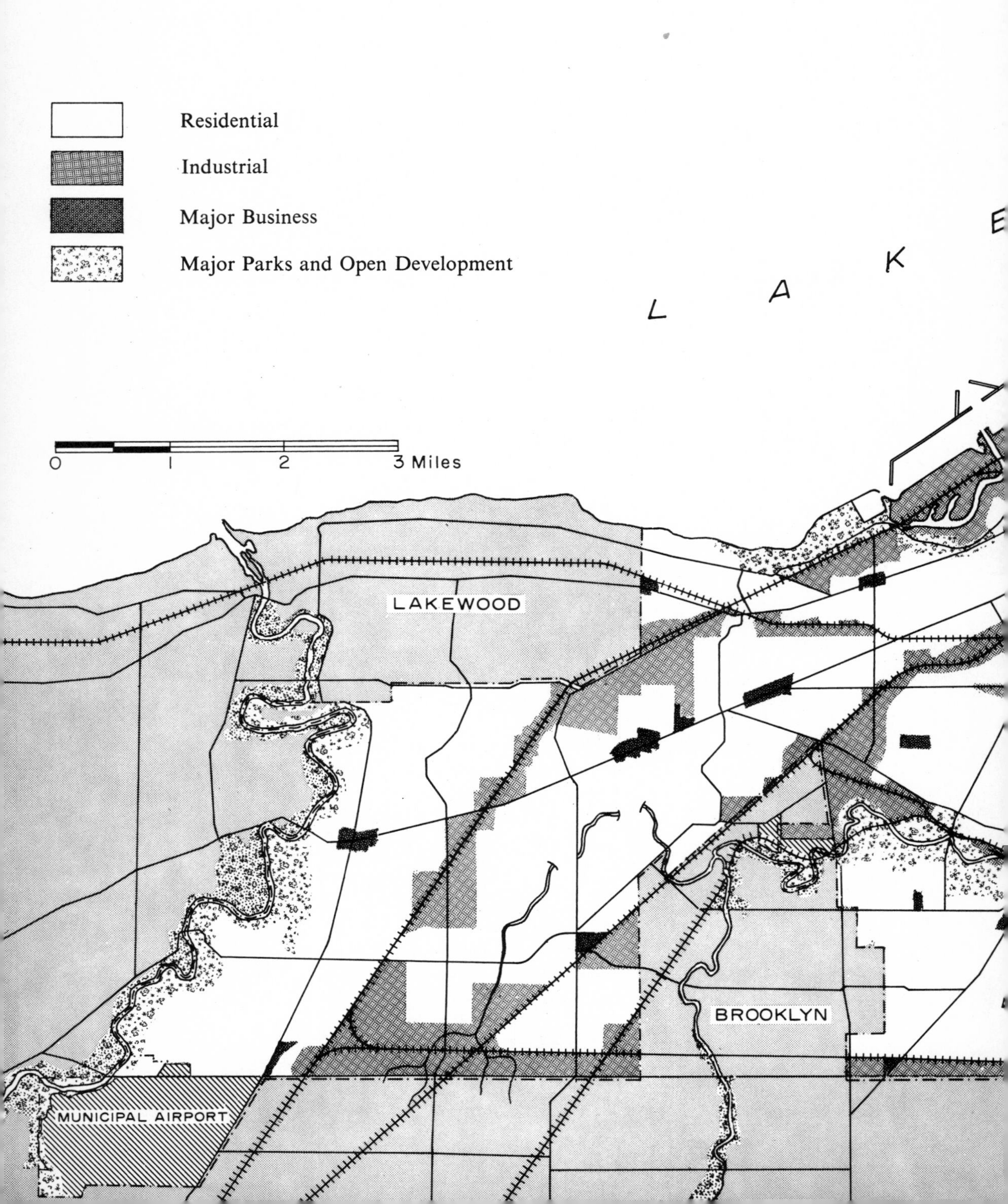

E R I E
DOWNTOWN
AIRPORT
EAST CLEVELAND
CLEVELAND HTS.
SHAKER HTS.
NEWBURGH
HTS.

first, with the help of a unified, simplified drawing, all of the physical elements dealt with in the working-and-living-areas section. As shown on pages 164–165, the initial six subsections of the main body of the Cleveland document illustrate the sequence of plan presentation I have suggested, and the drawing, which is the first plan drawing in the document, is an excellent example of a straightforward simplification of a very complex set of proposals. Each separate physical element dealt with in this plan chapter also requires a plan drawing in order to clarify the relationships among the proposals concerning the subject matter of each physical element. The use of such separate drawings for each physical element considered is now widespread. Very few plan documents, however, make use of a simplified drawing for the basic physical elements dealt with in the working-and-living-areas section of the plan in the manner done so successfully by the authors of the Cleveland plan. The Berkeley and Philadelphia plans are less effective than they might have been because they did not follow the Cleveland example.

The subject matter of the general-plan sections dealing with commercial and industrial activities is superbly handled in the Philadelphia plan document. The actual presentation of the plan proposals, however, is too complex and detailed to fit the general-plan concept advocated in this book. These sections of the Philadelphia plan should be familiar to every student of contemporary planning, however, because of their outstanding technical quality and because they are of such basic importance to the general plan.

In recent years as a result of widespread urban-redevelopment activities and the preparation of what are called "community renewal programs," it has been suggested that such programs should receive special attention in the general-plan document. They obviously will influence the nature of the plan proposals and the rate of plan effectuation. But, as illustrated by the Cleveland and Berkeley documents and, in particular, the Philadelphia document, I believe it best to deal with such new activities and programs within the context of the essential physical elements dealt with in the plan. The four drawings from the Philadelphia plan shown on pages 167–170 indicate plainly that citywide urban-renewal policies were carefully considered in the preparation of the residential-element portion of the plan. Renewal policies for the other physical elements dealt with in the working-and-living-areas section of the plan are treated in the Philadelphia plan document in the same manner as in the residential-element subsection of the plan.

The Cleveland plan, as shown on pages 172–173, illustrates a different method of acknowledging the importance of what is known in today's pro-
(*Text continued on page* 171.)

RESIDENTIAL-AREAS ELEMENT OF THE GENERAL PLAN

(From *Philadelphia Comprehensive Plan,* 1960, page 87.)

PROPOSED DISTRICTS AND COMMUNITIES

The Plan proposes the organization of residential areas into a system of neighborhoods, communities, and districts in order to enhance the local civic identity which now exists in many parts of the City. Physical elements which can be used to promote a feeling of local identity are arterial streets, expressways, and large parks, all of which provide boundaries, and clusters of shopping and community facilities, which provide places where residents of an area come in contact with one another. Fifty-six communities are proposed, having a population range of 25,000 to 50,000 people. These communities form ten districts, in which population ranges from 150,000 to 300,000 people.

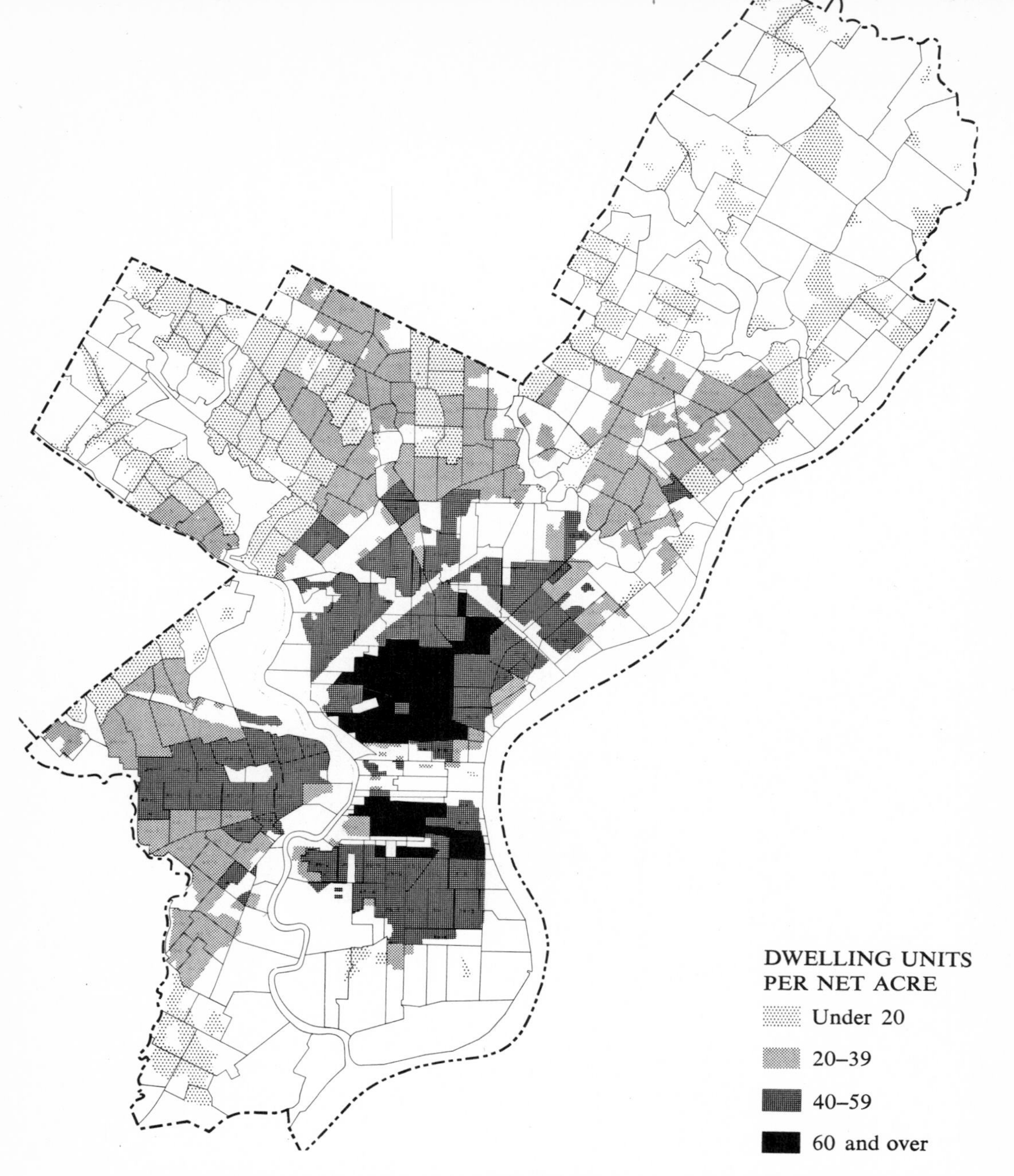

RESIDENTIAL-AREAS ELEMENT OF THE GENERAL PLAN

(From *Philadelphia Comprehensive Plan,* 1960, pages 82, 83.)

RESIDENTIAL DENSITY 1950 (BY CENSUS TRACT)

In 1950, dwelling unit density by Census Tract varied from less than one to over 100 units per net acre. Average density in the City was 29 units per acre. The dense development of inner areas dates from the pre-automobile era. Today, detached houses are built at 6 to the acre, twin houses at 12. Row houses and two-story "garden apartments" average 25 per acre, while "C-1" rows are developed at 15 to the acre. Three-story "walk-up apartments" may reach 55 per acre. Elevator apartments can be built at densities as low as those of single houses or as high as 500 units per acre; when converted to apartments, these structures may have densities as high as 150 dwelling units per acre.

RESIDENTIAL DENSITY PLAN

The Plan allows for a total of 660,000 dwelling units at an average density of 25 per acre. High density (60 and over) is planned for most of Center City, along subway lines, and other areas of special transportation advantage; high-medium density (40–59) within an area three miles from Center City and adjacent to commuter rail lines farther out; low-medium density (20–39) in an area three to six miles from Center City and adjacent to rail transit stops farther out; low density (under 20) in other areas of the City. Exceptions occur where existing development is good although at higher or lower density than optimum, where an institutional facility creates a special demand for housing, or where transportation facilities are not equivalent to those of comparable locations.

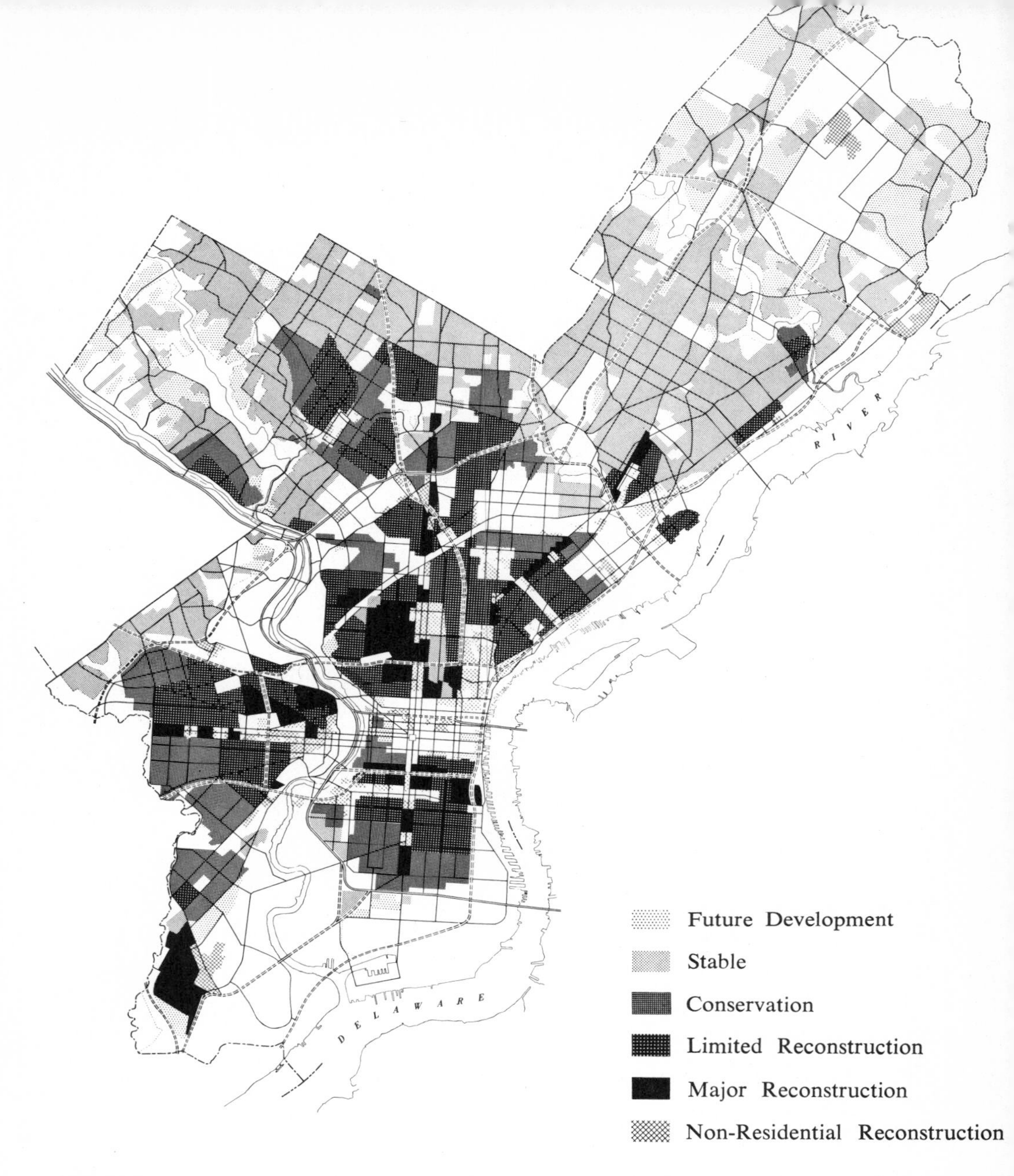

RESIDENTIAL-AREAS ELEMENT OF THE GENERAL PLAN

(From *Philadelphia Comprehensive Plan,* 1960, page 88.)

RESIDENTIAL TREATMENT PLAN

About 65,000 units of the 1950 housing stock must be cleared and 130,000 units rehabilitated to eliminate substandard housing conditions. Changes in land use will take 23,000 of the units to be cleared and 60,000 of the units needing rehabilitation, leaving 42,000 substandard units to be cleared and 70,000 to be rehabilitated. Major reconstruction (clearance of one-third or more of the dwelling units) is proposed for 5½ square miles; limited reconstruction (clearance of one-tenth to one-third of the units) for 15 square miles; and conservation for 11 square miles.

fessional terminology as "the community-renewal program." It is a significant example because the technical work on the Cleveland plan was carried out between 1942 and 1949, several years prior to the enactment of the federal urban-renewal legislation that has been so influential recently. The Cleveland general-plan proposals shown on pages 172–173 are placed in the document at the end of what I refer to as the working-and-living-areas section. In this location they serve as an excellent summary of some of the most important proposals affecting all of the physical elements dealt with in this plan chapter and set the stage for consideration of the subsequent sections of the chapter.

(c) The Community-Facilities Section. This section of the plan chapter should describe the general location, character, and extent of the citywide systems of community facilities proposed to serve the spatial organization of primary economic and social activities delineated by the proposals in the preceding section. It should include all public and private facilities of a community-service nature, such as public parks and private hospitals, that require relatively large amounts of land or significant concentrations of activities that have not been covered in the preceding section. Although the facilities systems dealt with in this section will be determined primarily by the requirements of the working-and-living-areas proposals, physical-design proposals in the remaining three sections of this plan chapter will impose limitations and requirements that will influence the final location and the general character and treatment of some of the community facilities proposed. The decisions made in the civic-design section, for example, usually will determine to a very large extent the location and orientation of the civic center, certain key features of the park system, and the ways in which some of the larger school and recreation activities are combined and situated.

Citywide plans for parks and recreation facilities have been prepared and used by a large number of city governments. The necessity for treating these physical elements in the general-plan document is well accepted and many good examples exist. On page 175 is a redrawing of the plan for parks and recreation areas for San Francisco which was completed by the professional city-planning staff in 1954. It is a particularly good example because the drawing shows the parks and recreation areas in relationship to the most important proposals of the working-and-living-areas section of the *San Francisco Master Plan*. The Cleveland general-plan document contains a fully developed section on parks and recreation areas,

COMMUNITY RENEWAL AND THE GENERAL PLAN

(From *Cleveland Today . . . Tomorrow: The General Plan of Cleveland,* 1950, pages 20–21.)

Redevelopment Areas—proposed for residential use

Redevelopment Areas—proposed for nonresidential use

Conservation Areas—corrective action required

Protection Areas—mainly protective measures required

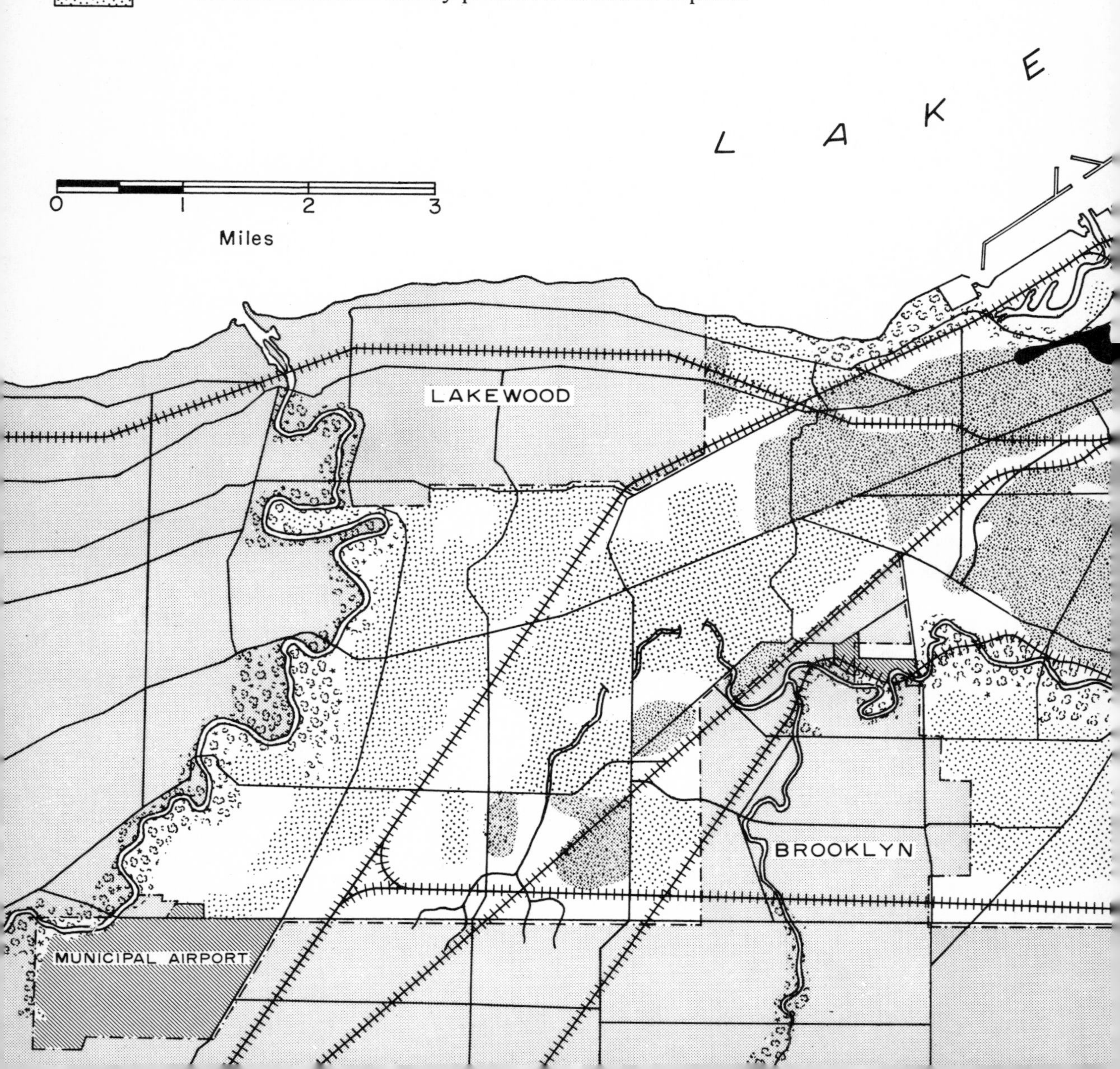

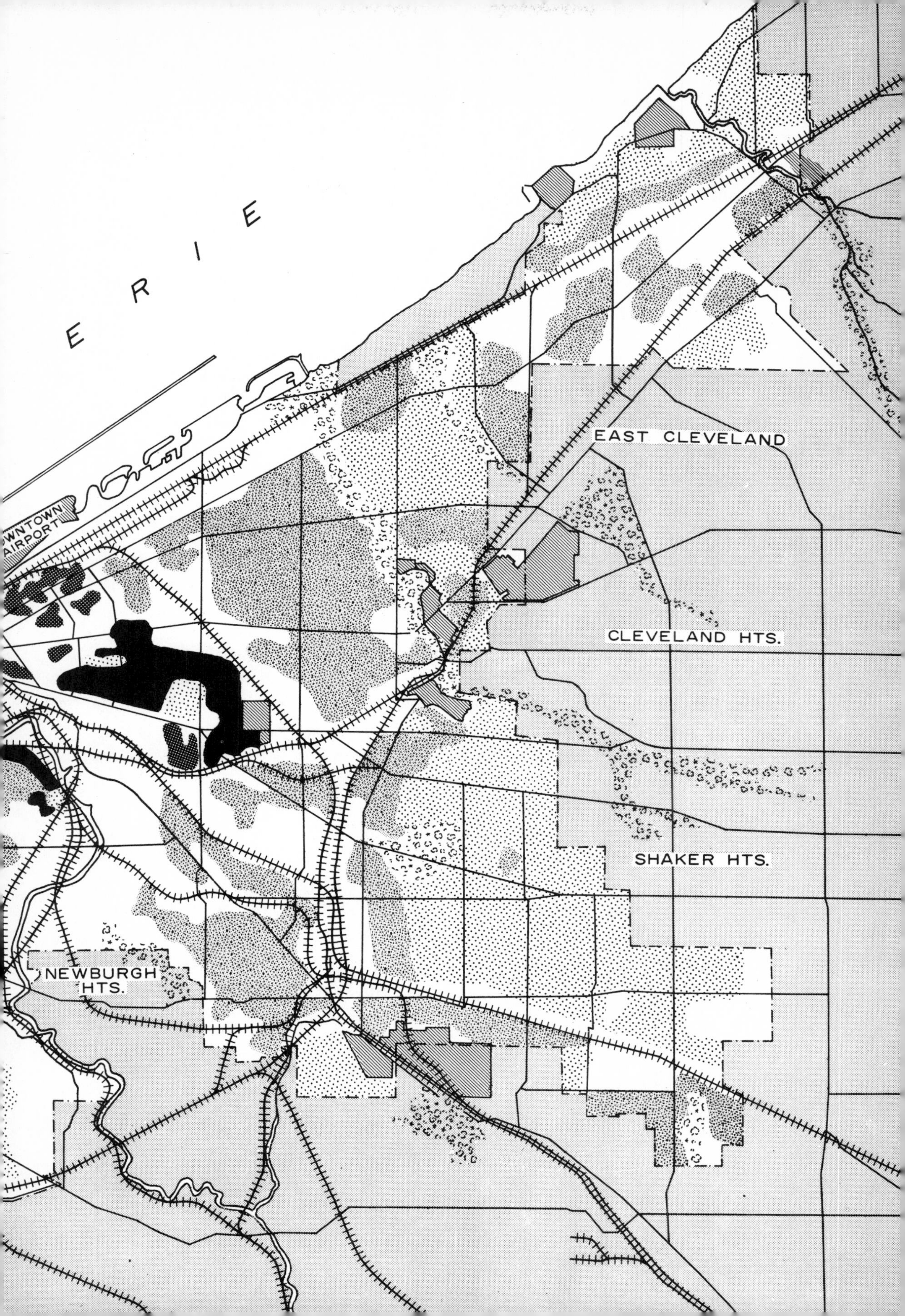
E R I E
DOWNTOWN AIRPORT
EAST CLEVELAND
CLEVELAND HTS.
SHAKER HTS.
NEWBURGH HTS.

the importance of which is indicated by proposals for land acquisition which call for adding 1,500 acres to the existing system of 3,030 acres, an increase of almost 50 per cent. The Philadelphia plan illustrates particularly well one of the reasons for dealing with those physical elements that are concerned with community facilities in one section of the plan document. As shown on page 155, the Philadelphia plan proposes to concentrate a number of community facilities at 10 district and 56 community centers located throughout the city.

The phrase *community facilities* as used in this book is meant to be interpreted broadly. It should include not only the kinds of public community facilities that our society takes for granted, such as schools, parks, playgrounds, libraries, police stations, hospitals, health centers, art galleries, and fire stations. It should also include private facilities of a community-service nature, such as churches, stadiums, schools, golf courses, and cemeteries, and should relate these facilities to the major physical-design proposals made in the working-and-living-areas section of this plan chapter. Every community has traditions and values that will determine the relative importance to be assigned to the different physical elements of the community dealt with in this section of the plan.

(d) The Civic-Design Section. I believe that one of the most important but least-recognized reasons for the rapid development of city planning in the United States, once it gained a foothold in local government after World War II, is the basic human need for visual beauty. Every city dweller provides silent but powerful support for civic work aimed at the creation of a more beautiful city. A city-planning profession whose efforts result in the gradual reorganization of our cities so that they are simply more efficient, more obviously better organized only for the practical social and economic necessities of urban life, will not be accepted for long. If city planners restrict themselves to these limited objectives, they will sooner or later be removed from the key role they now occupy and will be replaced by men capable of creating beautiful as well as functional cities. Because there seems to be a danger that this may happen if the design quality of contemporary city-planning and civic-development work is not raised, the organization of the general-plan document calls for a separate section devoted solely to the civic-design policies and features of the plan.

The civic-design section of the general-plan document has been placed fourth in the sequence of the six sections of this plan chapter because it is dependent primarily on the features of the plan dealt with in sections (b)

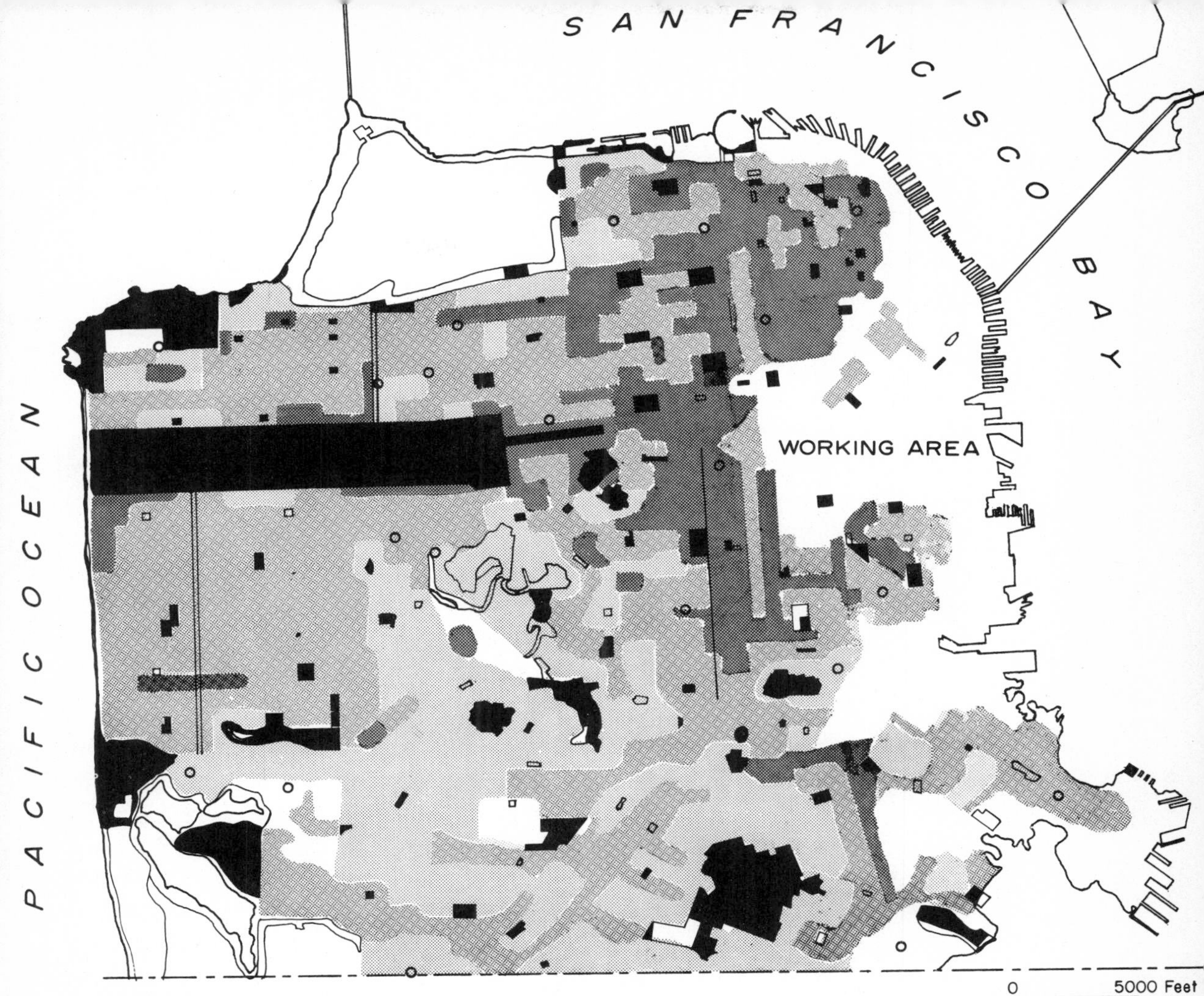

PARK-AND-RECREATION-AREAS ELEMENT OF THE GENERAL PLAN

PARK AND RECREATION AREAS

- Existing Area
- Proposed Area
- General Location

POPULATION DISTRIBUTION

- Moderately Populated
- Densely Populated
- Very Densely Populated

In 1954 the San Francisco Department of City Planning published a document entitled "A Report on a Plan for the Location of Parks and Recreation Areas in San Francisco." The above drawing is based on Plate G in this Report. It illustrates clearly the particular importance of the relationships between the working-and-living-areas element of the general plan and the park-and-recreation-areas element. Official documents describing and summarizing the main ideas in the Report were subsequently adopted by the San Francisco City Planning Commission.

and (c), although, of course, the circulation-elements section of the chapter must also be considered in determining civic-design policies and features. Working with the proposed general layout of the major commercial, industrial, and residential districts, with the related community facilities and public open-space system, and with the visually ever-present circulation elements, the city planner creates a synthesis that will assume a three-dimensional form. This community form is perceived, consciously or unconsciously, by every citizen. As a whole, it gives him a sense of the way in which his city is organized in relation to its site; he is made aware of the fact that his city exalts its natural geographic setting, simply accommodates itself to it, or debases it.

The over-all structure and form of the city create in the mind and emotions of the citizen a sense of individual dignity and well-being, or they create a sense of dullness, confusion, or degradation. As he moves about the city daily, he also experiences the more generally understood reactions to an immediately perceived surrounding. He is aware of the parts of the city—its main streets, its hivelike "downtown" central district, its civic center, its shopping districts, its industrial districts, its parks. The civic-design section of this general-plan chapter is concerned with these two kinds of aesthetic experiences. It should attempt to bring out the major physical-design proposals that have been made concerning the form of the city as a whole considered in relation to its site and the key features and parts of the city that are individually of special significance to the over-all design.

The creative effort involved in the work done during the general-plan design stage which produces a synthesis that satisfies the city's functional requirements and also results in a significant form, aesthetically, is not an effort that can be made methodically, step by step. It is an effort that depends on inspiration, a highly developed sense of fitness and beauty, and an unusual identification with both the social community—its values, its aspirations, its historical traditions and associations—and with the distinctive, special qualities of the natural geographic setting of the community. But once the creative synthesis has taken place, the dominant qualities and features of the resulting design for the physical organization of the city can be identified and judged. The roles played by the key features of the design in creating a city that will have unity, variety, order, and balance can be described and talked about, and the functional and symbolic importance of these features can be consciously linked with their importance as elements of the over-all design. Unless this synthesis is achieved, in as direct and natural a way as it has been achieved for centuries by the governing groups in the more self-confident urban communities elsewhere in the world, we will fail to tap the great reservoir of community pride and support that exists in every American city for carrying out necessary public and private projects in ways that will enable them to fit into the over-all design for the city as defined in the civic-design section.

Although some of the outstanding postwar city-planning programs were led by men whose professional abilities and motivations compelled and enabled them to accord civic design the highest level of concern, no contemporary general-plan documents that I am aware of offer good examples of how to deal with this aspect of city planning. The works of Frederick Law Olmsted and Daniel Burnham are still unequalled. I have no doubt, however, that the present upsurge of interest in the civic-design aspect of general-plan work, and in this aspect of city planning and architectural practice in general, will once again enable us to focus our attention openly and confidently on general-plan proposals aimed at aesthetic objectives.

(e) The Circulation Section. The subject matter of this section includes all of the physical circulation systems needed to enable people and goods to move about freely within the city and its regional environs. It is placed fifth in the sequence of the six sections that together contain the general physical-design proposals of the plan because it is, in my judgment, a secondary section. It is dependent on the preceding, more important sections. The major circulation requirements of the community are determined basically by the spatial relationships between the primary urban-activity centers, and these are determined by the proposals expressed in the working-and-living-areas, community-facilities, and civic-design sections of this plan chapter. There will always be exceptions to this general rule. Topographic features will limit the number of possible routes and locations for transit lines, subways, and freeways, for harbors and railroads, and for other physical elements of the over-all system of circulation facilities. But within such limitations there usually are a number of significant choices that can be made. The point I wish to emphasize here is that, as a general principle, circulation facilities should be designed to accommodate the fixed activity centers and civic-design features of the general plan, rather than the reverse.

The circulation section of the general plan consists of the primary and secondary street systems, the regional freeway and parkway systems, major off-street parking facilities, and air, rail, and water terminals and routes. It also includes the local and metropolitan public-transportation systems, truck terminals and routes, and the systems of pedestrian ways that are of such vital importance especially to the central district of the city, to high- and

PUBLIC-TRANSPORTATION ELEMENTS OF THE GENERAL PLAN

(From *Cleveland Today . . . Tomorrow: The General Plan of Cleveland,* 1950, pages 36–37.)

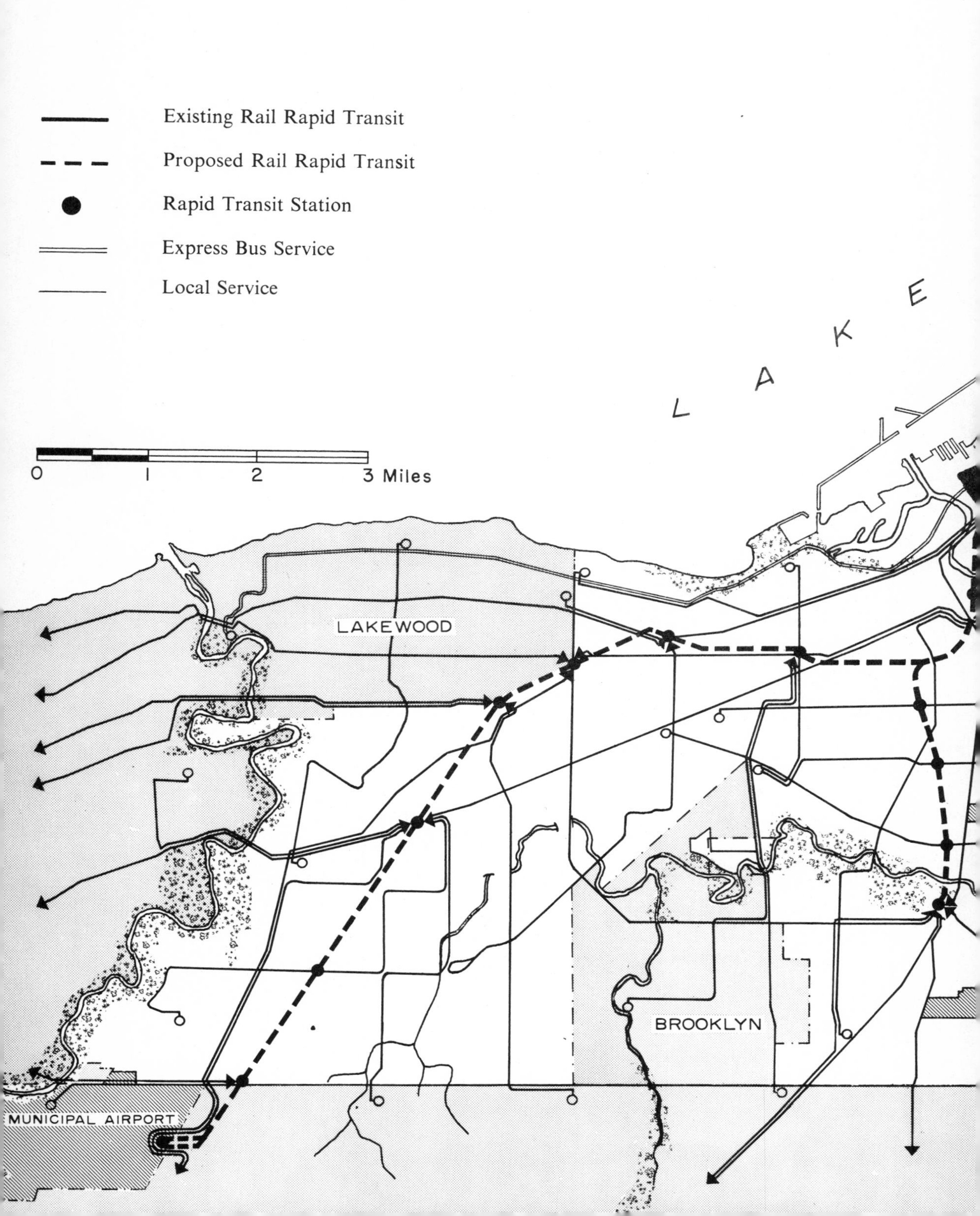

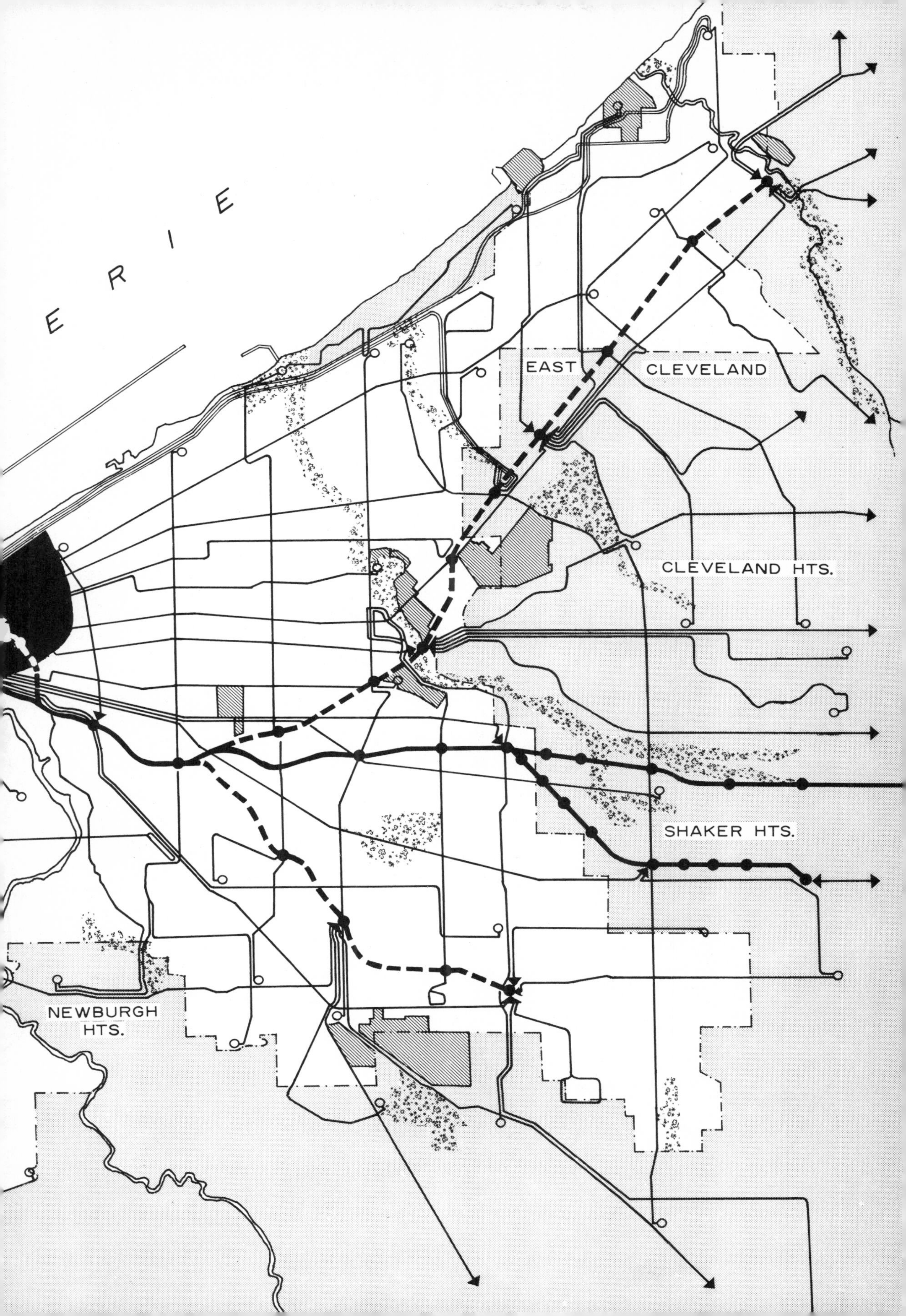
E R I E
EAST
CLEVELAND
CLEVELAND HTS.
SHAKER HTS.
NEWBURGH
HTS.

low-density residential districts, and to certain park and recreation features. The city-planning profession is only beginning to give proper attention to the latter group of circulation facilities. Viewed and planned in their proper subordinate relationship to the primary requirements of urban life, as suggested here, carefully coordinated circulation systems offer tremendous possibilities for increasing the economic and cultural productivity of our cities and metropolitan regions.

The amount of land needed to enable the convenient movement of people at peak hours during the regular work week, and to and from entertainment centers and outdoor recreation areas in the evenings and on weekends, is relatively very large. Usually more than one-fourth of the total land area of the community is required. Because of the close functional interrelationships between the several kinds of transportation systems needed, the large scale and high cost of these facilities, and the secondary relationships they have in common to the subject matter of sections (b), (c), and (d) of this chapter of the plan document, it is advantageous to present the circulation elements in a separate section.

The Cleveland, Berkeley, and Philadelphia plan documents all deal with the circulation elements in the manner suggested. The public-transportation element as dealt with in the Cleveland plan, however, is exceptional because, as shown on pages 178–179, it illustrates so well the vital importance of the metropolitanwide system of local public-transportation routes. Very few published general-plan documents show by means of a unified drawing the relationship of local public-transportation routes to the proposed rapid-transit and express-bus routes.

(f) The Utilities Section. Every modern community is dependent on an extensive, costly, fixed, underground network of utilities. This section is intended to simplify the community-facilities section, where essential public and private utilities are usually considered, by providing a separate place in which to deal with utilities. The utilities section includes primarily those community services that are, or should be, provided for in pipelines, conduits, or wires that are underground. It includes the water-distribution, storm-drainage, and sewage-disposal systems and the gas, electricity, and telephone pipeline and conduit systems. There is an overlapping with the community-facilities section of the plan with regard to the features of these systems that require relatively large land areas, such as sewage-disposal plants, refuse dumps, pumping and generator stations, and water-storage reservoirs.

Planning for these utilities in an economical manner frequently imposes what may seem to be and sometimes are hard and fast limitations on the way in which a city can be organized physically. Financial and technical feasibility factors must be taken into account in every case where it seems necessary, for other reasons, to plan for development in ways that will require complicated, special utility-system designs, such as those made necessary by tidelands development and hilltop concentrations. The functional requirements of the essential utility systems are obviously important. But these requirements must not dominate the other more important requirements of the over-all design. For this reason, and because they are, after all, underground, they should be grouped together and placed last in the sequence of the six sections that make up the chapter of the general plan that deals with general physical-design proposals for the community.

As indicated earlier, the special conditions existing in a particular community may suggest the regrouping of certain physical elements dealt with in that community's plan into one or two additional sections. For example, a community having an unusual concentration of public or specialized private institutions, such as a university town, a community with a very large medical center, or a state capital, may find it helpful to present the proposals of the plan concerned with such a major physical element in a separate section. Similarly, a community owning large tidelands areas might consider it necessary, in order to focus attention effectively, to present the tidelands physical-design proposals of the plan in a separate additional section.

The main point of the basic six-section scheme for organizing this chapter of the general plan is simply that the key physical elements dealt with in the major physical-design proposals—elements that must be provided for in every general plan—should be identified and described in such a way that the citizen reader will be able to understand the logical relationships between them. This requires discussion of the large number of individual physical elements in a way that will clearly indicate their dependence on one another.

(5) Conclusion and Appendices

Many general plans published during the past twenty years include a final chapter in the main body of the document restating the uses of the plan. Having reached this point, the reader will be familiar with the plan, and he will understand its practical utility in a way that was not possible before. Examples usually are given that illustrate how the plan will be used by private builders and investors, by federal, state, and special-district governmental agencies, and by the departments of the municipal government itself. This is an obvious thing to do. I think it is more important than it may seem to be simply because it is so obvious. Such examples are particularly helpful to incumbent councilmen and city-planning commissioners in the educational work that only they can do with the freshman members of their respective bodies.

The following quotations from the 1962 Chico and 1950 Cleveland general plans are drawn from the final chapters of these documents, each of which is titled "From Plan to Reality." The Chico document, in emphasizing the responsibility of the city council for the plan and the need for "keeping the plan current," states:

> Now that the General Plan has been adopted by the City, it is the official policy guide for the development of Chico. But membership on the City Planning Commission and the City Council will change and so may public policies and physical conditions. A plan that is not periodically re-examined by the Commission and Council soon will become obsolete. Any major proposal in conflict with the plan calls for review of the reasons for the pertinent features of the plan. If the new proposal is found to be superior, the plan should be amended. The procedure for amending the plan prescribed by state law requires at least one public hearing before the Planning Commission and one before the City Council. Regular annual review of the plan in connection with the annual consideration of the capital improvement budget is a good way to keep the plan current. At least once every five years, and possibly more often if the community is growing rapidly, the plan should be thoroughly restudied.

The Cleveland document concludes with an explanation of the ways in which the proposals of the plan can be carried out:

> . . . There are many ways . . . to help bring about the improvements that the Plan recommends.
>
> An important step is the making of detailed community plans for each section, working with local groups. Another is changing the zoning map to carry the land-use plan into effect.
>
> Many parts of the General Plan can become reality only by spending public money. Some parts affect Cleveland alone, like playgrounds and local main streets. These can come just as quickly as Cleveland voters decide they want them by approving bond issues and tax levies. Other parts of the Plan, like freeways and redevelopment of slums, need additional funds from County, State, and Federal sources.
>
> Public improvements, of course, should be scheduled in the order of their importance to the community. We must also be careful that our public spending, year by year, leads steadily toward the accomplishing of the Plan. These two

goals are the aim of the Capital Improvement Program which, as called for by the Charter, the Planning Commission submits to the Mayor each year. The Program presents recommendations for public construction and land buying for the next six years. It has been of more and more influence on the City government and the people in recent years.

The General Plan can be just as useful to private individuals and companies. A prospective home buyer can make a better choice among sites by knowing their nearness to future playfields, freeways, transit, etc. Business and industry can take a like advantage of the City's plans in shaping their own future.

The thoroughness and the speed with which the General Plan is carried out depend upon all of us as citizens and property owners of Cleveland. If we agree that our city must be a better place for people to live, and if we agree that the design for better living presented in the General Plan is the goal toward which we should work—then the Plan will become a reality. We can reach it through the democratic workings of our City government, and the will of the community.

There is a need, finally, to include in the official document, in the form of appendices, certain kinds of background information that cannot be fitted into the necessarily simplified description of the plan given in the main body of the document. This need has become more and more evident as a result of our experiences since World War II. Earlier practice was characterized by the publication of separate reports containing detailed background information on the plan. Some, but not all, of the information in these reports was usually needed if the plan itself was to be understood. Every active city-planning program will always find it necessary to publish reports supplementing the official general-plan document. The general-plan document itself, however, should contain whatever detailed information is actually needed to enable the plan to be properly understood. If this essential information cannot be presented in the main body of the document, it should be included in the form of appendices. No fixed list of the types of information that should be included in this way can be made. But general practice indicates that there is a need for a carefully selected bibliography, and for tables and summaries of factual information dealing with such basic subjects as land-use acreages and percentages, economic growth and decline indices, and population figures and forecasts.

I also believe there should be an appendix presenting city-planning enabling legislation, in the form of specific charter provisions, city-council ordinances, and state and federal legislation, together with a brief historical account of the reasons for the development of the local, state, and federal governmental policies and procedures defined by these legislative and constitutional provisions.

The General-Plan Document

Finally, I believe there is a need at this stage in the development of city planning as a governmental and professional activity to include in the plan document a discussion of city-planning methods and techniques. During the next twenty to thirty years, while the city-planning profession completes the final, awkward stages of its initial general-plan preparation work, there is bound to be a certain amount of mystery surrounding the work of the professional staff. The way in which the basic policies are translated into general physical-design proposals should be described just as clearly as it is possible to do so. If additional discussion of the policies themselves, especially those that deal with nonphysical factors, seems to be needed, it should be included here. The more definite technical procedures used in working out the adjustments between the different physical elements dealt with in the design proposals, particularly between the living-and-working-areas, community-facilities, and circulation sections, should be described and explained. A general knowledge of these procedures, and of the meaning of concepts such as "population-holding capacity" should be sought, even though it is unlikely that many readers will want to know about them. Some readers, however, will have unnecessary doubts about the plan and the work of the professional staff if the most important steps in the plan-making procedure are not explained. Their critical attitude must be respected; it is indispensable in gaining the kind of self-reliant understanding of the plan that will be needed if the plan's crucial, tough proposals are to be supported and carried out.

CONCLUSION

I COMPLETED THE first draft of this book in 1955 while on sabbatical leave, but I was not satisfied with my work. In the intervening years the subject of the general plan has continued to hold my attention. During this period I have been able to participate in the work of governing the physical growth and development of an American community at the legislative level. This sustained experience as a municipal legislator has enabled me to test my previously developed concept of the general plan and to work out and experiment with new ideas designed to improve the concept.

As a result of a second opportunity, in the spring of 1962, to concentrate and reflect on the subject, I found that my convictions concerning the importance of what I had written about the primary legislative uses of the general plan, in particular, had become stronger. In bringing this statement to a close, therefore, I wish to express the hope that what I think I have learned concerning the great practical value of a general plan for individual city council members, who want to govern well the physical development of their community, as set forth in Chapter III, "The Legislative Uses of the General Plan," will be carefully considered by my colleagues in the city-planning profession, and by the political, civic, and governmental leaders of the cities of the United States.

I believe that every city council in the United States today has among its members men and women who are perfectly capable of understanding what a general plan is. I believe that when they see how reasonable and practical and valuable the basic concept of the general plan is, they will never again govern in quite the same way.

Conclusion

Once the simplicity of the general-plan concept is appreciated, the practical benefits will become apparent very quickly. Major conflicts involving community-development policies will be resolved. Major capital-improvement programs will be agreed upon, financed, and carried out. A great new era of civic design will be fostered and sustained. I believe that all of these things will occur sooner or later, since I believe in social progress. But in our society, with our philosophy of democratic self-government, these things will happen sooner if we will trust our elected representatives and assist them, by helping them to develop an urban general plan that they can use, to do well what they must do in any case.

A BIBLIOGRAPHIC ESSAY ON THE URBAN GENERAL PLAN

By HOLWAY R. JONES

INTRODUCTION

THE GENERAL plan, as T. J. Kent, Jr., defines it, is "the official statement of a municipal legislative body which sets forth its major policies concerning desirable future physical development; the published general-plan document must include a single, unified general physical design for the community, and it must attempt to clarify the relationships between physical-development policies and social and economic goals." Keeping this definition in mind, the compiler has attempted to link together, in the form of a bibliographic essay, some of the major evolutionary steps in the formation of an urban general-plan theory. The academician will immediately recognize the difficulties in attempting to "pull out" the significant writings on this subject. City planning's early leaders viewed the city essentially as "mechanistic." Their backgrounds being in architecture and engineering, it is not surprising that this should be so. What is surprising, perhaps, is that these professions should so long have dominated the field. Only in recent years have social scientists' analytical techniques found universal application in city planning and come to be essential tools in the professional planner's equipment, with the result that the "mechanistic" view has been "humanized" and social values placed in better balance. . . .

Because the compiler is treating the evolution of an idea, the subject is approached in the traditional manner of the historian—chronologically. It is realized, of course, that this method has certain limitations in that no idea simply "pops out," whole and new born, without a long period of gestation and that often it is difficult to say when, in the time scale, an idea becomes influential. In most instances, however, date of publication can be assumed to be the effective date of transmission, and this date is used throughout the bibliography.

Another important limitation is that this bibliographic essay deals only with the United States. Obviously, as any historian will be quick to criticize, the germ of the "city plan" as a concept goes back in Western thought to Hippodamus of Miletus (born c. 480 B.C.) and actually may be traced back much earlier to the civilizations lying along the Tigris-Euphrates, Nile, and Indus rivers.

The compiler is indebted to T. J. Kent, Jr., who not only made a number of helpful suggestions for the original edition of this essay,* but desired that it be included with the present book. Melvin Webber also helped to clarify a number of points.

---

* "A Bibliographic Essay on the Evolution of an Idea," Part III, *The General Plan in the Urban Planning Process,* Exchange Bibliography No. 21 (Oakland: Council of Planning Librarians, July, 1962), pp 22–40. Minor changes have been made, by the author and Mr. Kent, in the version of the bibliographic essay appearing here to assure its appropriateness and currency in relation to the present book.

GENERAL REFERENCES

To appreciate the significance of the general-plan concept one must first become acquainted with the broad sweep of town and city development in the United States and, more specifically, early American attempts to plan the urban environment. The first 26 references set the stage.

1. Adams, Thomas. *Outline of Town and City Planning: A Review of Past Efforts and Modern Aims.* New York, Russell Sage Foundation, 1935. 368 pp.

   This is an excellent summary of the evolution of city planning in the United States. See particularly pp. 118–129 and 161–251 for developments before and after 1900.
2. Bridenbaugh, Carl. *Cities in the Wilderness: The First Century of Urban Life in America, 1625–1742.* Second edition. New York, Alfred Knopf, 1955. 500 pp.
3. ———. *Cities in Revolt: Urban Life in America, 1743–1776.* New York, Alfred Knopf, 1955. 434 pp.

   The first of these two thoroughly documented studies emphasizes the evolution of democratic urban life in the five largest towns on the North American continent, while the second recognizes two persistent themes: "The astonishing expansion of all the activities of urban existence" and the revolt of urban citizens against the "old" ways of doing things.
4. Comey, Arthur C., and Max S. Wehrly, "Planned Communities," in *Urban Planning and Land Policies,* Vol. II of the *Supplementary Re-*

port of the Urbanism Committee to the National Resources Committee. Washington, D.C., Government Printing Office, 1939, pp. 1–161.

Case studies of 144 communities which "have actually been constructed from the start according to a more or less comprehensive physical plan." Selected bibliography, pp. 153–161.

5. Conklin, Paul K. *Tomorrow a New World: The New Deal Community Program.* Ithaca, N.Y., Cornell University Press, 1959. 350 pp.

   A history of the New Deal community program with background material on the influence of the garden-city movement.

6. Gallion, Arthur B., and Simon Eisner. *The Urban Pattern: City Planning and Design.* Princeton, N.J., Van Nostrand, 1963. 435 pp.

   An interesting resume of the history of the development of city planning, primarily from the point of view of an architect.

7. Green, Constance M. *American Cities in the Growth of the Nation.* New York, John de Graff, 1957. 258 pp.

   Brief historical sketches of the rise of certain characteristic American cities: New York, Philadelphia, Baltimore, Charleston, Boston, Cincinnati, St. Louis, New Orleans, Holyoke, Naugatuck, Chicago, Denver, Wichita, Seattle, Detroit, and Washington, D.C. Author has recently completed a much more detailed study of the nation's capitol.

8. McKelvey, Blake. *The Urbanization of America, 1860–1915.* New Brunswick, N.J., Rutgers University Press, 1963. 370 pp.

   Urban growth, its character and causes, are analyzed by the author, who places special stress on the relations between this growth and other aspects of American history.

9. Schlesinger, Arthur Meier. *The Rise of the City, 1878–1898* (A History of American Life, Vol. 10). New York, Macmillan, 1933. 494 pp.

   The author contends that these two decades mark the era of decision between an essentially urban world and a rural world.

10. Tunnard, Christopher, and Henry Hope Reed. *American Skyline: The Growth and Form of Our Cities and Towns.* Boston, Houghton Mifflin, 1955. 302 pp.

    The thesis of this book is that the American city is very much the product of definite forces which have given it a unique form and pattern. These forces and their consequences are traced from the colonial mercantile town of the 1600–1700's to the regional city of the mid-twentieth century.

11. Wade, Richard C. *The Urban Frontier: The Rise of Western Cities,*

1790–1830 (Harvard Historical Monograph No. 41). Cambridge, Mass., Harvard University Press, 1959. 360 pp.

An account of the rise and development of Ohio Valley cities—Pittsburgh to St. Louis.

12. Weber, Adna Ferrin. *The Growth of Cities in the Nineteenth Century: A Study in Statistics* (Cornell Reprints in Urban Studies). Ithaca, N.Y., Cornell University Press, 1963. 495 pp.

    Considered a classic on the statistical history of worldwide urbanization, the second half of the book, on "causes of the concentration of population, urban growth and internal migration, the structure of city populations, the natural movement of population in city and in country, and general effects of the concentration of population," is exceptionally useful although originally published in 1899.

13. Wissink, Gerardus Antonius. *American Cities in Perspective: With Special Reference to the Development of Their Fringe Areas.* New York, Humanities Press, 1963. 320 pp.

    A study of the development of American cities through the eyes of an unusually perceptive European visitor.

REFERENCES ON CITY-PLANNING PROGRESS IN THE UNITED STATES

14. Meyer, H. H. B., editor, "Check List of References on City Planning," *Special Libraries,* Vol. 3 (May, 1912), pp. 61–123.

    General references and listings by localities. Section on periodical articles with the first entry dated 1861.

15. American Institute of Architects. Committee on Town Planning. *City Planning Progress in the United States, 1917,* edited by George B. Ford. Washington, D.C., Journal of the American Institute of Architects, 1917. 207 pp.

    The first comprehensive view of city-planning progress.

16. Kimball, Theodore, editor. *Municipal Accomplishment in City Planning and Published City Plan Reports in the United States.* Published under the auspices of the National Conference on City Planning, 1920. 79 pp.

    Compiled largely from data assembled by the Detroit City Plan Commission.

17. Nolen, John, "Twenty Years of City Planning Progress in the United States: President's Address," *Proceedings of the 19th National Conference on City Planning, 1927,* pp. 1–44.

18. Chamber of Commerce of the United States. Civic Development Department. *City Planning and Zoning Accomplishments.* Washington, D.C., 1928. 102 pp. mimeo.
19. Hubbard, Theodore K., and Henry Vincent Hubbard. *Our Cities Today and Tomorrow: A Survey of Planning and Zoning Progress in the United States.* Cambridge, Mass., Harvard University Press, 1929. 389 pp.

    Based on field surveys made by Howard K. Menhinick, who visited about 120 cities and 15 counties and regions in all parts of the United States.
20. "Short List of Typical American City Plan Reports," in *Manual of Information on City Planning and Zoning,* by Theodore Kimball (Cambridge, Mass., Harvard University Press, 1923), pp. 43–46; and in *Planning Information Up-to-Date,* by Theodore K. Hubbard and Katherine McNamara (Cambridge, Mass., Harvard University Press, 1928), pp. 12–14.

    An excellent selected list of representative plan reports "notable as exemplifying general principles of city planning or as a collection of highly specialized illustrations or statistics . . ."
21. "How Cities Are Preparing for the Post-War Period," *Planning: Proceedings of the Annual Meeting Held in Chicago, May 1–3, 1944.* Chicago, American Society of Planning Officials, 1944, pp. 31–117.

    A review of planning progress and future programs in 16 cities over 300,000, 4 cities under 50,000, and 4 cities between 50,000–300,000 population.

ANNUAL REVIEW OF CITY-PLANNING PROGRESS IN PERIODICALS

22. *Landscape Architecture:* April, 1912; April, 1913; January, 1915; January, 1918; January, 1920; January, 1921; January, 1922; January, 1923; and January, 1924.
23. *National Municipal Review:* January, 1913; July, 1914; July, 1915; July and October, 1916; September, 1917; November, 1918; January, 1920; January, 1921; January, 1922; February, 1923.
24. *City Planning:* April, 1925; April, 1926; April, 1927; April, 1928; April, 1929; July, 1930; April, 1931; April, 1932; April, 1933; April, 1934.

The above references represent a selective listing designed to give the city planner an appreciation of the historical roots of today's modern American metropolis. For those who wish to delve more deeply into this subject and city planning generally, the following sources are recommended:

25. Bestor, George C., and Holway R. Jones. *City Planning: A Basic Bibliography of Sources and Trends*. Sacramento, California Council of Civil Engineers and Land Surveyors, 1962. 195 pp.
An annotated bibliography of 1,215 items.
26. Mackesey, Thomas W. *History of City Planning* (Exchange Bibliography No. 19). Oakland, Calif., Council of Planning Librarians, 1961. 65 pp.
For references on American city planning, see pp. 35–49.

EVOLUTION OF AN IDEA

FROM THE day the first colonist stepped ashore in the New World, town planning became a necessary part of survival. Between 1630 and 1650 seven New England villages were laid out and many others soon followed. Although in some cases we do not know who these early planners were, it is apparent from the original plan drawings still extant that a concept of "town plan" as a vehicle for decisions about private and public uses of land must have existed. Certainly these plans were not general, long-range, or comprehensive in the modern sense, but they were plans that established patterns—and in some cases these patterns are still predominant in the twentieth-century city. L'Enfant's plan for Washington, D.C., is an outstanding example of this, as is James Oglethorpe's layout of Savannah, Georgia.

With the many examples of early plans in colonial America, it seems all the more incredible that it should have remained until the latter part of the nineteenth century for a planner to state, "When a man or company wish to begin a new or valuable business, they can adapt their wants to the city plan." Yet, according to Thomas Adams (*Outline . . .* , p. 171), Robert Morris Copeland was "probably" the first to use the phrase, "city plan," in this way. We, therefore, cite his "general plan"—so the drawing is marked—as one of the early statements of the use of a plan. To Copeland, it was "fallacious" that one could not "foresee sufficiently the future requirements of business to wisely provide for them."

27. Copeland, Robert Morris. *The Most Beautiful City in America: Essay*

and Plan for the Improvement of the City of Boston. Boston, Lee and Shepard, 1872. 46 pp.

Certainly other early plans for American cities could be cited, but in the period prior to the modern concept of the general plan, perhaps only one other need be mentioned. Following the classic World's Columbian Exposition of 1893, business leaders in Chicago became convinced that their city needed a plan. They turned to Daniel Burnham, who had been the leading spirit behind the fair and whose experience subsequently had included the preparation of plans for Manila and San Francisco. The happy result was "the first comprehensive plan for the orderly development of a great American city"—a plan destined to have an impact far and wide on city planning in this country.

28. Burnham, Daniel H., and Edward H. Bennett. *Plan of Chicago Prepared During the Years MCMVI, MCMVII, and MCMVIII,* edited by Charles Moore. Chicago, Commercial Club, 1909. 164 pp.
    See also the interesting article by Robert L. Wrigley, Jr., "The Plan of Chicago: Its Fiftieth Anniversary," *Journal of the American Institute of Planners,* Vol. 26 (February, 1960), pp. 31–38; and the special issue of *Architectural Forum,* Vol. 116 (May, 1962), which is entirely devoted to Chicago and its shaping by Burnham.

But although Burnham's Chicago plan was comprehensive, it was not in any sense a general plan by modern definition. For the genesis of the modern concept we must turn to a famous name in landscape design and city planning—Frederick Law Olmsted, Jr., son of the man who first proposed preservation principles for Yosemite Valley. The father's best known work is Central Park in New York City. The son, whose training at the hands of his father must have been exemplary, expressed his ideas in two addresses before the National Conference on City Planning: The city plan is a document intended to assist in making possible the "intelligent control and guidance of the entire physical growth and alteration of cities." It should embrace "all the problems of relieving and avoiding congestion" as well as providing a forecast of "the probable future requirements of land for collective uses," and, finally, it is "a device or piece of administrative machinery for preparing and keeping constantly up to date, a unified forecast and definition of all the important changes, additions, and extensions of the physical equipment and arrangement of the city which a sound judgment holds likely to become desirable and practicable in the course of time . . ."

29. Olmsted, Frederick Law, Jr., "Reply in Behalf of the City Planning Conference," *Proceedings of the Third National Conference on City Planning, Philadelphia, May 15–17, 1911*. Boston, 1911, pp. 3–13.
30. ———, "A City Planning Program," *Proceedings of the Fifth National Conference on City Planning, Chicago, May 5–7, 1913,* pp. 1–16.
31. ———, "Introduction," in John Nolen, editor, *City Planning: A Series of Papers Presenting the Essential Elements of a City Plan*. New York, D. Appleton & Co., 1916. (See also revision published in 1929.)

Two contemporaries of Frederick Law Olmsted, Jr., shared in the development of the general-plan concept. One of these was Edward M. Bassett, seven years his senior, who, as Chairman of the New York City Heights of Buildings Commission and the related Commission on Building Districts and Restrictions (1913–1916) as well as the Zoning Commission (1916–1917), was very influential in establishing the nation's first comprehensive zoning ordinance. Although reports of these Commissions and his own speeches before the various sessions of the National Conference on City Planning reveal a lawyer's analytical approach to zoning problems, he apparently was also developing his concept of the master plan during this early period. This is first clearly stated in a small publication of the Regional Plan of New York and Its Environs in which he introduces his notion of the master plan as a guide for comprehensive planning to be more fully explored in his book published twelve years later.

32. Bassett, Edward M. *Recent New York Legislation for the Planning of Unbuilt Areas, Comprising the Text of the City and Village Planning Laws of the State of New York, a Description of Their Origin and Purposes, and Suggestions as to How They Should Be Administered* (Bulletin No. 11). New York, Regional Plan of New York and Its Environs, 1926. 30 pp.

The second contemporary of Olmsted was Alfred Bettman, three years his junior. As a leader in Cincinnati civic and political life, he became convinced of the need for city planning and brought to the task his broad understanding of civic affairs and specialized knowledge of the law. Thus, although Bettman's training and experience was very different from Olmsted's, the two men developed very similar thoughts about the master plan, and, as Kent has pointed out, undoubtedly were influenced and stimulated by one another. Bettman's chief contribution, at this period, was his clear understanding of the essential technical elements of the plan.

33. Bettman, Alfred, "The Relationship of the Functions and Powers of the City Planning Commission, to the Legislative, Executive, and Administrative Departments of City Government," *Planning Problems of Town, City, and Region: Papers and Discussions at the Twentieth National Conference on City Planning Held at Dallas and Fort Worth, Texas, May 7 to 10, 1928,* pp. 142–159.

The next step in the evolutionary process was the appointment by U.S. Secretary of Commerce Herbert Hoover of a nine-man Advisory Committee on City Planning and Zoning. Olmsted, Bassett, and Bettman were members of this Committee and share, in large part, responsibility for key statements in this influential document. The significance of the Standard Act is recognized by [a number of] later writers on city planning legislation and administration. . . .

34. U.S. Department of Commerce. Advisory Committee on City Planning and Zoning. *A Standard City Planning Enabling Act.* Washington, D.C., Government Printing Office, 1928. 54 pp.

The immediate effect of the Standard Act was to encourage a number of state enabling acts and revisions, patterned in large part after it. Nevertheless, progress toward refinement of the general-plan concept continued to be made. Bettman sharpened his own ideas of the master plan and, in 1931, clearly distinguished between the master plan and official map:

> The master plan and official map are therefore two different concepts, with different purposes and results. They are different in time, the master plan necessarily preceding the official map, which is of greater degree of definiteness and involves a greater degree of surveying and engineering detail which, as a practical matter, becomes justified only as the means of the carrying out of the master plan and therefore necessarily made subsequent to the master plan and at a time nearer to the actual time intended for the accomplishment of the planned improvement.

35. Bettman, Alfred, "City Planning Legislation," in John Nolen, editor, *City Planning: A Series of Papers Presenting the Essential Elements of a City Plan.* New York, D. Appleton & Co., 1929, pp. 431–471.

36. ———, "Master Plans and Official Maps," *Planning Problems of Town, City, and Region: Papers and Discussions at the Twenty-Third National Conference on City Planning Held at Rochester, N. Y., June 22 to 24, 1931,* pp. 50–71. Reprinted in *City and Regional Planning Papers,* edited by Arthur C. Comey. Cambridge, Mass., Harvard University Press, 1946, pp. 37–41.

In 1935, four planning-minded lawyers published a definitive set of model laws for planning cities, counties, and states. Bettman re-emphasized the contrast between master plan and official map, calling the former a "plastic" document, the latter a "rigid" one. The term "master plan" was defined (p. 40), but perhaps the most valuable contribution to an understanding of the concept was Bettman's discussion, pp. 57–62, 77–78, 95–96, and 115–117.

37. Bassett, Edward M., Frank B. Williams, Alfred Bettman, and Robert Whitten. *Model Laws for Planning Cities, Counties, and States Including Zoning, Subdivision Regulation, and Protection of Official Map*. Cambridge, Mass., Harvard University Press, 1935. 137 pp.

By the latter half of the depression decade, the master-plan concept as a "guide for comprehensive [physical] planning" had advanced far enough so that one of its first advocates felt he could devote an entire volume to the subject. Bassett's study is basic to an understanding of the evolution of the master-plan concept, particularly pp. 61–143. The author discusses the needs and purpose of the master plan, what it should contain, and the development of the term. Cincinnati, says Bassett, was the first city to appoint a planning commission with power to establish a master plan and was the first large city officially to adopt its plan (1925); however, widespread use of the term "master plan" did not come until after the publication of the Standard Act (1928), which set the pattern of state enabling legislation for several years to follow. Bassett discusses the Standard Act and confusions arising from it; this is followed by a discussion of several state and local acts which introduced modifications (the Pennsylvania, California, Massachusetts, New York enabling legislation for counties and the New York City Charter effective on November 3, 1936).

38. Bassett, Edward M. *The Master Plan; With a Discussion of the Theory of Community Land Planning Legislation*. New York, Russell Sage Foundation, 1938. 151 pp.

Just prior to America's entry into the war, Professor Robert A. Walker, then an Associate Administrative Analyst, Office of Budget and Finance, U.S. Department of Agriculture, published his influential book in which he undertook the task of analyzing the composition of city-planning boards in an attempt to determine why they had not met with greater success. His book adds very little to general-plan theory (see pp. 119–122), but his indictment of the lay commission in planning and his preoccupation with city planning as a staff department in municipal government has influenced a whole new generation of professional city planners. In 1950 Walker reissued his book with two new chapters, one on "Developments During World War II and Its Aftermath" and another reappraising the nature of the planning function.

The second edition brought forward a number of critical comments. Rexford Tugwell, former Governor of Puerto Rico and an influential figure in the New Deal days of the Resettlement Administration, and a political scientist, Edward C. Banfield, suggested that there may be another "conception of the planning profession, if not its practice," called "developmental planning." John T. Howard, Chairman of the Department of City and Regional Planning, Massachusetts Institute of Technology, disagreed with both Walker and his reviewers in his "In Defense of Planning Commissions."

39. Walker, Robert Averill. *The Planning Function in Urban Government* (Social Science Studies No. 39). Chicago, University of Chicago Press, 1941. 376 pp. Second edition, 1950.
40. Tugwell, R. G., and E. C. Banfield, "The Planning Function Reappraised," *Journal of the American Institute of Planners,* Vol. 17 (Winter, 1951), pp. 46–49.
41. Howard, John T., "In Defense of Planning Commissions," *Journal of the American Institute of Planners,* Vol. 17 (Spring, 1951), pp. 89–94.

Also to make its appearance just as war engulfed the United States was Ladislas Segoe's *Local Planning Administration,* published by the International City Managers' Association. This book, now in its third edition, edited by Mary McLean and considerably changed from the original 1941 printing, strengthened the Walker thesis during the important expansion decade of the fifties following the war.

42. Institute for Training in Municipal Administration, Chicago. *Local Planning Administration,* by Ladislas Segoe with the collaboration of Walter F. Blucher, F. P. Best, and others. Chicago, 1941. 684 pp. Third edition edited by Mary McLean, Chicago, 1959. 467 pp.

After several years of experience with the Standard Act and its consequences, Bettman reversed a position he had held earlier and wrote into his draft of a model urban redevelopment act, prepared as Chairman of the American Society of Planning Officials' Committee on Urban Redevelopment, a definition of the essential physical elements that should be dealt with in the general plan. Two years later the model act was issued in revised form.

43. "Report of the Committee on Urban Redevelopment" at the annual Business Meeting, American Society of Planning Officials, *Planning, 1943: Proceedings of the Annual Meeting Held in New York City, May 17–19, 1943*. Chicago, American Society of Planning Officials, 1943, pp. 93–103.
44. Bettman, Alfred. *Draft of an Act for Urban Development and Redevelopment*. Chicago, American Society of Planning Officials, 1943. 14 pp. mimeo.
45. ———. "Revised Draft of an Act for Urban Development and Redevelopment," in Arthur C. Comey, editor, *City and Regional Planning Papers*. Cambridge, Mass., Harvard University Press, 1946, pp. 259–275.

POSTWAR EXPERIENCE

WITH THE end of World War II in 1945 and the subsequent national readjustment of this country's economic and social life, cities faced a sudden upsurge in the need for city planning and construction of public works of all kinds. Professional city planners and educators began to take a hard look at city planning's newfound status; they began to question old concepts and, at the same time, to evolve new procedures and methods. The influence, too, of the federal government in making funds available for redevelopment and urban planning stimulated thinking significantly. It is no wonder, then, that the . . . fifties and early sixties produced a number of excellent contributions to urban-general-plan theory and practice, perhaps one of the most significant being Cincinnati's new general plan of 1948, the first general plan for a large city to be adopted by a city council.

46. Cincinnati (Ohio) City Planning Commission. *The Cincinnati Metropolitan Master Plan and the Official City Plan of the City of Cincinnati, adopted November 22, 1948*. Cincinnati, 1948. 175 pp.

After five years of debate, Congress passed the Housing Act of 1949 on July 15. Although subsequent legislation, particularly that of 1954, considerably modified provisions relating to urban renewal and planning, this Act contained the first federal approach to the idea of the general plan. Section 105, Title I, required that the redevelopment plan conform "to a general plan for the development of the locality as a whole." However, no definition of a general plan was included in the Act. As the Division of Slum Clearance and Urban Redevelopment began to put Title I into operation, the Housing and Home Finance Agency found it necessary to call in S. B. Zisman and others to define the elements necessary for a general plan. The result of this work was published first as a departmental memorandum and more formally stated in the Division's manual.

47. U.S. Housing and Home Finance Agency. Division of Slum Clearance and Urban Redevelopment. *The General Community Plan—A Preliminary Statement*. Washington, D.C., 1950.
48. U.S. Housing and Home Finance Agency. Office of the Administrator. *Slum Clearance and Urban Redevelopment Program: Manual of Policies and Requirements for Local Public Agencies*. Book I, Part 2, Chapter 2, "Community Planning," Section 2, "The General Plan." Washington, D.C., n.d. 3 pp. loose-leaf.

While federal personnel labored over the application of the general-plan concept to redevelopment plans and procedures, a practical city planner with many years' experience and a professional society publicly stated their views. Bartholomew urged that the planner not lose sight of his major task—the production of a good city plan. He discusses his concept of what the "good" city plan should contain and has a number of things to say about the timing and production of planning documents. The following year the Board of Governors of the American Institute of Planners officially endorsed the draft of a booklet on city planning which was subsequently published by the Chamber of Commerce of the United States.

49. Bartholomew, Harland, "The Plan—Its Preparation, Composition, and Form," *American Planning and Civic Annual, 1951*. Washington, D.C., 1951, pp. 97–102.

    Reprinted in Herbert L. Marx, Jr., *Community Planning* (New York, Wilson, 1956), as Vol. 28, No. 4, of the Reference Shelf, pp. 72–79.
50. Chamber of Commerce of the United States. Construction and Civic Development Department. *City Planning and Urban Development*. Washington, D.C., 1952. 47 pp.

    A concise statement of the nature and purpose of the general plan in contrast to the "official map" appears on pp. 23–24.

Zisman's contribution has already been referred to. . . . In 1954 Kent addressed the California Biennial Institute of Mayors and Councilmen, and for the first time outlined his ideas on the legislative uses of the general plan.

51. Zisman, S. B., *The General Plan in the Redevelopment Program* (Re-

development Information Service Publication No. 5). Chicago, National Association of Housing Officials, November, 1952. 8 pp.

Mr. Zisman stresses "the fact that ultimately the best redevelopment grows out of, and is in fact part of, the general plan."

52. Kent, T. J., Jr., "Guiding City Development: A Major Responsibility of the City Council," *Proceedings, 4th Biennial Institute of Mayors and Councilmen*. Berkeley, League of California Cities, 1954. 17 pp.

The legislative break from the Standard Act in California came in 1955 with the adoption of an amendment to the City and County Planning Enabling Act which explicitly defined the essential physical elements to be dealt with in the general plan (Article 7). Citizen awareness of the new California concept was enhanced with a colorful and well-illustrated brochure on city planning published by the state legislature.

53. California. Laws, Statutes, etc. *Laws Relating to Conservation, Planning, and Zoning . . .* Sacramento, Printing Division, 1955. 146 pp.

See particularly pp. 9–11.

54. California. Assembly. Interim Committee on Conservation, Planning and Public Works. *Planning for Growth: A Report on the Status of City and Regional Planning in California*. Sacramento, Legislative Bill Room, 1955. 84 pp.

See particularly pp. 22–23 ("Nature and Function of the Master Plan"), pp. 24–25 ("Steps in Preparing the Master Plan" and "Elements of the Master Plan"), and pp. 26–31 for examples of experience in Berkeley, Richmond, and Los Altos, California.

The history of the general-plan concept indicates that the lawyer is in a peculiarly advantageous position to contribute to the theory of city planning. Bassett, Bettman, Frank B. Williams, and, more recently, Charles M. Haar have made major contributions. Among these, the latter has been most influential in his writings on the general plan. Haar emphasizes that the content of the master plan has changed from strict adherence to seven activities as proposed by Bassett to broader concepts including classifications which are co-extensive with the responsibilities of the local planning agency. The influence of federal agencies in setting up standards as a prerequisite for financial aid, says Haar, is exerting pressures "from the top" and is going to have an increasing effect on the content. The author discusses these tendencies and concludes that they are the result of a growing realization of interdependence of modern society on all activities affecting land use. In a second article, published the same year, Haar discusses the concepts of the master plan, what the master plan means to the city planner, what it means to property interests, the criteria for a statutory checklist, and the written master plan.

55. Haar, Charles M., "The Content of the Master Plan: A Glance at History," *Journal of the American Institute of Planners,* Vol. 21 (Spring-Summer, 1955), pp. 66–70.

56. ———, "The Master Plan: An Impermanent Constitution," *Law and Contemporary Problems,* Vol. 20 (Summer, 1955), pp. 353–418.

Contains a valuable appendix summarizing information on planning commissions, preparation of master plans, content, and analyzing the acts in terms of how they translate plans into action. A fifth chart deals with the legal impact of the master plan.

In 1956 the Cambridge city-planning consulting firm of Adams, Howard, and Greeley was commissioned to survey the work program, functions, and organization of the Los Angeles Department of City Planning and to recommend ways of improving the effectiveness of the Department and its program. Although the city had had an active planning program for many years, its failure to produce a general plan led to confusion and uncertainty, said the consultants. It is not surprising, therefore, that this analysis—especially in light of the background and experience of the three members of the firm—strongly recommended the preparation and adoption of "a single master plan" and emphasized this by adding, "and cease the misleading practice of identifying each component plan as itself a master plan."

57. Adams, Howard, and Greeley. *Report to the Board of City Planning Commissioners, City of Los Angeles, on the Los Angeles City Planning Department, 1956.* Cambridge, Mass., November, 1956. 175 pp.

Two other lawyers who examine the content of the general plan and whose analyses are especially revealing are J. B. Milner and Allison Dunham. Milner critically discusses the legal and administrative problems of the master plan, stressing its importance as a significant legal document distinct from and equal to zoning law and subdivision control; he reviews Canadian practice and shows how confusion has arisen regarding the role of the master plan. Dunham's analysis attempts to reconstruct a theory of the master plan in order to make clear the separation of the responsibilities of a "central planner" from those of a departmental official and of a private landowner. He criticizes Bassett's concept as "too narrow because it excludes from city planning all development plans . . . (other than location) of public and private users of land resources; too physical because it emphasizes location and thereby ignores numerous socioeconomic forces; too rigid because a city is a dynamic place; and too detailed because a master plan ought to be confined more to general principles." While the author claims that recent city-planning literature shows a marked tendency to depart from the Bassett view (in part due to the planner's confusion over the terms "plan," "forecast," and "proposal"), he also feels that there is a theory which supports Bassett. The key to Bassett's concept, writes Dunham, is the factor of external impact of one public work upon another, although he also stresses the zoning plan as a device which determines "where various types of private development should not be located." Dunham develops this thesis to show that "what is needed is a philosophy delineating the reasons for interference by central planners with the decisions of others."

58. Milner, J. B., "Introduction to Master Plan Legislation," *Canadian Bar Review,* Vol. 35 (December, 1957), pp. 1125–1175.
59. Dunham, Allison, "City Planning: An Analysis of the Content of the Master Plan," *Journal of Law and Economics,* Vol. 1 (October, 1958), pp. 170–186.

Like his partner, Harland Bartholomew, Eldridge Lovelace believes the fundamental job of the city planner is to prepare a city plan; indeed, he believes so strongly in this central concept that he urges the title, "Director of the City Plan," for the chief planning officer. On the other hand, Dennis O'Harrow, Executive Director, American Society of Planning Officials, takes quite a different view.

60. Lovelace, Eldridge, "1. You Can't Have Planning Without a Plan. 2. Needed: One-Dimensional City Plans. 3. The Flexible City Plan is No City Plan at All," *Journal of the American Institute of Planners,* Vol. 24, No. 1 (1958), pp. 7–10.
61. O'Harrow, Dennis, "Magic and Master Plans," American Society of Planning Officials *Newsletter,* Vol. 25 (February, 1959), p. 9.

    See also the April, 1959, issue for reactions.

Hugh Pomeroy, Director of Planning for Westchester County, New York, at the time of his death, shares with T. J. Kent, Jr., the idea that the master plan is an essential guide for its chief client, the city council. Kent's teaching colleagues, Francis Violich and Corwin Mocine, also share his concepts about objectives, organization, and procedures; but the former, of course, applies them to very different local-government situations in Latin America.

62. Pomeroy, Hugh R., "The Master Plan—Its Importance and Its Implementation." Address given before the Pennsylvania Planning Association Annual Meeting and the Local Government Conference on Planning, Philadelphia, November 14, 1958. 20 pp. mimeo.
63. Violich, Francis, "The Urban General Plan as an Instrument for Guiding Urban Development: a Working Outline for the Seminar on Urban Planning," Inter-American Housing and Planning Center, Bogotá, Colombia, October 5 to 30, 1958. Berkeley, Department of City and Regional Planning, University of California, May 1, 1958. 27 pp. mimeo.
64. Mocine, Corwin R., "The Master Plan—Its Form and Function," *Arizona Review of Business and Public Administration,* Vol. 10 (July, 1961), pp. 13–14.

Perhaps the most significant book of an epochal decade for city planning is Charles M. Haar's *Land-Use Planning*. His theme is much broader than city planning; he deals with the whole subject of property law in its contemporary setting with emphasis on urban land in metropolitan areas. But he reviews the history of the assumptions and goals of city planning, utilizing material which he developed earlier in various law journals, relating his discussion to important law cases and including a "brilliantly argued debate" in which "an attorney and a city planner discuss some fundamental issues concerned with the role of the city council, the role of the professional city planner, and the role of the master plan" in the city-planning process.

65. Haar, Charles M., "The Master Plan: An Inquiry in Dialogue Form," in his *Land-Use Planning: A Casebook on the Use, Misuse, and Re-Use of Urban Land*. Boston, Little, Brown and Company, 1959, pp. 730–744.

Reprinted in *Journal of the American Institute of Planners,* Vol. 25 (August, 1959), pp. 133–142.

With his election to the Berkeley City Council in 1957, T. J. Kent, Jr., was in a position to develop his ideas concerning the role and function of the general plan in a practical way, giving his statements a cast of political pragmatism often lacking in a purely scholarly approach. Twelve years' teaching experience also greatly aided this process. Among his students who have contributed richly, in their own right, to the theory of the general plan, Alan Black stands out as the most important in recent years.

66. Kent, T. J., Jr., "The Legislative Functions of the General Plan," *Proceedings, 8th Biennial Institute of Mayors and Councilmen.* Berkeley, League of California Cities, 1960. 14 pp.
67. ———, "The City General Plan: Its Technical Elements and Legislative Functions," in California Governor's Conference on California's Urban Areas and the State Highway System, *Papers.* Sacramento, State Department of Public Works, 1960, pp. 32–35.
68. Black, Alan. *The Functions of the Urban General Plan.* M.C.P. Thesis. University of California, Berkeley, 1960. 136 pp.

Robert C. Hoover of Wayne State University rejects the "fourth power" concept of Tugwell as well as Haar's "master plan as an impermanent constitution." It is also certain that his proposals would not fit the definition of general plan suggested by Kent. Hoover would have an elected "Metropolitan Direction-Finding Commission" prepare a 25-year "body of socio-physical end-directions; an executive-prepared 10-year plan for services and physical development; a legislatively-prepared 5-year growth policy and a 5-year socio-physical development plan, the latter to be re-enacted annually."

69. Hoover, Robert C., "On Master Plans and Constitutions," *Journal of the American Institute of Planners,* Vol. 26 (February, 1960), pp. 5–24.

The final entries in this bibliographic essay are, appropriately, official general-plan documents that offer significant evidence of the reality and validity of the general-plan concept. They focus on major physical-development problems and opportunities; they deal with a common set of essential physical elements; they are long-range, comprehensive, and general; and they are presented in unified, single documents available to the public. These plan documents are significant also because they are concerned with cities representing a wide range of sizes and located in different regions of the United States. Finally, the documents are significant because they are the result of sustained political and professional programs: the civic and professional leaders responsible for these urban general plans were, in each instance, individuals who had gained the respect of their colleagues as a result of many years of work in municipal government and city planning.

70. Cleveland City Planning Commission. *The General Plan of Cleveland.* Cleveland, 1950. 48 pp.

71. Berkeley City Planning Commission. *Berkeley Master Plan*. Berkeley, California, 1955. 111 pp.

72. Philadelphia City Planning Commission. *Comprehensive Plan: The Physical Development Plan for the City of Philadelphia*. Philadelphia, 1960. 105 pp.

INDEX

INDEX